SECRET SEXUALITIES

M000202610

Groundbreaking in its historical range, vast sources and scholarly research, *Secret Sexualities* contains rare primary texts, published together for the first time. It takes a bold approach in not discriminating between issues of sex, sexuality and gender. The 'body' is as important as its desires and its sexual practices.

This timely work is supported by a general introduction which provides a theoretical framework. The texts range from trial records and newspaper items to medical pamphlets and anatomical treatises.

Ian McCormick provides substantial texts which deal with anatomy and medicine. Discussion of the construction of eunuchs and hermaphrodites provides a rare insight into the complex relationship between the monstrous body, sexuality and gender.

Classical texts have also been included where they provide insight into the construction of a lesbian culture along with a range of sapphic texts dealing with cross-dressing, mannish women, and female husbands.

Secret Sexualities: A Sourcebook of 17th and 18th Century Writing is essential reading for students and researchers studying this period.

Ian McCormick is a Senior Lecturer in English Studies at Nene College of Higher Education.

SECRET SEXUALITIES

A sourcebook of 17th and 18th century writing

EDITED BY
IAN McCORMICK

London and New York

First published 1997
by Routledge
11 New Fetter Lane, London EC4P 4EE

Simultaneously published in the USA and Canada
by Routledge
29 West 35th Street, New York, NY 10001

© 1997 Ian McCormick
Ian McCormick asserts his moral right to be identified as the editor
of this work

Typeset in Scala by Solidus (Bristol) Limited

Printed and bound in Great Britain by
Clays Ltd, St Ives plc

All rights reserved. No part of this book may be reprinted or
reproduced or utilized in any form or by any electronic,
mechanical, or other means, now known or hereafter
invented, including photocopying and recording, or in any
information storage or retrieval system, without permission
in writing from the publishers.

British Library Cataloguing in Publication Data

A catalogue record for this book is available from
the British Library

Library of Congress Cataloguing in Publication Data

Secret & Sexualities : a sourcebook of 17th and 18th century
writings/Ian McCormick.
p. cm.
Includes bibliographical references and index.
ISBN 0–415–13953–8 (hardbound). — ISBN 0–415–13954–6 (pbk.)
1. Gays' writings, English. 2. English literature–
Early modern, 1500–1700. 3. English literature
–18th century. 4. Lesbians–Literary collections.
5. Gay men–literary collections.
I. McCormick, Ian,
PR1110.G39R68 1996
96–16053
CIP
820.8 '0920664–dc20

ISBN 0–415–13953–8 (hbk)
ISBN 0–415–13954–6 (pbk)

TO MY PARENTS

CONTENTS

ACKNOWLEDGEMENTS x

GENERAL INTRODUCTION 1

1 **ANATOMIES** 13
  Introduction 13
  Degrees and Symptoms of the Venereal Disease 15
  A Treatise of Hermaphrodites 18
  Eunuchism Displayed 21
  The Nature of Hermaphrodites 34

2 **CRIMES AND PUNISHMENTS** 49
  Introduction 49
  The Fall and Great Vices of Sir Francis Bacon 52
  Mervin, Lord Audley, Earl of Castlehaven 53
  The Case of John Atherton 62
  The Trial and Conviction of Several Reputed Sodomites 64
  A Notorious Gang of Sodomites 66
  The Trial of Lord Duffus for Sodomy 67
  Thomas Rodin, Alias Reading, for Attempting Sodomy 69
  Trial of William Brown 71
  The Trial of Mother Clap for Keeping a Sodomitical House 72
  The Trial of Gabriel Lawrence for Sodomy 73
  The Trial of William Griffin for Sodomy 75
  The Trial of George Kedger for Sodomy 77
  The Trial of Thomas Wright for Sodomy 78
  The Trial of George Whittle for Sodomy 80
  Proposals for Castrating Criminals 83
  A Dissertation upon Flogging 84
  Mr Swinton Accused of Sodomitical Practices 85
  The Wadhamites: A Burlesque Poem 100
  A Court Martial 104
  The King versus Wiseman 104
  A Full and Genuine Narrative of the Confederacy 106
  The Trial of Richard Branson 109
  Short Extracts 114

3 REPRESENTATIONS   117

Introduction   117

Sins of Sodom   121

Mundus Foppensis   124

The Levellers   126

The Women-Hater's Lamentation   130

The Mollies' Club   131

Sir Narcissus Foplin   134

Reasons for the Growth of Sodomy   135

A Learned Dissertation upon Old Women, Male and Female   143

A Genuine Narrative   147

Hell upon Earth   147

Lord Hervey   150

A View of the Town   151

The State of Rome under Nero and Domitian: A Satire   152

The Pretty Gentleman   153

Two Young Gentlemen   158

The Destruction of Sodom Improved   161

Love in the Suds   162

The Latin Epitaph on Bob Jones   168

The Times   169

The Fruit Shop   172

4 SAPPHIC TEXTS   175

Introduction   175

The Man-Woman   177

The Womanish Man   179

A Dialogue between Cleonarium and Leaena   181

A Serious Proposal to the Ladies   182

Sappho   183

Blest as the Immortal Gods Is He   184

The Fable of Iphis and Ianthe   184

Venus in the Cloister; or, the Nun in her Smock   187

Roxana   198

Monsieur Thing's Origin   198

The Unaccountable Wife   202

Letter from a Young Lady   204

The Toast   207

Travels in Turkey   209

The Progress of Nature   210

CONTENTS

A Spy on Mother Midnight   212
The History of the Human Heart   215
Memoirs of a Woman of Pleasure   216
Tonzenie   220
Catherine Vizzani   222
A Discovery of a Very Extraordinary Nature   234
The Adulteress   235

GLOSSARY   237

NOTES   241

BIBLIOGRAPHY   249

INDEX   255

ACKNOWLEDGEMENTS

The texts used in this book, together with the supporting materials, could not have been prepared without the assistance of a number of libraries. In particular, I should like to thank staff at the British Library; the Bodleian Library, Oxford; the Brotherton Library, Leeds; Leicester University Library; Birmingham City Libraries and Jane Marshall, at Nene College Library, who efficiently obtained a number of monographs and inter-library loans during my work on the book. David Fairer was an inspiration during my doctoral research. I should also like to thank Ian Firla who organized a portable computer which proved invaluable. Iain Macpherson, Nadia Valman, Tim Meldrum, Michelle O'Callaghan and my colleagues at Nene College were a support at crucial stages of my work. The project could not have been completed without the assistance of research funding from Nene College. James Armstrong knows his important contribution to the project; his friendship was a strength throughout. Finally I should like to thank my partner, Stuart McQuade, for his continuing support.

GENERAL INTRODUCTION

The variety of topics and the range of rhetorical strategies included in this sourcebook reflect the uncertainty and instability of fixed categories of sex, gender and sexuality during the seventeenth and eighteenth century. The period was marked by the unresolved tensions of ancient and 'modern' practices. It is tempting to seek out forerunners of late twentieth-century thinking, but the period was also the preserve of classical learning; the authority of influential medieval and Renaissance texts and commentaries was just as important as 'direct' empirical observation. Attitudes to sexuality were often brutal by our standards, but they were also multiple, contradictory and fanciful. The diversity of the rich textual heritage from this period mirrors our own condition insofar as we are faced with a variety of critical terminologies, models, strategies and prejudices that obstruct or enhance the possibility of knowing 'sexuality'. Faced with such a heterogeneity of materials there is a serious danger that the object of study itself fragments into random groupings of particularities. Yet diversification of sexualities has been matched by expanded policing, observation and control; secret acts are viewed in the open forum of the confession, the law court, or the psychiatric session. Nonetheless, sexualities – in all their historical constructedness – shift beyond our grasp, refusing to yield up a stable cognitive core. Jeffrey Weeks, for instance, has warned that

> There is no essence of homosexuality whose historical unfolding can be illuminated. There are only changing patterns in the organization of desire whose specific configurations can be decoded. This, of course, propels us into a whirlwind of deconstruction – for if gay identity is of recent provenance, what of heterosexual identity. (1985: 6)

In recent years there has, nonetheless, been an explosion of ideas concerning sexuality. The drive to classify constructions of sexuality has itself become a theoretically problematic enterprise. Recently, 'queer', for instance, has been used to name a specific defiance of settled orthodoxies of sexual identity. Accordingly, the starting point for 'queer theory' is, in Moe Meyer's words 'an ontological challenge to dominant labeling philosophies' (1994: 1). This strategy takes up Weeks's 'whirlwind of deconstruction' by contesting the binary opposition between (among other things) homosexuality and heterosexuality. These terms are not simply 'mirror' images; nor do they precisely and exclusively delineate a site of struggle. Moreover, it is not sufficient to work from a model of empowered

1

and disempowered, particularly when we begin to discern intimations of the latter producing the former. In a general cultural framework Stallybrass and White have noted that what was designated as 'low' – as dirty, repulsive, noisy, contaminating results only in a problematic and paradoxical exclusion: 'Yet that very act of exclusion was constitutive of its identity. The low was internalized under the sign of negation and disgust. But disgust always bears the imprint of desire. These low domains, apparently expelled as 'Other', return as the object of nostalgia, longing and fascination' (1986: 191).

To complicate the issue further, different varieties of same-sex relations and significations circulate simultaneously; the control of them may take the form of hangings, imprisonments, or fines; of censuring and censorship; satire and silence. In another sense, the categories of transgressive or 'secret' sexualities cannot simply be opposed to 'open' and accepted forms of sexual interaction. The complex positioning of spectator, reader or voyeur participate in the demolition of naive oppositional accounts. In a range of texts included in this sourcebook, the secret is shared with the reader before the cross-dressed female courts and sleeps with her same-sex partner; narratives of sex between nuns violate a sacred space almost as much as the intrusive eyes of the titillated heterosexual reader; a prostitute enjoys same-sex fun with her fellow sex-workers, but expresses horror when she herself is the secret observer of male same-sex activities; writers lift the petticoats of eunuchs and hermaphrodites playing out a double logic of exhibitionism and secrecy, public and private responsibilities. An expanded notion of heterosexuality emerges as the privileged space of overlapping and intertwined desires. Yet as the contemporary critic or reader reappropriates transgressive sexual narratives, the tired monological discourse of heterosexuality shifts to the margins.

Three assumptions have tended to organise the discussion of these issues: that sex is simply fixed at birth; that gender is the product of arbitrary cultural differentiations constructed upon sex, serving to distribute power unequally; that sexuality is concerned with the object of one's desire, normally gravitating towards one of the opposite sex, within a western patriarchal system. Yet these settled partitions between sex, gender and sexuality are open to challenge. The idea that 'sex' is a simple biological given, for example, has been contested in the work of Thomas Laqueur. He argues that before the Enlightenment (and in some later texts) 'To be a man or a woman was to hold a social rank, a place in society, to assume a cultural role, not to be organically one or the other of two incommensurable sexes. Sex before the seventeenth century, in other words, was still a sociological and not an ontological category' (1990: 8). Exploring the differences between sex and gender, Eve Kosofsky Sedgwick has recently suggested that these terms seem 'only to delineate a problematical *space* rather than a crisp distinction'

(1990: 29). She proceeds to argue that sexuality has often been confused with sex across 'the array of acts, expectations, narratives, pleasures, identity-formations, and knowledges, in both women and men, that tends to cluster most densely around certain genital sensations' (31). Other categories such as race or class might themselves be important in the construction of sexuality. Characteristically, multiple configurations of power begin to shift sexuality to the margins. Is is as though we can't decide whether sexuality is the container, or the thing contained.

There is a danger that we lose a working notion of sexuality; that it becomes simply the site visited or annexed systematically by other manifestations of power. Unstable and elusive, sexuality exists only as that which is read off (or against) structures that are more accessible as oppositional targets. As a result, there is a tendency to insist upon understanding sexuality as the product of, and resistance to, bourgeois construction of self (defined in terms of one rigid heterosexuality), which established its hegemony in the seventeenth and eighteenth centuries. In this regard, Moe Meyer has noted that queer theory

> signals ... an ontological challenge that displaces bourgeois notions of the
> Self as unique, abiding, and continuous while substituting instead a concept
> of the Self as performative, improvisational, discontinuous, and proces-
> sually constituted by repetitive and stylized acts. (1994: 3)

In terms of post-structuralist theory the shift in power is neatly played out between diversity and singleness. The transition from a monological and material account to a multi-layered, dialogical inclusiveness is attractive, despite the underlying materialism at work in the production of sexualities. Yet there is a danger of excessive simplification in tracking a single serpentine path to sexual transgression. In textual terms, sexuality accomplishes multiple digressions, inhabiting different social and cultural spaces not all of which are directly reducible to the economic base. As Weeks has noted, 'Capitalist social relations do certainly set limits and pressures on sexual relations as on everything else; but a history of capitalism is not a history of sexuality' (1985: 6). At the same time, we are warned not to treat power as a homogeneous force; rather, power 'can be seen as mobile, heterogeneous, insistent and malleable, giving rise to various forms of domination, of which the sexual is one, and producing constant forms of challenge and resistance, in a complex history' (9). For Michel Foucault, 'resistance is never in a position of exteriority in relation to power' (95); despite the regulatory powers of literary discourses, psychiatry, and jurisprudence – which acted upon 'perversity' – we must learn how these 'also made possible the formation of a "reverse" discourse: homosexuality began to speak in its own behalf, to demand that its legitimacy or "naturality" be acknowledged, often in the same vocabulary, using the same categories by which it was medically disqualified' (1976: 101).

The power of heterosexual norms has usually been equated with the priority of 'nature', or the natural, as the discourse that is best used to reinforce and privilege its representations. Nature is linked centrally with the notion of procreation as the prime end of human life; desires that move beyond this goal are, in a variety of ways, and in different degrees, transgressive. At another level, heterosexuality reinforces economic ideologies in its division of labour (through gender) and insofar as procreation mirrors production. Further to this, heterosexuality becomes the model for what we are essentially; it is fixed at the core of our being. Desires which do not focus exclusively on these neat sex–gender roles are therefore perverse, deviant, artificial constructions. Thus a main theme in the theory of sexuality has been the opposition between the essential and the constructed, between the natural and the artificial. Same-sex relations, and all that they signify, are therefore celebrated and reclaimed in all their artificiality and constructedness; by the same token, heterosexuality is asked to reconsider its claims to an essential nature. At a theoretical level, it has been common for post-structuralist critics to work from a demolition of privileged, stable, 'origins' to a carnival of style, artifice, performance and play. Sodomy is a failure of significa-tion; the thing 'not to be named'; it is reduced to tittle-tattle, a luxurious froth, civilization's most recent and most dangerous invention. Paradox challenges purity in a new aesthetics of sexuality.

For Freud, the notion that heterosexuality was safely grounded in nature, as the natural and inevitable direction of sexual development required explanation. In *Three Essays on Sexuality* he noted that it was not a self-evident fact that men should find a sexual interest in women. Freud also argued in an *Outline of Psychoanalysis* that sexual life began soon after birth; that the 'sexual' was a broader concept than the 'genital'; that sexual life was concerned primarily with obtaining pleasure from the body, often beyond the needs of reproduction. Detailed case studies appeared to complicate and infinitely expand the range of sexualities. According to Eve Kosofsky Sedgwick, psychoanalytic theory, 'if only through the almost astrologically lush plurality of its overlapping taxonomies of physical zones, developmental stages, representational mechanisms, and levels of consciousness, seemed to promise to introduce a certain becoming amplitude into discussions of what different people are like' (1990: 23–4). Yet in certain respects Freud's work proved to have a strictly normative effect with the subsequent development of ego-psychology, in which the analyst deployed or offered his or her own harmoniously balanced ego as a goal, as a means of restoring the patient's damaged or perverted ego. The goal was to return the patient to an integrated, healthy state, purged of the disorientating 'illness' of homosexuality. Psycho-analysis may serve as an obstacle to understanding sexuality, but Freud's theories were, nonetheless, revolutionary in their time and continue to stimulate, if not determine, new directions in thinking about sexuality. Freud's approach often appeared scientific, but we might also consider his work as a decoding of cultural phenomena. In the period covered by the extracts collected in this sourcebook, myths, stories, translations, newspaper items, crime reports and authoritative learned citation were used as much as empirical observation to understand the nature and production of sexualities. Historical classifications were often temporary and momentary, and they may often appear as alien or as exotic as some of Freud's, if perhaps for different reasons.

In Weeks's view, desire 'cannot be reduced to primeval biological urges, beyond human control, nor can it be seen as a product of conscious willing and planning. It is somewhere ambiguously, elusively, in between, omnipotent but intangible, powerful but goal-less' (1985: 157). The essentialist model is prescriptive or normative, but fails to do the conceptual work involved in the adequate description of how desires function, and how sexualities are made. Moreover, the terminologies used in the essentialist and the constructivist model have been interrogated. Eve Kosofsky Sedgwick offers the alternative model of the 'minoritizing' and the 'universalizing', arguing that 'it can do some of the same analytic work as the latter binarism, and rather more tellingly' (1990: 40). In part, her proposal serves as a return to the political question, to the pressing need to think about the distributions of power in the organization of sexuality. According to Marcuse capitalist society was grounded in sexual repression; its survival hinged on postponed gratifications. Mass factory work was dull because it involved division of labour as its efficient process. At the same time, sexuality was reduced to the functions of the genital zones, simplifying the body's surfaces to a productive focus. In Marcuse's analysis, Freud and Marx are married to explain the emergence of heterosexuality. For post-structuralist theorists such as Deleuze and Guattari, our latent and shattered drives might be reclaimed enabling us to create new networks for desire, and different ways of coming together. But as Weeks notes, 'this flux is too much for capitalist society to endure, for it simultaneously encourages and abhors this chaos, and cannot live with the infinite variety of potential interconnections and relationships' (1985: 173).

With respect to theory, the chaotic flux is much in evidence. Eve Kosofsky Sedgwick, for instance, has attacked the assumption that homosexuality today 'comprises a coherent definitional field rather than a space of overlapping, contradictory, and conflicting definitional forces'. We are left, therefore, without any platform on which to stand, let alone any capacity to position ourselves securely. As a result, past constructions of sexuality may be even more difficult to grasp, either on their own terms, or on ours. Nonetheless there have been a number of attempts to provide explanatory models which posit defining moments in the history of sexuality. For Foucault, late nineteenth-century homosexuality was characterized (in 1870)

> less by a type of sexual relations than by a certain quality of sexual sensibility, a certain way of inverting the masculine and the feminine in oneself. Homosexuality appeared as one of the forms of sexuality when it was transposed from the practice of sodomy onto a kind of interior androgyny, a hermaphrodism of the soul. The sodomite had been a temporary aberration; the homosexual was now a species. (1990: 43)

For many critics the past merely offers alien constructions of sexuality rather than possible identifications and sympathetic, celebratory encounters. Katz draws one lesson from his history of sodomitical sin: 'that the distant past has only a negative, contrasting relation to the present; our own contemporary social organization of sex is as historically specific as past social-sexual forms. Studying the past, seeing the essential differences between past and present social forms of sex, we may gain a fresh perspective on our own sex as socially made, not naturally given' (1994: 58). Following on from Foucault, some theories have explored how sodomy, for instance, was largely determined by civil or canonical codes. For Foucault, 'sodomy was a category of forbidden acts; their perpetrator was nothing more than the juridical subject of them' (43); for Cohen the early modern period saw the creation of 'a juridical space within which popular representations of "the homosexual" could be legitimately written in late Victorian Britain' (1989: 184). For Foucault, the nineteenth century saw the emergence of the homosexual as 'a personage, a past, a case history, and a childhood in addition to being a type of life, a life form, and a morphology, with an indiscreet anatomy and possibly a mysterious physiology. Nothing that went into his total composition was unaffected by his sexuality' (43). The model may be disputed in its details, but there is also the more general problem discerned by Eve Kosofsky Sedgwick that 'one model of same-sex relations is superseded by another, which may again be superseded by another. In each case the superseded model then drops out of the frame of analysis' (47).

Before the seventeenth century, sodomy was not even precisely differentiated from its demonic associations with werewolves, heretics, sorcerers, and the like. Increasingly, however, it came to be linked with pride, excess of diet, idleness, and contempt of the poor. Yet the moral charge served to attack both the individual and that of which he was a part. As Alan Bray notes, 'It was the Court – the extravagant, overblown, parasitic Renaissance court – not homosexuality which was the focus of their attention. What homosexuality provided was a powerfully damaging charge to lay against it; at what should have been the stronghold of the kingdom, there was only weakness, confusion, and disorder' (1988: 37). Yet there were shifts in the specific positioning of sodomy with respect to the sense of what constituted sin and crime at the end of the eighteenth century. Transgressive categories had to be rethought; as Cohen notes, the relationship between sin and the crime itself was problematized (1989: 192). Moral supervision could not be supplied adequately by the Church, and that vacuum was filled by the societies for the reformation of manners. Cohen argues that these were 'instrumental in propagating a new technology for moral enforcement and in attaching this technology to the exercise of the state' (194). Towards the end of the eighteenth century there was a shift from the notion of an offence against the 'spiritual aspect of man' to a violation against the person. By the nineteenth century sodomy is not to be mentioned because it violates certain standards of 'decency' (198–200). Cohen concludes that by 1885, 'This metonymic slide from the act to the actor can be seen to have subsumed the moralistic (knowledge) effects emerging from earlier interpretations of sodomy in defence of a normative familial ideology' (203). Starting in the seventeenth century, Randolph Trumbach (1990), has argued that in 1670 sodomy was

> the province of the abandoned rake, who was also likely to be a libertine in religion and a republican in politics. The rake always took the active (or penetrator's) role in sodomy; his passive partner was a younger, late adolescent male. But the rake was also quite sexually interested in women and was in no way effeminate in behaviour or dress. (105)

Effeminacy, on the other hand, was associated with the fop. He was aroused by women but was not a sodomite. By 1710 Trumbach discerns the emergence of the effeminate sodomite or 'molly'. This shows 'the transition from one kind of sodomy to another, and from one gender system to another' (106–7). In this regard, the issue of class has become central to the analysis. As Thomas A. King remarks,

> in creating homosexuality as a non-identity ... the bourgeoisie were casting off onto the concept of homosexuality all the traits associated with the obsolete aristocrats – not only sodomy, but also arbitrariness, excessiveness, and, most emphatically, social impotency. For this reason, what was most bothersome about newly visible sodomites like the mollies was that they occupied this no-place, this lack, mimetically, as the basis of improvisations within an increasingly normative society. (1994: 40)

Elsewhere Trumbach has defined the 'molly' as an 'adult passive transvestite effeminate male' (1991: 112). Lately he has begun to explore how the reorganization of gender roles affected women. For Trumbach, 'women continued to be given legitimate feminine status more because of their sexual relations with men than because of their avoidance of sex with women' (1991: 113). Sexual relations between women were not covered by sodomy statutes and therefore 'the variety of sexual acts in which human bodies might engage guaranteed that there were four genders, two of them legitimated, and two stigmatized' (135). Accordingly, lesbian relationships emerge later than male same-sex relations: 'the sapphist role began slowly after mid-century, and could be seen enacted very clearly by some individuals in the last quarter of the century' (114). Trumbach's theory largely underestimates many texts which might be thought to suggest lesbian character-istics, or at least to problematize stable notions of sex, sexuality and gender. For Trumbach, finally, 'the majority of women who had sexual relations with women – and they must have been a very small libertine minority of all women – did not cross dress, and did not even take on masculine airs' (125).

The work of Eve Kosofsky Segwick may serve to stimulate a less systematic approach; surely, she argues, it would be sensible to work from 'the relation enabled by the unrationalized coexistence of different models during the times they do exist' (47). An accommodating strategy is offered by Emma Donoghue. Lesbianism, like male acts of sodomy was often constructed in terms of a diversity of transgressive or problematic associations. For Donoghue, 'the suspicious characteristics seem ... to have included spinsterhood, aristocracy, crossdressing or mannish style, general sexual looseness and a theatrical or artistic career' (1993: 19). But she begins her study with a sensible caveat: 'Lesbian historians can exhaust themselves looking for lesbian equivalents to particular aspects of gay history, for example sodomy trials or an early urban bar culture' (9). Donoghue discusses the literature of romantic friendship, building on the work of Lillian Faderman's *Surpassing the Love of Men* (1981), but she is considerably more expansive in the materials offered as constructions of female same-sex relations. She offers her book as 'a history not of facts but of texts, not of real women but of stories told about women, stories which reflected and formed both attitudes to lesbian culture and lesbian culture itself' (12–13). Although gender is central to her study she sees 'same-sex desire as disrupting the conventions of femininity rather than denying womanhood itself' (22). She shares with Martha Vicinus the view that lesbian history may be discontinuous and strange to the modern reader; we may not find heroines who naturally fit our modern views. Donoghue's manner of writing, and of research, carefully distances itself from phallocentric priorities and procedures: 'The researcher is not so much penetrating the past to find what she wants as making contact with it, touching the surface of her present interests to the details of the past; the more she touches, the more she will become sensitized to the nuances she is exploring. This friction between centuries can bring us a sense of intimacy with our foresisters, as well as great pleasure, and laughter when things fail to fit' (24).

The contours of the historical debate are now much clearer, and we can be self-conscious about the uses of history. For Cohen, 'what appears to be at stake in the historiographic debates about homosexuality is how we ought to comprehend the limits of its effectiveness for organizing our own engagement with and experience of the current historical moment.' (1989: 211). Jeffrey Weeks provides a number of approaches to history. As a 'lesson', it 'assumes a transparent and homogeneous past whose warnings can simply be read off. Unfortunately, "history" never moves along a single tramline'; as 'exhortation' ... 'the adjuration of the class, or nation, or gender, or oppressed minority to listen to its past, to find in its buried glories the moral example and histories of resistance to give us strength in our present difficulties'; as 'politics' history is used 'to provide a historical perspective on political decisions, and to see the present as historical' (9–10).

In one sense this sourcebook begins from Stallybrass and White's conclusion that 'Each place within the social ensemble is a particular site of production of discourse, a specific semantic field, but each domain in turn can easily be reconstructed within the terms of other domains and according to the hierarchies and ranks governing the social formation as a whole' (1986: 194). The statement serves as a useful programme for reading the sourcebook; extracts have been arranged and divided up, but an adequate and imaginative reading involves a series of intertextual interventions in which histories become stories, fabrications and reconstructions in lively debate with, and around, 'dominant' hetero-sexualities.

The majority of the extracts deploy notions of secrecy and openness. As I noted, this serves to position reader, writer and text in complex and often contradictory ways. Moving beyond Stallybrass and White's history of the 'low' I would argue that we have to negotiate a notion of the 'monstrosity' of the subject matter. In this regard the monster could be taken in a strictly etymological sense as that which is shown (Latin *monstrare*, to show). But the monster was also a warning, a portent of things to come. It properly belonged in the category of the preternatural, somewhere between the natural and the supernatural, as that which remains, the unexplained. Yet monsters are also still within nature, they are products of Nature's playfulness. She tires of the exhausting, repetitive injunction rigidly to repeat the same forms; she therefore plays in her creation, producing monsters (sports of nature). For the early scientists such as Bacon, the observation and explanation of nature's secret and sportive pathways is offered as the prerequisite for progress. Yet these secret observations lead into the social and cultural as art competes with nature in the production of forms, behaviour and relations not previously opened out. Moreover, secrecy is important on the way to individuation. As Russel Meares has noted, 'The attainment of the concept of secrecy brings another major change in relating to others ... The child begins to know that secrets are disclosed in a developing dialogue with others who can be trusted to share and respect them' (1993: 14).

One aim of this volume is to provide a range of texts that supply a sense of the diversity of thinking about sexuality in the seventeenth and eighteenth centuries. G.S. Rousseau has noted that homosexuality 'created a rich literary heritage in the Enlightenment, the omission of which renders serious discussion of sexuality primitive' (1985: 133). Although he admits that 'The literary record may ultimately prove a slippery handle to unlock the mysteries of gender stereotypification and societal repression' (133), he concludes that 'literature broadly conceived ... remains one of the most sensitive barometers – however inaccurate its measurements and distorted its antennae – of the climate of opinion and feeling in an age' (161). A variety of literary figures, major and minor, remain to be reclaimed and acclaimed in terms of a transgressive sexuality. Nor can we ignore the European dimension; David Foxon has stated that 'it becomes clear that the English were very well aware of the outburst of erotic writing that took place on the continent in the mid-17th century, were quick to import and naturalize it in England, and ran the risk of successful prosecution in doing so' (1963a: 22). The extent to which these texts were owned, distributed and read still requires detailed research, and is further problematized by the way we should position ourselves to them in our own time. A sexuality sourcebook for this period must, to a large extent, work as a satire on the object of its knowledge, given the lack of affirmative self-representations. Deciding which readings of the documents included here were open to the individual at the time is just as difficult to establish as knowing which we may import, and clarify, from contemporary theory. To what extent, if any, did the seventeenth- or eighteenth-century reader come to these texts with our sense of their social or institutional constructedness? Twentieth-century readings become deeply hypothetical and parenthetic; the records and reports of people who experienced a difference from heterosexuality is very different from our own, and may shift again as our own views shift. The discourse of effeminacy has not disappeared from gay lifestyles; camp is being reclaimed (and reconstructed); reassignments of sex continues to excite curiosity, but these do not have precisely the same placing as eunuchs and hermaphrodites in the earlier period. Similarly, the role of effeminacy was not necessarily positioned then as it is now in terms of other discourses and debates. As previously noted, reproduction as the ultimate ground and goal of sex, identity, and futurity was not so settled an assumption as it might first seem. Theological absolutes are not necessarily challenged by direct opposition, so much as by the interference and intervention of a range of discourses of the artificial, the exotic, the monstrous, the status and power of which is difficult to assess, given the variety of readers of these texts and the different reasons for their acts of reading. Some texts worked in the world of the imaginary, of the fantastic, in a distant, corrupt pagan past, but these frameworks need not demolish their multiple challenges to orthodoxy. Texts could be censured or censored, but illegalities also served as sites for the construction of different identities. Revealing and concealing the diversity of desire is everywhere manifested in the texts included in this sourcebook. This is, in a sense, a documentary sourcebook from behind; like the many writers included, the compilation and the reading of this book necessitates peeping through curtains and turning back sheets. Deconstructing what we think we see may well involve reconstructing ourselves in surprising and unanticipated ways.

1 ANATOMIES

Introduction

The interest in secret anatomy, masquerading often as medical literature, cannot be separated from the erotic nature of the material which could be exploited and marketed. The renewed interest in anatomy at the end of the seventeenth century was reflected in the progress and discourse of science. Yet this very discourse was in itself gendered; it was not uncommon (in a metaphor that goes back to Francis Bacon) to construct Nature as a female whose clothes must be torn away in order to uncover her most secret operations. The tearing away of the veil of disguise (with an undercurrent of violent unmasking) served to heighten desire for the erotic other; it was also a device designed to insulate and reinforce the novelty of the subject matter, protecting the author's soundness as a privileged narrator. The anticipation of possible censure partly served as a procedure to advertise the erotic material by pointing to its possible prohibition.

Explanations for anatomical defects are given as the excess of seed, the woman's imagination, divine punishment, the health or shape of the womb, melancholy and lechery. Bearing in mind Sedgwick's judgement that 'biologically based explanations for deviant behaviour ... are absolutely invariably couched in terms of "excess," "deficiency," or "imbalance" – whether in the hormones, in the genetic material, or, as is currently fashionable, in the fetal endocrine environment' (1990: 43) it can be seen how far modern debates have a source in the early discourse of monstrous sexuality. The monstrous body was never simply a body but a site for the circulation of a range of social, cultural and psychological narratives.

The heterogeneous variety of explanation and construction was especially evident in discussions of hermaphroditism. These relied heavily on the reproduction of earlier traditions of thought, chiefly patching them together, anthologizing them, with little attention to internal conflicts and contradictions in the material assembled. Yet classical texts spoke in a variety of voices. As sources of authority they could therefore be put to different uses, according to the whim of the commentator. Sexuality was already having its transgressive history written for it from a wide range of theories that stretched from the ancient past to the limits of the known world, across time and across space. The publications that discuss eunuchs also demonstrate that spatial or temporal displacements exotically complemented one another.

The investigation of hermaphrodites as grotesque digressions promoted a multi-layered discourse that later critics sought to simplify. James Parsons's *A Mechanical and Critical Enquiry into the Nature of Hermaphrodites* appeared in 1741 and George Arnaud's *A Dissertation on Hermaphrodites* in 1750. James Parsons argued simply that 'if there was not so absolute a law with respect to the being of only one sex in one body, we might then indeed expect to find every day many preposterous digressions from our present standard'. A discourse based on excess and lack was frequently deployed to encompass a range of phenomena; crucially, it also served as the framework for later taxonomies of sexuality. Such instances of anatomical excess and lack appeared in moments of nature's 'sportive-ness', resulting in the addition or subtraction of body-parts between the sexes. Important here was the notion of nature's boredom with the rigidities of the systematically worked out creations, existing merely to be replicated. Such boredom was relieved by fantastic invention which was the source of variety. But the value of nature as a normative system was in danger of invalidating itself by abdicating its own laws, running the risk of inconsistency. There was a profound respect for the authority of nature, yet there was a sense of awe at nature's capacity to move outside herself, contradicting her self-constituted identity by excursions into the unnatural. Another important point was that these monstrous disfigurations were enforced: they were not an act of choice or conscious self-fashioning. The proper response to them was therefore compassionate but also remedial, calling for correction and introducing (*naturalizing*) the professional duties of the surgeon. Despite being (in these terms) a sport of nature (*lusus naturae*), the hermaphrodite remained within the broader category of nature and must act according to her laws.

Much of the material was inherently homo-erotic and, like the pamphlets on sodomy, was effectively marketed by promoting an insider's knowledge of a secret world. These publications typically demonstrate an obsession with the phallus but also indicate a pressing fear of castration and social emasculation; they also express a heightened desire for the ambiguous category which results. Again, writers are primarily concerned with a slippage of categories in which the convenient binary opposition of male and female has broken down. Such material is generally concerned with the exotic 'Other', the aberration which paradoxically reinforces the normal. The exotic serves to emphasize cultural difference by anatomical means. As John Marten notes, 'The men of *Guinea* ... have a great *yard* [penis], much surpassing our countrymen, whereof they make great account.' The obsession with eunuchs perhaps reflected in a different fashion the need to define virility against its 'other'.

Degrees and Symptoms of the Venereal Disease

John Marten or Martin was a popular writer on medical matters and a quack doctor. Foxon notes that there was an early prosecution of the author 'being evil disposed and wickedly intending to corrupt the subjects of the Lady the Queene . . .' (1963a: 31). Much of the material was borrowed from earlier works by Sinibaldus's *Geneanthropeiae* (1642) and Venette's *Tableau de l'amour* (1687). Text from *A Treatise of all the Degrees and Symptoms of the Venereal Disease* (1708).

The *testicles* or *stones* are accounted among the principal parts of generation, and that justly; and though they are not necessary to the life of man, yet they are to the conservation of the *species*; and indeed by the loss of them a man receives very great prejudice, both as to the strength and activity of his body, and also as to the acuteness of his reason and understanding, as appears by *eunuchs*, who are not of such penetrating judgements, but more effeminate than those not castrated or gelt, and not so robust, hardy, masculine, or courageous.

In Herbert's *Travels*[1] it is said that most of the men of the Cape of Good Hope are *semi-eunuchs*, one *testicle* or *stone* being ever taken away by the nurse, either to distinguish them from ordinary men, or that Mistress Venus allure them not from Pallas.

How sheepish and womanish does a *castrated* man, deprived of his manly parts, appear? How dead and withered, cold in love affairs, beardless and effeminate, is he? Women shun his company, laugh at him, ridicule and deride him as not fit (indeed he is not) for their conversation and company; for those members are accounted, and not without reason, the principal and most pleasing members of the whole *microcosm* or body of man; (more especially by the women kind) a man of a squeaking voice, without a beard, is ashamed of himself, because taken notice of by the women, for women like not effeminate faces, though otherwise perhaps well provided, but when a man is deficient below stairs, how wretchedly disgraceful is he?

The *yard* or *penis* is a peculiar instrument whereby to convey the *seed* . . . into the *womb* of the women, as also to convey the urine out of the bladder. I need not stand here to tell where it is placed, or to set forth the various names invented by lascivious persons, neither give a description of it, as to its thickness or length, only that it differs much in divers men, and in short men, and those given much to venery,[2] it is generally observed to be larger than in others; I say I need not set forth those matters here, but it is necessary to observe that it is neither boney, as in *dog, fox, wolf*; nor *grisly*, nor *fleshy*, but that it is framed of a peculiar substance . . .

The men of Guinea . . . have a great *yard*, much surpassing our countrymen, whereof they make great account, and although it varies much according to the race of families, and course of life, yet frequent *coition*[3] very much contributes to its length, and magnitude; but sometimes, it being beyond the ordinary length and bigness, is attended with some inconvenience; for the magnitude, grossness, foulness and too great length is a hindrance to fruitfulness.

Sir John Mandville in his *Travels*[4] ... tells us that in the Isle of Hermes the men's members hang down to their shanks, insomuch that they are obliged (those of them that know better manners) to bind them straight and anoint them with ointments made there for to hold them up, whereby they may live more civilly. The reason, says he, of these dilated members, are supposed to be by the reason of the heat of the climate dissolving the body.

Ctesias[5] reports and *Martial*[6] alludes to the same, that the ancients, to prevent young effeminate *Inamorato's*,[7] especially *Comoedians*, from using untimely *venery*, and breaking their voices, were wont to fasten a ring or buckle on the fore-skin of their *yards*.

Concerning this art of infibulation,[8] or buttoning up the *prepuce*[9] with a brass or silver button both sides of the glans, a kind of rational invention, it was borrowed, I suppose from the Egyptians or Arabians ... There are some among them, who, by a serious vow of chastity, would gain and preserve an estimate of purity, and in that portion of their foreskin, reserved after their circumcision, being bored through, do wear a huge unmeasurable great ring.

The milder sort of cannibals, who inhabit beyond the Tropic of Capricorn, not only bore their lips and ears to put in ornaments, but in their abominable pride, and boldness, they pierce their genitals, to adorn them outwardly with most precious stones. But enough of these absurd foolish customs.

Nature seems not so wanton in any part of her works as in the make of the *yard*, especially the *prepuce*, because there seems to be no necessity for it: in some it is very troublesome, from hence perhaps arose the necessity of circumcision so generally practised in all eastern parts of the world, as is among the Jews to this day. History tells us the Egyptians were the first that circumcised their *virilities*, and said they did it more for cleanness than any thing else ... Moses Aegyptius says, that circumcision helpeth to bridle and restrain inordinate lust, and concupiscence[10] of the flesh; but the contrary doth appear, for no nation is more given to carnal lust than the Egyptians, Saracus and Turks, that are circumcised; and that the Egyptians and other nations did adore that part, and make an idol of it, under the name of *Priapus*,[11] and did carry it about in open show in their wicked idolatrous solemnities.

I have read that the Turks, Persians, and most oriental nations, use *opium* to force or stimulate venery, though I don't think it so much to invigorate them to the act, as to prolong the act, and spin out the motions of carnality, lengthening the titillation of lust, as opium will do in some, there being some luxurious lechers that think nature too sudden in the evacuation of the semen.

The *clitoris* ... is sinewy, of a hard substance, in form much resembling the *yard* of a man, from that with two pairs of muscles, and suffers *erection*, and falling as that doth; and is that which causeth lust in women, and gives delight in the act of copulation; for without this, a woman never desires copulation, or hath pleasure in it, or conceives by it. In some women, especially those that are very lustful, it is so vastly extended, that it hangs out of the passage externally, and so much resembles the yard of a man, that by some they have been called *Fricatrices*,[12] and accounted *Hermaphrodites*, and we have read that such have been able to perform the actions of a man: but however it is, this is certain: that the bigger the *clitoris* in women, the more lustful they are, and even so salacious, as sometimes especially, as scarcely to be satisfied by several men; for which their lascivious temper, in Creophagi in Arabia, I have read they circumcise them ...

Many women also in Ethiopia and other places, have suffered themselves to be circumcised, or cut, the part being over-great and exceeding its natural bigness, led to it by this reason: that as men have a *prepuce*, so women after the same manner have a *glandulous* flesh in their *genitals*, not unfit to be circumcised. And that the women of the *Cape of Good Hope* do the same for *ornament*, and some upon a religious account ...

Though by the way, I believe in some countries there are *Hermaphrodites*, and we read that in Florida and Virginia, there are a nation of them, which have the generative parts of both sexes ... but it seems they are a people that are hated by the very Indians, and by them made servile, to carry burdens, and do offices instead of beasts, they being very strong, and able-bodied. For an *hermaphrodite* is looked upon as a creature of vile deformity, bringing a shame upon both sexes; and in olden times wherever found, were either drowned or made away with, such amphibious creatures being by them not thought fit to live.

Beyond the Nasamones, and about Matchlies, there are ordinarily found hermaphrodites which so much resemble both sexes, *male* and *female*, they have carnal knowledge one of another, interchangeably by turns ... [A]n *hermaphrodite* who was accounted for a woman, and was married to a man ... bore some sons and daughters notwithstanding was wont to lie with the maids and get them with child.

I have read of a remarkable account of an *hermaphrodite*, in a certain city of Scotland, that went for a maid, yet got her master's daughter with child, who lay in the same bed with her; she was accused of the fact in the year 1461, found capable, convicted and condemned before the judges, and suffered death, by being put in the ground alive.

Women have *testicles* or *stones*, as have the men; but they differ from men, first, as to the place, they being within the belly of the woman, but without in man,[13] secondly, in magnitude; for they are less in women than in men, thirdly; in form, for they are uneven in women, but are smooth in men. Fourthly, they are depressed or flattish in women, but oval in men, and also are more soft than men's are: their use is the same that they are in men ...

I have heard of women's being *castrated*, as well as men; and that Andramistes, the King of Lydia, was the first that made women *eunuchs*, after whose example the women of Egypt were sometimes *spaded*.[14]

The end of *spading* women might be the same as *castrating* men, in order to rend them *sterile*, and consequently they envy others; though many, as history tells us, did it or suffered it to be done to abate their undaunted *lusts*, and some in order to prolong their youth, and that they might also perpetually use and enjoy their health, in a flourishing condition of body.

A Treatise of Hermaphrodites

The author vacillates between the innocence of his text and a sense that it might encourage same-sexual relations. On one level he provides an 'innocent entertainment'; on another he is a voyeuristic, titillated participant in what he describes. Sometimes he argues that women may participate in an equal pleasure; elsewhere female hermaphrodites 'can give as much pleasure as men do, but cannot receive in any proportion the pleasure themselves'. In another section of the *Treatise* we encounter Diana and Isabella who appear to be bisexuals rather than *tribades*. Text from *Tractatus de Hermaphroditis: Or, a treatise of Hermaphrodites* ... (1718). Attributed to Giles Jacob. The text was published as *A Treatise of Hermaphrodites* (1718) with John Henry Meibomius's *A Treatise of the Use of Flogging in Venereal Affairs*. See Donoghue (1993: 25–58); Jones and Stallybrass (1991: 80–111); Shapiro (1987); Friedli (1987).

My design in the following sheets is merely as an innocent entertainment for all curious persons, without any views of inciting masculine-females to amorous trials with their own sex; and I am persuaded there will not be one single HERMAPHRODITE the more in the world, on account of the publishing this TREATISE.

It may be expected by some faithless persons, that I should produce an HERMAPHRODITE to public view, as an incontestable justification of there being creatures of this kind; but as I have not authority to take up the petticoats of any female without her consent, I hope to be excused from making such demonstrable proofs; and if I had such a power, the sight might endanger the welfare of some pregnant female, whose curiosity would spur her to a particular examination.

THE intrigues of my HERMAPHRODITES are indeed very amazing, and as monstrous as their natures; but that many lascivious females divert themselves one with another at this time in the city, is not to be doubted: and if any persons shall presume to censure my accounts, grounded on probability of truth, I shall be sufficiently revenged in proclaiming them, what my HERMAPHRODITES are found to be in the conclusion – Old Women.

I confess, all histories of extraordinary conceptions from these intrigues, or by women without actual copulation, are equally fabulous with those of the engendering of men: it would be as surprising to find a man with a teeming belly, as to see a woman increase there merely by her own applications.

I doubt but this small TREATISE may put some persons upon a previous examination of robust females, that they may be at a certainty with respect to mutual enjoyment; but I would not have them rashly conclude from large appurtenances only, that they are unnatural, but on the contrary, agreeable companions.

To conclude, I fear not the censure of HERMAPHRODITES, nor of those that would be such to satisfy their vicious inclinations; neither am I under any apprehensions from the censure of our reforming zealots.

I doubt not but there are many persons in the world of both species, particularly of the female sex, who would willingly assume to themselves the parts belonging to hermaphrodites, if they could have a vigorous use of the members of both sexes, upon any lustful inclination; a lascivious female would be transported at the thoughts of acting the part of a man in the amorous adventure, and a lecherous male would propose equal pleasure in receiving the embraces he used to bestow; but though most persons agree that women have the greatest sense of enjoyment in the act of copulation (as without all question they must, by the situation and disposition of the parts), yet they would be more forward in satisfying this brutal curiosity than those of the opposite sex. Men are more easy to be limited in the pleasures of Venus than women; as they are endued with more reason, so they are generally easily satisfied in those enjoyments, which were chiefly designed for the propagating of their species.

Intrigues of hermaphrodites and masculine females

The hotter the climate, the stronger the inclinations to venery. When I was formerly in Italy, there happened a notable adventure in the neighbourhood of Rome, between a certain Lady called Margureta, one of a noble family in the Papal Dominions, and a lady of France, whose name was Barbarissa: these two females were in their statures very near equal to the largest sized male; they had full and rough faces, large shoulders, hands and feet, and but slender hips, and small breasts: in short, they resembled men in all respects, but their dresses, their gaits[15] and voices, and indeed they were suspected to be hermaphrodites. These Ladies, I am informed, paid frequent visits to each other, and 'twas always observed, that nobody was admitted to their splendid entertainments, which heightened the curiosity of a servant in the family of Margureta to attempt a discovery of their intrigues, they always locking themselves in, the moment they had dispatched their suppers: in order to this, on a time, this servant, called Nicolini, with a piercing instrument of iron, and the assistance of an artificer, ingeniously made a communication for the sight into the next room, by working a small hole through the wainscot, opposite to the bed, in the chamber wherein the two masculine Ladies accustomed to solace themselves. At the next meeting, Nicolini, to his no small surprise, had a prospect of the two females embracing each other, with a succession of kisses, of no short duration. After this they both drew up their petticoats, and, exposing their thighs to view, they mutually employed their hands with each other, in the same manner, and with the same force of inclination, as a juvenile gallant would make his approaches to what he most admires in a beautiful Belinda, at the same time continuing the closest salutations; at last one of the females threw herself down upon the bed, and displaying herself commodiously, the other immediately begun the amorous adventure, covering her companion so effectually, that Nicolini could not possibly discover any farther particulars: they had not continued their sportings long before Margureta, which officiated now instead of the man, arose from Barbarissa, and turning towards the window with her clothes up in her arms, Nicolini immediately discovered something hang down from her body of a reddish colour, and which was very unusual: they both panting, and almost breathless, retired from the bed to a table, where they sat down and refreshed themselves with sufficient quantities of generous wine. About an hour after this, they began to renew their frolics, and it being Barbarissa's turn to caress, who was not so masculine as Margureta, to incite the falling down and erection of her female member, she turned over a large book, amply stored with obscene portraitures, wherein the amorous combat was curiously described in the utmost variety of postures which were ever practised, or the head of a youthful and ingenious painter could invent; but this not having the effect expected, Margureta stripped herself naked, as did likewise Barbarissa, and both dancing about the room, they gave each other repeated strokes with their hands on their white posteriors; and this likewise failing to move Barbarissa, Margureta opened a cabinet, and taking from thence a large birchen rod, she flogged Barbarissa lustily, her buttocks seeming to yield that amorous discipline; upon this, something appeared from the privities of Barbarissa, like unto what

Nicolini had observed of Margureta, and they instantly put on their loose gowns, and ran to the bed, where Barbarissa embracing her companion, did her work effectually. After their sportings were over, that each had returned the favours received, they decently dressed themselves, and sat them down again to the table, where, after drinking a bottle or two of the richest Italian wines, they kissed each other in the most loving manner, and Margureta rang the bell for Nicolini to light Barbarissa downstairs, who immediately taking leave of Margureta, was carried in a chair to her place of residence.

The story sufficiently shows the unnatural intrigues of some masculine females, where by the falling down and largeness of the clitoris, they have been taken for men, as mentioned in my descriptions of the hermaphrodites, and are capable of every action belonging to a man, but that of ejaculation.

Eunuchism Displayed

The text was partly a satire on the fashion for castrated opera singers; it also explores the legal question of marriage; the nature of manhood; the history of eunuchs. A vast array of sources is used, together with a range of stories and contrasted points of view. Text from *Eunuchism Display'd, Describing all the different sorts of Eunuchs etc.* (1718) by Charles Ollincan or Ancillon. Originally published as *Traité des Eunuques* (1707).

The motives that engaged me to write the ensuing treatise were very singular. It is not long since we saw several Italian eunuchs (Masters of Music) who made a very great figure, as they might very well do, getting such considerable sums of money from those who they could not have imagined were endued with so little reflection, till they had happily experienced it.

These unexpected favours puffed them up with a vanity which is ever peculiar to eunuchs, and some of them had got it into their heads that truly the ladies were in love with them, and fondly flattered themselves with mighty conquests. But alas! our ladies have not so little natural philosophy but they know how to make a just distinction, and have too fine a gout to be satisfied with mere shadow and outside.

But notwithstanding ... it is certain there has been an exception to the general rule, for one of these singers, it seems, with his fine songs and address, had so far engaged a young LADY of a considerable fortune that she began to yield to propositions of marriage, which the Signor had the modesty to make to her, and who probably might have carried his point, had it not been happily prevented by the care and vigilance of a relation, whose quick judgement and penetration soon discovered that affair. He communicated the matter to me, and desired I would give him what assistance I could in writing, which he might make use of, from time to time, as occasion should offer, to hinder what both he and his lady called such a marriage which could not but be attended with dismal consequences.

It is somewhat difficult, I must confess, to talk of eunuchs, without saying something that may shock the modesty of the fair sex ... and in respect of the ladies, such care is taken, that when any thing must be expressed freely, and in its natural terms, it is always in Latin, a language they are generally unacquainted with.

Marriage being the gift of God, and his work who has united thereby two sexes, and who considering that it was not good that man should be alone, gave him a helpmeet, and commanded them both to increase and multiply, and imprinted in them an eager desire to unite themselves together for the propagation of their species. This union therefore ought by no means to be casual or in common, like that of beasts (which have no understanding). But it ought to be a conjunction, chaste, religious and holy, full of piety and heavenly benediction, having for its end only to execute the command of God, who is its author and protector.

Now what I propose in this treatise is to see amongst what kind or sort of marriages we must place those of eunuchs. This then is the general plan I design to follow, to make a full ecclaircissement (as the French call it in this matter) and regulate it by a decision certain and incontestable. This treatise then shall be divided into three parts.

1   In the first, I shall examine what an *eunuch* is, and how many sorts of eunuchs there are, what rank they have held, and do now hold in ecclesiastical and civil society, and what consideration men have had, and actually now have for them.

2   In the second, I shall examine what right they have to marry and whether they ought to be suffered to enter into that state? And,

3   In the third, I shall endeavour to solve all difficulties and objections which can be brought against those maxims and decisions I have advanced and established in this treatise.

It is now above 4000 years since mention was first made of eunuchs in the world; both sacred and profane history take notice of an infinity of these sort of people, which were looked upon by the ancients to be neither men nor women, but were called a third sort of men; *Tertia Hominum Species*: which, bating the unphilosophicalness of the expression, gives us no ill idea of the value and esteem people had for eunuchs in former times. We have heard mention made of great numbers in all ages, and in all countries, and therefore we have no reason to doubt that there have been such people in the world, and that there are to this very day.

Most of the learned believe, that *Semiramis* Queen of the Assyrians[16] ... was the first that introduced this kind of mutilation; and they ground their opinion on the authority of *Ammianus Marcellinus*[17] [who] gives us to understand that there were multitudes of eunuchs in her time, that they looked pale and wan and deformed, all their features and lineaments distorted, and that when ever any one went abroad, and saw whole herds of these mutilated and maimed wretches, he could not but detest the memory of *Semiramis*, that old Queen, who first of all made young boys undergo castration.

Others say[18] that she dressed herself in man's clothes and brought her son up like a girl, on purpose, least the Assyrians grown ashamed of being governed by a woman, might set her son upon the throne to her prejudice. Others, somewhat differing in opinion, will have it that her son being the same size, and having a voice exactly like her own, she put herself in man's clothes; and to secure herself the government, gave it out that she was the son to Ninus and not his widow.

Diodorus Siculus[19] reports ... that this Queen ... abandoned herself to all manner of pleasures, and made choice of the handsomest and best-proportioned men of her army to serve her, but that all those who were admitted to her bed, were afterwards put to death by her order. But it is more probable she had them made eunuchs through an effect of jealousy, least after having received from her the greatest favours, they should go and have engagements with other women.

Vossius[20] is of the opinion that the Persians were the inventors of this wicked and detestable custom, and that the Latin word *spade*, which comprehends several sorts of eunuchs, was taken from a village of Persia called *Spada*, where he fancies the first execution of this nature was made ... I shall only say, that the first eunuch mentioned in the holy scriptures was Patiphor ... who bought Joseph from the Midianites ... and it is observed ... that Nebuchadnezzar caused all the Jews, and all other prisoners of war, to be gelt or cut, that he might have none to attend him in his private service but eunuchs.

Lucian[21] in his dialogue of *Eunuchs* gives a very short definition of them. He says that an eunuch is neither male nor female, but a prodigy in nature. This definition of Lucian is too general, it ought to have been more exact, that it might have given us a particular notion or idea of what he designed to define. Let us see if we can give a better.

An eunuch is a person which has not the faculty or power of generation. In short, eunuchs are such *qui generare non possunt*, as the civil law expresses it. Such who can by no means propagate and generate, who have a squeaking languishing voice, a womanish complexion, and a soft down for a beard, who have no courage or bravery of soul, but ever timorous and fearful: in a few words, whose ways, manners and customs are entirely effeminate.

But if an eunuch was thought to be such a wretched despicable thing, in regard of his body, much more was he in respect of his mind. Let us see what St *Basil* in the primitive church thought of eunuchs:

> If you want witnesses (says he), do not produce slaves or miserable eunuchs, an abominable tribe, who are past sense of honour, who are neither men nor women, whom the love of sex has rendered mad or furious. They are jealous, despicable, fierce, effeminate, gluttons, covetous, cruel, inconstant, suspicious, furious, insatiable. They cry (like children) if they are left out of an entertainment; and to say all in one word, they are condemned to the knife as soon as born, and from such crooked wretches must we expect an upright mind? The knife indeed has made them chaste, but this chastity is of no service to them, their lust makes them furious, which yet is impotent, sterile and unfruitful.

Perhaps this description may be thought to be too sharp and satirical, as proceeding from a person who was highly angered and provoked, and consequently ought to be suspected; but I shall instance one, whose testimony can by no means be liable to suspicion, being a person entirely disinterested, who not only confirms this description, but also adds new circumstances which make eunuchs yet more frightful and horrid, and this is Ammianus Marcellinus, who says 'That when Numa Pompilius, and Socrates said anything that was good of an eunuch, nobody believed them, for they thought they told nothing but a company of lies.' ... One may say of eunuchs the same that is usually said of bastards: that for the most part they are very bad, but that sometimes we may chance to find one that may prove good for something. And as Ammianus Marcellinus says ... Roses grow amongst thorns, and some wild beasts grow tame.

How many different sorts of eunuch there are

According to St Matthew's gospel ... there are some eunuchs which are so born from their mother's womb; and there are some eunuchs which were made eunuchs of men; and there be eunuchs which made themselves eunuchs for the kingdom of heaven's sake. But the subtlety of men's wits, by reason of later events, have found out more particular distinctions than our Blessed Saviour was pleased to make use of. There have been found to be different sorts or species of eunuchs ...

I   The first is those which are born so, and these are *absolutely* and properly eunuchs.

2   The second is those who either by force, or by their own consent, or with their own hands have been despoiled of all that which makes man and his virility; so that they are incapable of doing any act, and are obliged to let their urine pass through a pipe of metal, which they apply to the place of that which nature had given them, and is since cut off; and this section sometimes happened to people on account of some distemper, which obliged the surgeon to perform this melancholy and dismal operation . . . But this sort of mutilation was not only practised in cases of necessity (as in distempers otherwise incurable) but also on persons of sound health, as we shall see by and by, and was heretofore one of the functions of a surgeon.

3   The third class is of those whose testicles by a detestable art have been made so frigid as at last quite to disappear and vanish. This is done by cutting the vein that conveyed their proper aliment and support, which makes them grow lank and flabby, till at least they actually dry up and come to nothing. Sometimes they used to give a certain quantity of *opium* to the persons designed for castration, whom they cut while they were in dead sleep, and took from them those parts which nature took so great care to form; but it was observed that most of those that had been cut after this manner died by this narcotic.

4   The fourth class is those that are called *spadones*, who are born with such ill disposition of parts, or of so cold and frigid a temperament, or who have been rendered so through some misfortune, that they are incapable of generation.

There were besides these, others who were called eunuchs in a figurative sense, inasmuch as they kept themselves entirely chaste, and made no more use of their parts of virility, than as if they really had none, as we may believe has been sincerely practised by some, both of the Latin and Greek church, and which likewise may be charitably supposed of some of the fellows of both our universities.[22]

Of eunuchs that are born so

I am very well persuaded that it is not impossible but certain human creatures may come into the world destitute of those parts which are proper for generation. We see every day children born, some without their eyes, ears, hands, or some other part of their body; and therefore it may possibly happen that some may be born without those parts I just now mentioned.

Nature which every day produces so many monsters might very well form one of this sort. I know the naturalists say that there never yet has been an example of this kind; and in reality, *Pliny*,[23] who recounts so exactly, and so fully, such a vast number of monstrous human figures, which have been produced all the world over, makes no mention of such as I have mentioned.

However, I can truly say, I saw one, and perhaps it has been seen all over Europe; for the parents of this creature, having observed that the public would be pleased with such a singular piece of curiosity, and that thereby they might get considerable sums of money by showing it about from place to place, and from one country to another, I do not doubt but accordingly they carried it to all the principal parts of Europe.

When I saw it, it was at Berlin, in the year 1704. He was one of those cripples whom the French call un cu de jatte, and we in English have no name for, and was carried in a box upon a man's back; but with this difference: that those whom the French call by that name have neither legs nor thighs that they can make any use of, but draw themselves along upon their backside in a kind of wooden bowl-dish or platter; this that I am now speaking of had no back-side at all, that is, no hips or buttocks. His head was well fashioned, his face sweet and pleasant, of a brown complexion, and his hair chestnut; and though he was then above 20 years of age, yet had no manner of beard, or the least sign he would have any. His arms and hands were very well proportioned, his body handsomely enough shaped; he was between 2 and 3 foot high, he supported himself on a kind of block of wood, or rather the trunk of a tree, and walked (if I may be allowed the expression) upon his hands. He had two passages, as other men have, for nature to discharge her excrements; that before was very small and short, and below it hung a kind of cod, or *scrotum*, very lank and flabby, in which I could find not so much as the least sign of a testicle. I informed myself very particularly of his parents if he was actually born so, and they seriously assured me he was absolutely and entirely so, as nature had formed him. Now as I know that we ought not always to judge ill of the virility of a man who has no visible testicles, because it sometimes happens that they remain higher up in the body, and do not come down by some obstacle or impediment which hinders their descent, those men nevertheless that are in this case ought not therefore presently to have their virility called in question, for it has often been found that such persons who have had those parts thus hidden have been as perfect as other men, and have had all the other necessary token to prove their manhood.

It was this reason that I more curiously and attentively examined this person, and, finding besides all the marks of a *real* eunuch, I had all the reason in the world to conclude he was so in effect, and that he was properly one of those eunuchs that in the language of the holy scripture *have been eunuchs from their mother's womb*.

This therefore is a plain proof (abstracting from revelation) that there have been eunuchs so born, whatever the naturalists say to the contrary. Christianity has had also her eunuchs, though much against her inclination, for the Christian church abhors and detests that abominable practice. However, it is certain that Valesius, a native of Arabia, began a sect, and he was far from believing that mutilation was an obstacle or impediment to the priesthood, according to the canons of the Council of Nice, that on the contrary, he maintained it absolutely necessary, and that a man ought not to exercise that change without it ...

A second motive that induced people to make eunuchs was that they might have fine voices, and which would be much longer preserved by castration.[24] *Macrobius*[25] gives very good reasons why eunuchs have fine voices ... and this is the chief end the Italians at this day propose to themselves in cutting young people. But without entering into those reasons of *Macrobius*, which are very long and tedious, I shall only say that I know it to be fact that there can be no finer voices in the world, and more delicate, than some eunuchs' ...

Others have been forced into *eunuchism* as a punishment for some crime; for it was a common practice to punish malefactors, either for desertion or mutiny in the army, or any notorious crime, with this sort of punishment, which they looked upon as a note or mark of the highest shame and infamy.

But besides, there have been likewise other motives, as raillery, resentment and insult; to prove which may be instanced a history, wherein is recounted a very particular case, which, because it is so unpleasant, I shall now relate it.

That history[26] tells us that in the reign of Henry 1st of France, 'In the wars between the Greeks and the Duke of Benevento, the Greeks treated the duke very ill. Theobald or Tibbald, Marquis of Spoleto, his ally, came to his assistance, and took several Greeks prisoners, whom he commanded to be castrated, and then sent back in that condition to the Greek general, and said they should tell him that he did it to oblige the emperor, who knew he had a very particular love for eunuchs, and that he would try very speedily if he could not make him a present of a greater number, the marquis resolved to keep his word, and, having several other prisoners, was one day going to execute that fatal resolution when there came a woman, whose husband was one of them, running through the camp and, crying most pitifully, begged she might speak to Theobald. The marquis having asked the reason of her sorrow, my lord, says she, I am astonished to think such a hero as you are should amuse your self in making war with poor women, now the men are not in a condition to resist you. Theobald replied, that since the time of the *Amazons*,[27] no one, as he ever heard, made war with women; my lord, says the Greek, can you wage a more cruel war against us than to deprive our husbands of that which gives us health, pleasure and children; when you do this, you make us, not them, eunuchs; you have for several days past taken away from us our baggage and cattle, and I never made any complaint, but (and then she looked very wistly at the marquis, says the history) the loss of those goods you have taken away from a great many women of my acquaintance being irreparable, I could not help coming to implore the compassion of a conqueror. This honest speech of the poor woman so well pleased the whole army that they not only gave her back her husband, but everything else that had been taken from her. But as she was going away, the marquis asked her what she would consent should be done to her husband in case he was found again in arms. He has eyes (says she hastily), a nose, hands and feet, these are his goods, and you may take them away from him if he deserves it, but if you please let that alone which belongs to me.

Others have been made eunuchs by way of reprisal or retaliation of which Herodotus[28] gives us a very curious example. 'Hermotimus, says he, a native of Pedasus, the most considerable amongst the eunuchs of Xerxes, of all men revenged himself the best of that injury, and which was after this manner. He had been taken prisoner, and soon after was sold to Panione, of the isle of Chio, who traded in eunuchs, and castrated all the beautiful boys he could purchase, to sell them afterwards at a good price in Ephesus and Sardis, because in those parts eunuchs were much esteemed on account of their honesty and fidelity, and the confidence that might be reported in them in all cases of moment whatsoever: now at this, Panione, who had bought Hermotimus, as I said before, made a livelihood of this execrable and infamous practice, he made him undergo the same fate with a great many others. But Hermotimus was not unhappy in all respects, for being sent to the King of Sardis, with other presents, he so well behaved himself in that court, that in time he grew much more in the good graces of that prince than any of the other eunuchs. When the king with his troop left Sardis, and was marching to Athens, Hermotimus was sent about some affair of consequence to Atarne, a place in Mystia, where he found Panione, whom he presently knew, and addressed himself to him with all the complaisance in the world, with the highest expressions of civility and testimonies of friendship. He told him first that 'twas to him he owed all his advancement and prosperity in the world; and then promised to show him all the marks of his esteem he had for him, and that he would in a very singular manner show his acknowledgement and gratitude for all the benefits he had received from him, and live in an apartment of his house. Panione permitted himself easily to be persuaded by this discourse, and very readily brought his wife and children along with him to accept favours of Hermotimus; but scarce had they entered the house when Hermotimus spoke to him in these unexpected words. O thou most wicked of all mankind: thou hast hitherto gained a livelihood by a commerce the most detestable in the world. What injury hast thou ever received from me, or my parents, thou, or any of thy family, that thou hast brought to this wretched, miserable condition, in which from being a man as I was I am now become neither man nor woman? Dost thou think the gods could not see thy actions? As they are full of justice and equity, thou infamous artisan of misery and wretchedness, so have they this day put into my power to proportion thy punishment to thy crimes. After he had thus reproached the most unhappy Panione, he commanded his four sons (he brought with him) to stand before him, and made him geld his own children, and when that was done, forced the children to do the same ungrateful office to their father. Such was the vengeance of Hermotimus, and such the punishment of Panione.

All the world knows the history of Combabus, it is in Lucian; but Monsieur Bayle has published it in his historical dictionary with all its circumstances. Combabus was a young lord at the court of the King of Syria, well skilled in architecture. He was pitched upon by that monarch to attend his queen, Stratonice, in a long voyage which she was obliged to make in order to build a temple to Juno, according to the directions she had received in a dream. Combabus was young and handsome, and had got in his head, that the king would infallibly entertain some jealousy against him that he would dispense with him from undertaking that employment, but when he saw he could by no means prevail, he looked upon himself as a dead man if he did not take such care in his conduct as might not give occasion for the least shadow of suspicion. He only then begged of the king that he would be pleased to allow him seven days to prepare for his journey, and this he did after this manner.

As soon as he came to his lodgings, he bewailed the wretchedness of his condition, which exposed him to this dismal alternative, either to lose his sex or his life; and after having fetched a few bitter sighs, he cut his secret parts, and, having embalmed them, sealed them up in a box. When the time came that he was to undertake his journey, he presented the box to the king, in the presence of a great number of courtiers, and begged his majesty that he would keep it for him till his return, and told him that there was in it what was more valuable than gold and silver, and was as dear to him as his life. The king put his seal upon the box, and gave it to the master of the wardrobe to take care of it. This journey of the queen's continued three years, and what Combabus imagined he foresaw really came to pass, and the event plainly justified his precaution.

This action of Combabus gave birth to other motives for eunuchism. His intimate friends gelt themselves to be companions of his disgrace, and to comfort him according to the old maxim that it is a comfort to the unfortunate to have companions or partakers of their misery.

> For tis a comfort which the wretched know
> T'have others, like themselves, deep plung'd in woe.

[Montaigne][29] tells us of a certain peasant in his neighbourhood that made himself an eunuch... for mere passion and anger against his wife; this good man, as soon as he came home, was received by his wife, who was jealous of him to an extravagance, and was continually tormenting him with the usual welcome, and said anything against him that came uppermost, and as her jealousy furnished her with malicious abuses, he made no more ado, but immediately, with his scythe that he then had in hand, whipped off those parts which gave her so much umbrage, and without any more ceremony threw them in the good woman's face.[30]

[It] appears, both in sacred and profane history, that eunuchs have possessed the highest employments and offices in courts, and have had the ear and favour of their respective princes. I shall content myself with a few examples.

I shall say nothing of those odious motives which induced princes heretofore to be in love with eunuchs. All the world knows the history of Sporus, whom Nero caused to be gelt, and whose folly was so extravagant that he endeavoured to change his sex; he made him wear woman's clothes, and afterwards married him with the usual formalities, settled a dowry upon him, gave him the nuptial veil, and kept him in his palace in quality of a woman, which gave birth to this pleasant saying: that the world would have been happy had his Father Domitian had such a wife. In short, he caused his Sporus to be dressed like an empress, had him carried in a litter, and attended him to all the assemblies and public fairs of Greece, and at Rome to the Sigillaria, and squares of the city, where he kissed him every moment.

[These] eunuchs very often made such advantage of those favours that they insensibly became themselves, in effect, masters of the state and government, and frequently abused their great trusts, by which Christianity has too often smarted. Courts swarmed with this sort of people, who got themselves into all the principal posts and employments.

A convincing argument of this truth, may be drawn from the court of the Emperor Constantius, which was full of eunuchs, and they were masters of all affairs in the government. Of which court, we cannot draw a more natural picture than from what Monsieur Herman says, in his excellent *Life of St Athanasius*.

Befae, that Arian priest (says he) would presume to attack the emperor; he had the address to gain those that were about him; for the familiarity he had with the emperor, having made him known to the empress, he insinuated himself into the acquaintance of the eunuchs, and particularly Eusebius, who was at the head of that effeminate tribe, and one of the most wicked persons living. Having prejudiced this eunuch in his favour, by his means he soon gained the rest. In short, in time he infused his poison into the empress, and the ladies of the court, which made St Athanasius say the Arians made themselves a terror to the world, being supported by the interest and credit of the women.

After this it was no hard matter for him to gain the emperor, who was himself a slave to his eunuchs, of whom his court was full, and he followed in everything the advice and counsel of those lewd wretches.

But whatsoever credit and interest the inferior eunuchs might have, it is certain it was nothing in comparison to that of Eusebius, who was high chamberlain, or chief eunuch to the emperor; these, in respect to him, were but as little serpents that could only crawl and hiss, while Eusebius, like a dragon, held high his proud and lofty crest. [Historians] have given us likewise a full description of his excellent qualities. He was, say they, of an insupportable vanity, equally unjust and cruel; he punished, without examination, those that were convicted of no crime at all, and made no difference between the guilty and the innocent.

It was the eunuchs which caused all these disorders, and were the chief authors of all the excesses which others committed; and in reality it ought to be wondered at that as the Arian heresy made profession of denying the Son of God,[31] that it should support itself by the credit of eunuchs, who, being naturally unprolific and no less barren in their souls in relation to acts of piety and virtue than in the body, could not bear to hear the Son of God mentioned.

Alas, who will there be to write one day this history, and transmit to posterity a relation of so many sad and dreadful events? Who hereafter will believe that eunuchs, which we hardly trust with our domestic affairs, and whose service is liable in such cases to be suspected, being a sort of people that love nothing but their pleasures, and whose end is to hinder others from enjoying what nature has refused them, are now those who govern churches?

[Their] violences were so odious, even to the very pagans, that Ammianus Marcellinus writes thus of them: that being persons always fierce and ill natured, and having no domestic ties and obligations, and natural engagements like other men, they caressed their riches, which they looked upon as their dearest children.

If an extract of a letter written from Batavia in the Indies, dated the 27 November 1684 gives a true account of a certain adventure in those parts, as may very well be believed, since Monsieur Bayle has thought fit to relate it not as a thing fabulous but as if he believed it certain, so far ought we to be from suspecting the truth of it. There is somewhat very particular, which is this. 'Mreo, queen of the isle of Borneo, would have all her ministers be eunuchs. The Princess Eenegu, who disputed her right to the throne, on the contrary, would not suffer an eunuch at her court. But as we do not know what success the wars and contests of these two princesses may have, nor by consequence which of them at present enjoys the kingdom; so we are not certain whether the ministry of the isle of Borneo be composed of eunuchs or not.'

A man must have very little knowledge in the Turkish history that does not know that eunuchs are those who generally arrive to the highest posts of honour in the state.

The eunuchs having abused the favour of their respective princes, as we have seen in the foregoing chapter and made themselves so many merciless tyrants to their fellow subjects, it is not in the least to be doubted but these oppressed people had their oppressors in utmost horror, and who were consequently infinitely much more feared than loved.

But it is not the design of this treatise to discover what sentiments these people might have of their servitude or oppression, or the credit of these eunuchs that exercised so much tyranny over them. The question here to be examined is only what notion or idea the people entertained of such an eunuch, as an eunuch, and not of an eunuch as a tyrant.

And history informs us that they were not only utterly despised and hated, but that they could not abide so much as to see them.

Eunuchs according to the prophet Isaiah are only *dry trees*. They are *smitten* (as another prophet said of Ephraim) *their root is dried up, they shall bear no fruit*. Trees that ought to be cut down, and destroyed, and their remembrance be for ever blotted out; *why do they cumber the ground?* There is scarce anyone but would willingly give the first stroke to cut them down, or pluck them up by the roots, to abolish for ever this abominable practice out of the world; these are imperfect creatures, in a word, monsters, to whom nature indeed has been sparing of nothing but the avarice, luxury, or malice of men have disfigured and deformed.

If they have sometimes been raised to the highest pinnacles of human glory, and basked in the sunshine of this world; the people looked upon them as so many erroneous productions of the depraved and corrupted minds of princes who elevated them to those high stages of honour, and when they appeared in public, they only increased and augmented the hatred and aversion the people had for them amongst themselves, calling them women, &c.

Eunuchs were of such an evil augury amongst the heathens that Lucian in more than one place assures us that they made any people that met them turn suddenly back to their own houses, who would rather go home than prosecute their business that day, as having met what portended to them some disaster, or somewhat very unlucky. This is agreeable to what Pliny says in relation to animals having an aversion to any of their own species that should happen to be gelt. He observes, that if one gelds a rat, that he makes all other rats run away from him, and that they will sooner abandon their used haunts, than let him come amongst them.

A man who made an eunuch, was looked upon to be a *Notorious* or *Tableau*, as one that made a false or counterfeit deed; and the place where such action was committed was considered as a place where high treason had been committed.

But leaving these speculations, it is most certain the civil law looked upon this action of making eunuchs as abominable, and therefore never granted and allowed eunuchs the rights and privileges as other men had. For example, they were not permitted to make a will.

I own the Emperor Constantine, who gave them that privilege (for he did just as they would have him) put out an edict in their favour, whereby it was decreed that it should be lawful for eunuchs to make a will, or last testament as well as other people; and, on occasion, add codicils.

But all the learned in those laws are of opinion that this liberty was restrictive, and only concerned those eunuchs that were about his person or the empress; and it is certain in whatsover degree of favour the eunuchs were at court, yet they were still looked upon in reality to be no better than slaves; they were ever the sport of princes, who very often abused their services. And the same thing may be said of them as monkeys which ladies are so fond of, and dress them up in velvet and brocade.

They were uncapable of the privilege of adoption, the law being express against them in that respect ... However, I cannot but wonder that the Emperor Leo has re-capacitated them ... and the reason he alleges is very plausible, which is: that those who have lost the use of their speech, or are not able to bring words out of their mouths, so as to be understood, are by no means forbidden to make signs with their hands to supply the office of their tongue or write down how they would have their affairs managed. So neither should those who have lost their genitals, and so can have no children, for that reason, be debarred some other way, to make up their want of them.

It is certain the law has prescribed the age at which one may adopt in such manner that the proportion of ages should ever be observed; for it would be ridiculous that in adoption the son should be older than the father, or not so many years younger as might be according to nature; for these reasons it is said that adoption follows or imitates nature. But how would it imitate nature in this case of eunuchs to permit one who not only never was a father, but has not the capacity or parts requisite to make him so?

Besides it must be observed, that adoption originally was only permitted to those persons which once had children to comfort them, and in some measure to supply that loss; which privilege afterwards was extended to those who had no manifest impediment to hinder them from having children, but who in effect had the unhappiness never to have any; but it never was allowed women to adopt, because they were uncapable of the principal effect of adoption, which is *paternal power*, but yet sometimes they were permitted to adopt by dispensation, or by indulgence of the prince, and that they might be comforted for their dead children.

But surely it would be to abuse adoption to suffer these people who never had, or ever could have, any children to make use of that privilege. This is not to imitate or follow nature, but to surpass it; or rather insult and affront it, to give children to those who are despoiled of the means to produce any.

How then can a man so timorous and fearful as an eunuch is, serve as a support and assistance to a minor under his tutelage, who perhaps may, notwithstanding his non-age,[32] have infinitely greater courage and vigour of spirit than himself? I have often wondered how the civil law came to permit them to take up arms.

The conjugal combat is of a different nature from the military, and so are the arms; but as eunuchs are not accoutred with these, they are entirely in an incapacity of engaging in this agreeable warfare.

I shall conclude ... with some remarks which will not be foreign to the subject. I must say then that I have not pretended to write a natural history of eunuchs, or an exact relation of those people, as they have been considered in all ages and countries, the customs of nations, and times, differ very much; and to the shame of human reason be it spoken, we see that which was the common taste in one age, was disgust in another. This diversity appears everywhere amongst different people, who have different taste and genius. This deficiency, deprivation, or lack of virility, or manhood, is not equally opprobious in all places; in many places in the world it has rendered some people very considerable, which otherwise, would not have been in the least taken notice of.

It will be sufficient for me to conclude all what I have hitherto said on this subject: that there appears to be not any one ordinance, nor law, nor constitution, that regulates the marriage of eunuchs, which infallibly we should discover in either ancient or modern history, or in the compilers of the laws, if it had been permitted them to contract marriage, as we do actually find several laws in relation to their making themselves so, and concerning their power of making wills, adoption, and becoming guardians, &c. But on the contrary, we find laws which absolutely forbid and prohibit them to marry.

The Nature of Hermaphrodites

In this substantial extract, James Parsons explores a variety of classical and Renaissance authorities on hermaphrodites. He argues that these accounts are rife with errors and inadequate observation. He concludes that the hermaphrodite is in fact simply a female with an enlarged clitoris. Text from *A Mechanical and Critical Enquiry into the Nature of Hermaphrodites* (1741). See Cole (1930); Jones and Stallybrass (1991); Laqueur (1990); Shapiro (1987); Jacquart and Thomasset (1988); Friedli (1987: 234–60).

Though one may be informed of a matter which in itself is really fact, yet if an absurdity should arise in the narration, it would be laudable to enquire whether it is to be ascribed to the relater or to the thing told; but as there is nothing which, when true, can admit of any absurdity, there is therefore the greater right to be discontented with what is not easily understood; and it would be a crime to neglect taking notice of such accounts especially if anything monstrous or improbable is blended with them. Shall we, for example, sit down with some authors, and say that mares are always of both sexes; that the rhinoceros is always male; that the vulture is always female; that of all animals, goats, sheep, horses, men, and hares, are most liable to become hermaphrodites? and shall we go on to copy or quote them thoroughly lest by assenting to any part of them that does not square with nature and reason we shall find our judgements very deservedly arraigned, and the sagacious part of the world much displeased ... Such were the motives and considerations that prompted me to endeavour to wrest, from the jaws of scandal and reproach, poor human nature, which has, from time to time, suffered great disgrace, and many of whose innocent children have been punished, and even put to death, for having been reputed hermaphrodites; ignorance of the fabric of the body has been the first great occasion of those evils ...

What but ignorance or superstition could persuade men to imagine that poor human creatures (which were only distorted in some particular part, or had anything unusual appearing about them, from some morbid cause affecting them, either in the uterus, or after their births) were prodigies or monsters in nature? What, but ignorance and superstition, could urge men to make laws for their destruction or exclusion from the common benefits of life? In fine, what, but these very causes, could make several harsh laws continue still in force against them in many places, which suppose those women that happen to be *Macroclitorideae*,[33] to be capable of exercising the functions of either sex, with regard to generation; and, further, restrain them under severe penalties to stick to that sex only which they should choose? As if poor women could exercise the part of any other sex but their own.

The Romans, soon after the foundation of their city, had laws made against their *androgyni* remarkably severe; for whensoever a child was reputed one of these, his sentence was to be shut up in a chest alive, and thrown into the sea, which was so often put in execution as any of these unfortunate children were discovered. The inhabitants about the Gulf of Florida hold them also in great contempt, believing them to be something so evil as not to deserve the comforts of life; and though they do not destroy them yet they deal as badly by them, for when they go to make war, as many of these supposed hermaphrodites as can be found are obliged to carry their provisions, they are also compelled to bear the dead, and those sick of malignant diseases, to proper places, and attend them under very rigorous circumstances.

Nothing is more certain than that the causes abovementioned have had no small share in propagating a belief among the people of their existence; and this appears by a custom that long prevailed amongst the pagans in Italy, who, upon the birth of such children, as were thought hermaphrodites, always consulted their religions and wise-men what to do with *them*. A remarkable instance of this kind happened in a town in Campania in Italy, called Frusione, where a child being born of monstrous size, and another at Sinuessa whose sex was doubtful, insomuch, that they could neither judge it male or female, it was laid before the magistrates who immediately sent for some *aruspices*,[34] out of Hetruvia, and they pronounced it, 'Faedum ac turpe prodigium',[35] whereupon it was thrown into the sea according to the aforesaid law. But this was not enough, for as by the superstitions of the soothsayers and the pontifices,[36] such children were thought to portend some evil, there was a ceremony that always succeeded their destruction, which was performed by twenty-seven virgins, who marched in procession, singing about the city, and offered sacrifices to Juno, to avert the evil which they imagined was boded by the child's birth.

An hermaphrodite is an animal, in which two sexes, male and female, ought to appear to be each distinct and perfect, as well with regard to structure proper to either, as to the power of exercising the necessary offices and functions of those parts.

It would be an injury to truth to deny the existence of an hermaphroditical nature to all the animal world in general; but however I am inclined to believe it is only proper to some reptiles, and but a few of these.

If there was not so absolute a law ... with respect to the being of only one sex in one body, we might then, indeed, expect to find every day many preposterous digressions from our present standard. That there are certain limits set to the things of generation appears nowhere better than when animals of different species copulate; the animal that is the product of such a congress is in no wise capable of producing an offspring like itself, to this there is an absolute *ne plus ultra*, and why? Because, indeed if such were capable of generation, we should, by degrees, have a new set of heterogeneous animals upon earth ...

Whensoever the parts of both sexes are seen distinct in any subject, they are not in the same, but in different bodies preternaturally joined, and coalesced together in the uterus, by compression, heat, inflammation, or some other such accident; of this there was lately an example in town at Charing Cross, which had the heads separate, and the sexes appearing at considerable distance from each other. But who, with the least propriety, can call these an hermaphrodite, each body having its peculiar sex, and being morbid in their conjunction.

The notions that sprung up in the world concerning this matter were (no doubt) first taken from appearances that sometimes have happened of an extraordinary elongation in the clitorides of females; the first idea conceived from thence must have been that of a penis, and the appearance of a vulva joined to it raised an opinion of both sexes in the same body; hence proceeded the invention of a proper name for the surprising unity of both sexes in the same body; and hence the fictions of poets, which the learned are well acquainted with. It will not be difficult to account in some measure for the rise of such erroneous imaginations, if we only consider how ignorant the world was in former ages of the animal structure.

It is a matter of no small surprise, that authors never were able to take the least hint from the practice of the people of some of the Asiatic, as well as the African nations, concerning these Clitorides; for as in both these parts of the world, the women have them most commonly very long, and the people knowing that the length of them produces two evils, *viz.* the hindering of the coitus, and women's abuse of them with each other, wisely cut or burn them off while girls are young, and at the same time never entertain the least notion of the existence of any nature besides the female in those subjects who are thus deprived of that useless part. This knowledge is not confined to men of science alone amongst the Egyptians and Ethiopians, nor indeed amongst the Asiatics; for every parent knows when the child has this part longer than ordinary, and performs the operation at a proper time ...

There are many authors who have given histories of women that have been detected in the abuse of such large Clitorides, calling them Tribades, Confricatrices, and the like, the recital of one from Tulpius[37] may not be amiss, who after relating some passages transacted by one of these and a certain widow, makes this reflection, 'Though the clitoris for the most part lies hid, yet several have it so large, that they are thought by the ignorant to be transformed into men; but that this (whose history he writes) was in all respects a perfect woman, having only the clitoris half a finger's length.' And since this worthy author has given us this story so suitable to our present purpose, it will not be unreasonable in this place, to take some notice of a Memoir in the *Transactions of the Royal Society*,[38] presented by one Dr Thomas Allen, the subject of which he calls an uncommon *Lusus*,[39] and says 'This hermaphrodite is not to be reckoned amongst the Tribades of the Greeks, nor to be equalled by any description yet extant.' These Tribades were no more than women with clitorides larger than ordinary. Such of them as are so may be capable, perhaps, of that action from whence the name arose, whether they perform it or not; and by considering the sequel of this history, we shall find the subject he describes to be no other than a very woman, such as Tulpius has given the history of. He says, 'at six years of age, the child playing and wrestling with her fellow children, there appeared two tumours like hernias, but they proved testicles, differing from those of a man only in this: that each had his own scrotum; but in such a manner that the production of both formed the labia of the vulva ... She passed for a woman till the thirteenth year – when kneading of dough, all of a sudden, a penis broke forth, four inches long in an erection, situated as in a man.' It is no wonder she should pass for a woman, who, according to our author, had all the feminine parts to such perfection; and though the accretion and protrusion of the clitoris was never so sudden, yet there is not the least reason to ascribe to her a virile nature, because the female parts remained as perfect as before, without the least metamorphosis, and she had her menses regularly from her sixteenth during the following two years, at which time, says our author, they ceased, and she began to have a beard, hair on her body, voice, breasts, thorax,[40] ischia,[41] and many other things like those of a man. However, this sudden growth of the clitoris is not to be credited, for those who show a child of this nature will tell any lie to render the thing more surprising, as, for example, who by reading the bill of the little French girl could imagine any other than that, in an erect posture, she was only 16 inches high? Whereas when her limbs came to be viewed, the spectators found themselves mistaken, for the person never set forth in his bill that she sat when she was measured, or that her limbs were folded over each other. Hence it appears that the narrations of these kinds of things are always false, and the subjects never answer the character or description of them given by owners ... The inconsistencies that appear through this whole narration from first to last should promise no great credit, for it is entirely taken from the owner of the girl, and securely presented to the Royal Society, without the author's considering that no one part of his history can be reconciled to the known laws of the structure of the human body. I should not omit in fine to take notice of one word more: 'That at the sight of a woman her penis was erected, and became flaccid at the sight of a man'; from this I can conceive no other, than that she had more desire to the woman than the man; and yet after he says, she cast her eyes upon a handsome man and fell in love with him ...

It has been often argued by authors that these Confricatrices are more inclined to desire the access of women than of men, and being willing to savour the opinion of both sexes being found in one person, draw from that argument this conclusion: that therefore there must be as much of a masculine nature, as of a female, in them. To that it is answered: that they do not desire women more than men, from a mere natural inclination, but because by a gratification of this nature there is not so much danger of being exposed; therefore a congress like this is the more eagerly sought after and agreed on by two females so inclined, since by an over-long clitoris in one, both find their accounts answered, without fear of that accident, that is the necessary consequence of dealing with men; for that part being, as all allow, the seat of great titillation, it is no wonder it should be stimulated by being embraced in the vagina, nor that the receiver should also be effected by such frication,[42] as well as by a penis virilis; thus I hope it appears plainly that this conclusion is ill grounded.

Another argument made use of is: that those reputed hermaphrodites have beards like men and hair on some of their breasts. This can make but very little towards proving a masculine nature in them; so supposing some of these Fricatrices to have hair &c. as above, yet there are many women with hair between their breasts and on their chins, who deserve no such repute; one I have often seen whose arms to the fingers ends were covered with long black hair, having a beard also on her chin, who was the wife of a man of fortune by whom she had eight or nine children. I have also, at the Hotel de Dieu at Paris, seen a body opened that was hairy in the same manner, without any sign of a masculine nature whatsoever. Again, several women advanced in years have great quantities of hair on the chin, but the number of these as well as the former, among women, are but few; and those that are so ought no more to have any such character ascribed to them, on that account, than that many men who want beards should be said to partake of a feminine nature, and want the power of exercising the functions of a man; but daily experience shows us that these are as prolific, and produce as many signs of virility, as any others whatsoever.

Case of Anne, about 23 years old

He was tall and thin, having a masculine voice, a long head of hair, and only some softish hairs on his chin (for he used to pluck his beard with a tweezer as fast as it grew) he had no breasts, but was hairy about the pubis, and had a long penis, and the praeputium drawn back and well worn; he had no scrotum nor testes that were visible: under the penis, in the perinaeum, where the lithotomy is commonly performed there was a kind of chink, about half a finger's joint deep, &c. from all of which we judged him a man rather than a woman. Being asked concerning his venereal performances, he confessed, that he had cohabited with several whores, with a seminal ejection and much pleasure; and further, that whenever he had to do with any, or ever had an erection of his penis, a testicle swelled in his right groin (for sometimes the testes do not descend into the scrotum, but remain in the inguina[43]) which we perceived by touching, but that on the left side, nothing was to be perceived neither during the coitus nor otherwise; nor did anything ever flow from the aforesaid rima or chink.

Here was therefore a perfect man, mistaken for a female child at the birth, on account of the invisibility of the testes, and the appearance of that superficial chink in the perinaeum.

[Another] reason for such reports has been taken from boys having been concealed in female dresses, for some political or family occasions, and so continued under that acceptation, till either matters came to such a crisis as rendered their case less dangerous, or till beards and other signs of virility have occasioned a declaration of their true sex, and a change of habit. The vulgar now make a rumour of a miraculous change in children, whom they before accepted as females; the report takes wing, and is catched by several who commit the story superstitiously to posterity, without any manner of enquiry into the nature of the thing.

A case of this is cited in *Diemerbroeck*,[44] which happened in the time of Ferdinand I, King of Naples; it was of two children, who were called Carola and Francisca, and were reported to have changed their sexes upon the appearance of beards growing on them, which their mother gave out was miraculously done, upon which she changed their habits for those of men.

There was an opinion amongst the Greek and Arabian physicians, concerning a great analogy between the male and the female genitals as to their structure, who strenuously assert that these differ in nothing but their situation, that is, they compare the cervix and vagina uteri to the penis, and the fundus to the scrotum, only they are inverted or rather not protruded, and that which hinders their protusion in women, according to these authors, is the want of heat and sufficient force of nature. It would be a digression from our present purpose, if we should enter upon a comparative view of the parts of generation of both sexes, and endeavour to confute those chimeras, and therefore the use that is at present necessary to be made of this opinion is only to show that this was another origin from whence those reports of such metamorphoses have sprung and been encouraged, as well as any of those others already taken notice of. For admitting that hypothesis, *viz.* that every woman is a man, if she had but heat of temperament and strength sufficient to drive the inside of the uterus, &c. outward, and that that inversion should form a penis and scrotum, which was the general notion amongst some of the learned a long time after Galen.[45]

It will not be improper here to observe, that all these changes in the sex were most commonly said to be made from women to men; and I never could hear any account whatsoever of men's being changed into women, but two or three, one of which happened here in London; the story will not only be of use to our purpose, but a merry one, and therefore take it briefly as follows: at a great tavern in London, there lived, some few years ago, two drawers who were a considerable time servants in the house, and always lay together; one of them gets the other with child, who was with a great deal of shame and confusion turned away, and obliged then to put on women's clothes. The rumour of the drawer's being changed into a woman made a great noise all over the neighbourhood, and very likely would have been recorded for truth, if it had happened in an age a little earlier.

Here was a poor girl whose parents ignorantly believing she was a boy from the length of the clitoris, dressed her up, and employed her as such in the business of life; she no doubt believed herself so, until she was better instructed by her fellow-servant; and here is matter and foundation, altogether as probable and sufficient for poets or historians to build upon, as any heretofore taken notice of; and, in fine, hence it plainly appears that it is with equal right that human nature may be said to be capable of admitting of two natures, male and female, in one body, and of changing from one sex to the other.

Another is told by Caspar Bauhin[46] of a child who was baptised as a male, and was brought up a tailor by trade, went afterwards into the army, and served as a soldier both in Hungary and Flanders, married a wife, and lived seven years with her, at the end of which, our soldier one night rose from the wife, complaining of great pains in the belly, and in half an hour, was delivered of a daughter. When the story came before the magistrates, an examination was made, and the poor female soldier confessed herself of both sexes, and that a Spaniard had cohabited with her once (only) in Flanders, by which she proved with child; that the wife had concealed her want of what might be expected from a husband, with whom she never was able to act in any wise, during their (seven years) living together.

The author introduces the story in the following words. 'As the following history is of no small importance in explaining the nature of hermaphrodites, I have translated it thus from the German language.' From which words it appears, that he had a very just notion concerning them, and was far from making such things prodigies, being well versed in the knowledge of the animal structure that he counts the history of this, and another soldier ... sufficiently explicatory of the nature of hermaphrodites in general.

The parents of these could have no other motive for thinking these creatures boys than the length of the clitoris; which is plain from their bearing children when they came to age; and if anything of a masculine nature was in the soldier, it could surely in seven years' acquaintance have been exerted to the gratification of a wife, or would have produced some other effects very different from that of being got with child.

If hermaphrodites actually existed, surely there might have been before now some probable conjectures made to show the reasons or necessity of such beings upon earth, since so many authors have been busied about them from the beginning of the world. But there appears throughout their several opinions so general a train of absurdities that I cannot but wonder they were any more satisfactory to mankind in their days than they are to me at present. However, when the several causes laid down by certain authors from time to time, for the producing of those creatures, are considered, it will not be a difficult matter to point out innumerable errors amongst them, and deny that those causes can produce any such effect as a double nature in human bodies.

The first that I shall take notice of is that of Constantinus Africanus, who accuses nature of being hindered, or of forgetting its duty in the formation of the foetus, and by this mistake hermaphrodites are generated. 'It happens to some men, in generation, to have added to them those female parts, and to some women those masculine parts that are luxuriant in them, when nature is hindered, or grows forgetful; for when by any accident it happens thus, that superfluity of humid matter that usually contributes to either the inordinate size or number of any limb, goes to the formation of a member of any other nature without rule or order.'

Lemnius[47] ... is fond of giving another opinion of his own, which he supposes to account for hermaphroditism, and that is any unusual or indecent execution of the coition. 'Sometimes this infamous conception is formed from an indecent and unusual copulation, as when the man is supine, and the woman prone in the act, &c.'

Dominicus Terrelius[48] imagines the cause to be in the position of the female, immediately after the coitus. 'After a woman has received the semen virile into the uterus, care must be had of the perfection of her body; which ought not to be supine, because then the semen remaining in the middle of the uterus does not become either male or female absolutely, but both together, which is called an hermaphrodite.'

The opinion of Parmenides,[49] an ancient Greek author, appears in the following lines ... concerning hermaphrodites being produced. 'When the semina of a man and a woman are mixed together, the forming virtue, preserving a due moderation and temperature, will produce bodies properly made; for if there be an opposition of the said virtue in the mingled semen, she unhappily implants in the foetus a double sex.'

The principles laid down by Averroes[50] are no less particular than others just mentioned; he says, the semen muliebre[51] abounds with, or is constituted of, particles adapted to the nature of every member in the body, and in order to account for a superfluity of members in a body, he draws this conclusion from thence; that if the seminal matter in a female is more than is necessary for the formation of one child, and less than will make two, the superfluous part will form superfluous limbs to the one child, according to the nature of the particles it contains; that is, if it consists of particles fit for the head, there will be two heads, and so of the hands, feet, &c. And then he adds, 'The cause is much the same when the parts of generation of both sexes exist in any person.' And that, on the other hand, if there be a deficiency of the seminal matter, some limb or other must be wanting.

If this be thought a just hypothesis, then we cannot but suppose there is a great and most miserable restraint upon the whole animal part of the creation; for if it be absolutely necessary that such a certain quantity (and no more, nor less) is to be expended on the completing of a proportionable foetus, I am of opinion that not one-third of the animals of the world would escape being monsters; and the art and business of physicians would be more requisitely employed in ordering regimens, and calculations towards fixing the sustenance and other non-naturals, in such proportion to every animal, as should produce in each an exact quantity of seminal matter, than in curing diseases.

Peucerus comes into a class with Averroes but tacks some little addition to the doctrine of the latter, of a superabundance, or scarcity in any parts of the semen, their producing a superfluity or want of any of the members of the body; he says, 'If for making of two bodies the matter is deficient, but is too much for one, the vis plastica forms more limbs than are natural.' A little after he adds, 'In this manner hermaphrodites and Androgyni are begotten, who have the parts of both sexes; although one of them may be weaker and of less efficacy than the other, and sometimes it happens that one may be changed or quite abolished.' ... Indeed when he says that one of the sexes in an hermaphrodite is of no efficacy, he is right; for our reputed Androgyni, which are the Macroclitorideae, have one of theirs so, which is the clitoris; and consequently ought to be denied the character of an hermaphrodite; but when he says, one of the sexes is changed, he can, with less right, call them hermaphrodites. If one be changed, it must be to some other sex; and as there are but two, then there must be a male or female sex, upon the alteration, and all this, after they have become of this double nature, according to the cause in the first part of his opinion; for a change is consequent to the former state of the thing changed. But, in fine, when one sex is abolished, there ought to remain but a perfect man, or woman; how therefore can this most unaccountable variety be said to proceed from a redundancy of particles of any kind whatsoever.

Not a few old authors imagined there were several cells and ditches in the uterus for the reception of foetuses of the different sexes; and those who were of opinion that the cells were but seven, thought that three were on the right side for males; as many on the left, for females; and the seventh in the middle for hermaphrodites; which were generated, whenever the semen virile happened to fall into it. Another supposes but three, one on each side for the males and females, and the central cell for the Androgyni; and that 'Nature always intends the formation of a male, being inclined to form the best; that a woman is but a man, having accidental change in the parts, and is therefore a monster in nature; and that a male is always begotten, but because of the ill disposition of the matrix and the object it contains, and the inequality of the semen (whensover Nature cannot accomplish the formation of a perfect man) a female or hermaphrodite must be the consequence.'

If Nature intended the procreation of no sex but the male, there would have been no female; but if it was, at first, necessary, that a female should accompany the male in order to propagate their likeness and species, without which (it is evident) generation could neither have been begun nor carried on, the same necessity must always hold, and a race of females as well as males ought always to continue, in order to carry on that great work. How then are women monsters in Nature?

The first woman as well as the first man, when created, were endowed with different organs serving to generation, though in all other respects alike in their members; and since every woman afterwards had no difference in the formation of those parts, but must have been exactly the same with her female predecessors, even back to the first; by what reason can her parts be accounted monstrous or accidentally changed. Besides, whatsoever is monstrous in Nature ought to be of no further use in the economy of that particular system to which it may properly be said to belong, if in a natural state. But this hypothesis is of such a nature as scarce to be worth taking any more trouble to confute, being the product of a mere monster in Nature.

St Augustine,[52] who was more inclined to deal in matters metaphysical than natural, makes a long detail of several kinds of men, such as, those having but one eye in the forehead, pygmies, sciopoda's,[53] cynocephales,[54] and such like; and proposes this question: whether it was from Adam, or the sons of Noah, that such kinds of men have proceeded? But seems to believe that whatsoever they be, they were brought upon the earth by the special appointment of God. This he gives as the cause in general, but argues that the same will hold for those particularly believed to exist in this part of the world, as hermaphrodites, and those of a doubtful sex. 'The same reason that accounts for the monstrous births of men with us may serve to account also for those of nations that are so; for God, the creator of all, knew when and where everything should be created.' As yet we know not of any nation or genus of men heterogeneous to us in their form, although some have wrote concerning such; but later progresses and discoveries round the world, show us to the contrary; if such a nation was to be found, we might indeed with some reason suppose them to be a race, created on purpose by God; but we must not therefore assent to the Saint, in imagining God to be the intermediate author of any form in those poor children (commonly called monstrous) that might be painful or disadvantageous to their well-being and preservation; and therefore his comparison is not justly laid down, because, though the first semina of any species of animals are planted by the ordination of the Almighty, in an absolute manner in the beginning, from which they cannot digress in their successive generations; yet a woman, possessing all the greatest beauties and proportion in an hereditary succession, may bring forth a child, deformed in every member; which can reasonably be accounted no other than one accidentally injured in the uterus. A word or two more of this great man may be necessary here, to show that amongst those monstrous births we have enumerated from him, he was not less certain of the existence of hermaphrodites than of any other, which appears in these words, 'Although the Androgyni, which are also called hermaphrodites, are not often, yet, no doubt, they sometimes are, found, in whom the two sexes are so apparent, that it is uncertain from which they should be named; however the custom of speaking has prevailed that they should be nominated after the superior sex, which is the masculine, for nobody has ever said Androgynecas or hermaphroditas.'

These amount to the majority of physical causes, commonly assigned for the growth of hermaphrodites; many more as unreasonable as these might be drawn from the opinions of the astronomers, who have endeavoured to account for such births, by the motions of certain planetary bodies, that, they think, influence the actions of generation in a particular manner, and produce variety of monsters; but what are already laid down are fully sufficient to demonstrate the errors that reign through the whole; and that the existence of hermaphrodites being once granted amongst them, the greater number of authors strove to show the causes of their generation, the greater distance to which truth was banished on this occasion.

It is observable, that when authors are fond of having their readers believe what they assert, they generally favour their own opinions either in descriptions or figures, so much as even to stretch from the truth of the subject; which so far answers their ends as to beget in some people, indolently credulous, a belief of what they see, and leads them into an error. This will appear, by the following animadversions upon such authors as I thought would further answer our intentions on the present occasion.

Jacobus Rueffe[55] ... gives an account of a child which he calls an hermaphrodite as follows: 'In the year 1519, an hermaphrodite or androgynus was born at Zurich, well formed from the navel upwards, but having that part covered with a reddish fleshy mass, beneath which were the female parts, and under these, those of a man, in their proper situation.'

I confess the singularity of the situation of the female parts above the penis and scrotum renders me an infidel to the story, from the known impossibility of such a structure ... and we need no more wonder at the author's being fond of making it what he does, than at others, and not a few, who would turn the clitoris into the *penis virilis*, or whimsically turn boys into girls, and girls into boys, and therefore as he does not say, whether himself had seen it, or whether it was communicated to him, we must conjecture, that when a thing is received by hearsay, it is an easy matter to make a figure answerable to the report, and place parts of bodies in the situation that best suits our story.

In the same chapter this author says that many children are born, and even grow to considerable ages, whose sex is hardly upon inspection to be distinguished. The ignorant (says he) believe them to consist of both, but are much mistaken; then he pretends to have seen one of these doubtful cases in these words, 'I happened to see such an infant, whose sex was hard to be determined; testicles were indeed prominent without a penis; under the testicles there was a rupture or passage for the urine, but because of the want of the penis (nor was it totally absent, but turned inwards and bending downwards to the said rupture) Nature found this way for the exit of the urine. It was not baptized as a female, nor an Androgynus, but a male only.'

I cannot devise by what means credit should be given to such narrations as these, which so far digress from human nature's laws, when not accompanied with a very nice and particular anatomic description of such parts; and even that attested by numbers of persons equally skilled in the same science, or a public society of learned men, whose delight it is to enquire after truth and rectify superstitious allegations of all kinds, especially in natural history. At last this author, after informing us that the child was received and baptized by the people as a male, and not a female hermaphrodite, concludes the paragraph thus: 'But because such subjects are better perceived by the understanding, than by sight; I was not willing to represent it by any particular figure.' He was very much in the right not to give a figure of this subject from his imagination only, which, I am sure, he as well as several other authors have done before, without any other authority than the tradition of the people.

Reald Columbus[56] gives the story of what he calls the woman hermaphrodite first, which is much of a piece with that of the other authors mentioned hereafter. But if he had said at once that he had considered the cases of a man and a woman, he would have appeared a more judicious historian than he seems to be by adding the word hermaphrodite to either; which will be evident by the sequel of his account, *viz.* 'There was one of those Aethiopian women, called, by the Lombardians, Cingarae, who would neither perform as man nor a woman, for she unfortunately had both sexes imperfect; the penis not exceeding the size of one's little finger, in length or thickness, and the hole of the vulva was so narrow as not to be capable of receiving the top of the little finger. This wretch intreated me to cut off the penis, which she said, would be a hinderance to her in the coitus, and also desired I would enlarge the vulva, that she might be capable of receiving a man; but I dared not grant her request; knowing the danger the vessels were liable to, therefore I thought it could not be done without hazarding her life.'

There is not the least room to hesitate upon this case, with regard to the hermaphroditical character he gives her; for it is plain from her own desire, nothing but the properties of a female were in her. If otherwise, she would never

46

have begged him to cut off the part which our author calls a penis, but in truth the clitoris; and from her earnest entreaty to have her feminine parts dilated and made capable of receiving the necessary part of the contrary sex; for it is commonly the case in such women as have the clitoris longer than ordinary to have the orifice more or less covered with a thin skin arising from the perinaeum; this must have been the case with her, and the author might have gratified her by a chirurgical excision of that part, as safely as the Ethiopians and Egyptians perform the same upon their own children. And as to the membraneous covering to the orifice of the vagina, it might have been remedied by a snip of a scissors.

It is very observable that several authors, in treating of this subject, notwithstanding they run into such flourishing divisions of the word hermaphrodite, yet are commonly sure, before they conclude, to disown, or, in a great measure, contradict those very assertions which for art's sake, they at first ventured on. This shines in our present author [Johannes Riolanus],[57] who, after he has described the parts of generation, proceeds to recount the diseases of them which he calls his Consideratio Medica; and under that head, amongst the diseases of the urethra, he brings in some species of hermaphrodites, as though none were entitled to that character but such as had disorders in those parts proper to men; but from what he says of them, nothing can occur to any reasonable person but a notion of the real diseases of the parts, however he came to call them hermaphrodites, which name is applied here with as much impropriety as with any other author whatsoever.

The examination of any more authors upon this topic would amount to more pains than at present are necessary, and besides, repetitions could hardly be avoided if any more were called in question, since we find authors were so fond of running in the same path with one another; therefore the remarks that have been made on those already mentioned may, I hope, be sufficient (together with the rest that has been said) to answer the end of this treatise, which is no more than to illustrate the cause of the first rise of the notions of hermaphrodites among men; to show how credulous our ancestors have been of those chimeras, and how fond of encouraging their progress though in the meanest manner of arguing; to prove, by comparing all the opinions of authors, that no hermaphroditical nature can exist in human bodies; and, in fine, that those subjects hitherto so accounted were only females in all respects, superstitiously, and through ignorance, mistaken for those kind of creatures, or for men; which, with some other disorders of the pudenda of either sex, gave rise to the several divisions that afterwards sprung up concerning them; and as far from truth (or even rational conjecture) as any other error that ever was received by mankind.

All female foetuses, during the greatest part of the time of gestation, have the clitoris as large in proportion to their sizes, and sometimes larger, than the

Angolan woman before-mentioned, which is evident from several then showed together to the society; this, I am inclined to believe, is Nature's common rule all over the world. Now it is impossible that so many hermaphrodites should be found at once, since we have so very few instances among the European nations of those so reputed; though, as is before observed, they are common enough in Africa and Asia, in all those places especially that are nearest the equinoctial line; where the nonnaturals themselves conduce much to the general relaxation of the solids, and consequently, this unseemly accretion of that part.

2 CRIMES AND PUNISHMENTS

Introduction

Studies of sexuality have made extensive use of legal history, because the designation of certain kinds of sexual expression as criminal has been important for their self-definition. Trial records also have the advantage that they make an effort – at least on the surface – to confirm facts and are therefore important for reconstructing where sexual activities took place and among what classes of people. Yet such trial records should not be separated from imaginative and satirical accounts which deployed such public material. Reprints of trial proceedings were highly popular, and frequently appeared so as to coincide with current cases. Castlehaven's trial was reprinted at a time when sodomy was once again topical. Moreover, an important aspect of their marketing was the generation of moral outrage together with the excitement of presenting what had been secret to a public world.

According to the Preface to *Select Trials ... From the year 1720, to this Time* (1742) the narratives were designed partly to serve a moral function: 'Instruction, conveyed by example, makes a more deep and lasting impression in the mind, than that delivered by precept only.' Yet the didactic priority has to been seen in the context of another feature of the text: 'with the serious we shall intermix the pleasant, to divert, as well as instruct'. How criminal narratives overlapped with imaginative writings can be seen from the 'trial' of Robert Thistlethwayte, Late Doctor of Divinity, Warden of Wadham College. In this example, the legal discourse of evidence, witnesses and formal procedures was recomposed as a comic burlesque poem in *College Wit Sharpened* (1739).

Writing in his *Review*, Daniel Defoe devoted one of his issues to a brief but fascinating discussion of recent cases of sodomy and arson. Faced with the excitement and curiosity aroused by open trials and executions, Defoe found himself divided between the openness of trial reports and the need to conceal the very existence of such deviant activities. For Defoe, the incidence of arson and sodomy was novel, yet there was a marked contrast in Defoe's reaction to them. Arson required a 'large description' but Defoe wishes that in the case of sodomy the English would follow the Dutch, 'who in such cases make both the trials and punishments of such sort of criminals, to be done with all the privacy possible' (27

November 1717). He was anxious about the effect of the circulation of criminal narratives which served to embellish crime, exploiting novelty and surprise, scandalizing the reader. Defoe stated, therefore, that in the case of the crime of *sodomy*:

> I think 'tis in its nature pernicious many ways, to have this crime so much as named among us; the very discourse of it is vicious in its nature, abominable to modest ears, and really ought not to be entertained, far less should be so openly discussed, so publickly tried in the courts of justice, and the accounts of it exposed as a subject to the vulgar discourse of the people. (496)

Similarly, Daniel Defoe offers very little in the way of toleration:

> As for the persons, I leave them to justice. I believe, every good man loaths and pities them at the same time; and as they are monuments of what human nature abandoned of divine grace may be left to do – so in their crime they ought to be abhorred of their neighbours, spued out of society, and sent expressly out of the world, as secretly and privately, as may consist with justice and the laws. (496)

Behind these comments is the sense of a concealed category which called for, excited and sanctioned the need to unmask. Yet there was the subsequent danger of others imitating the crime. In this regard, Sedgwick has noted that, 'same-sex desire is still structured by its distinctive public/private status, at once marginal and central, as *the* open secret' (1990: 22).

The author of *Hell upon Earth* noted that the mollies went to their executions, 'unpitied and unlamented, loaded with the highest guilt ... The greatest criminal has some people that may drop some pitying expressions for his unhappy and untimely fate and condole his dismal circumstances; while those persons who fall by the laws of *Sodomy*, can expect neither pity nor compassion.' Sodomites could be hanged, fined, imprisoned, or placed in the pillory. In the case of the pillory it is worth noting that a hostile crowd could murder their victim (*Gentlemen's Magazine*, 3 April 1763; 10 April 1780); other punishments included being tied in a sack and thrown overboard on the high seas, or the amputation of ears (*Gentlemen's Magazine*, February 1745; 30 May 1752). Juries were encouraged to deal harshly where young men were involved (as in the *Trial of Richard Branson*, 1760), but internal procedures often prevented cases moving beyond the cloister (see the Wadham College scandal, 1739). Bribery was also a problem in dealing with convictions, as is shown in *The Confederacy* (1751).

Much of the material that is available on transgressive sexuality was governed and censored by its status as an unsympathetic third-person account. As a result, there are innate problems in attempting to reclaim the lost history of secret sexualities – as soon as these entered the public sphere they were channeled and filtered by ruling, hegemonic ideas. Many of the publications included in this selection are therefore concerned with a need to provide working categories, especially where a practical outcome is desired as in the case of *The King versus Wiseman* (1748). Similarly, a number of other trials are concerned with ascertaining exactly what kinds and degrees of sexual activity (especially anal penetration) had taken place – with a view to determining punishment.

The period from which I have chosen publications illustrates a transitional period in the history of sexuality. In the seventeenth century some of the most infamous sodomites such as Mervyn Touchet, Earl of Castlehaven (Francis Bacon's brother-in-law) had been aristocratic. This case had made legal history because the Lord Chief Justice concluded that a criminal participant could be a legal witness until he himself was convicted. Castlehaven was unanimously found guilty of rape, and a majority of the jurors found him guilty of sodomy. The other participants (FitzPatrick and Broadway) were later sentenced to death on the ground of their former testimonies against Castlehaven. The trial was an odd one because it was clear from the outset that Castlehaven's Roman Catholic tendencies were not in his favour.

The libertine period produced not only Rochester's *Sodom, or the Quintessence of Debauchery* (1684), but the case of Titus Oates who was convicted in 1685, and became notorious as a Roman Catholic, traitor and homosexual. Another aristocratic relationship that was opened out to the public was that between the Earl of Sunderland and Beau Wilson (1694). The interest in the private lives of these individuals was stimulated by the discovery of their correspondence, published as *Love-Letters Between a certain late Nobleman And the famous Mr Wilson* (1723). But increasingly, cases of sexual offences were dealing with members of the working class (artisans) and the lower-middle classes, rather than aristocratic libertines, and it is mostly from the province of the former group that extracts have been selected. This is illustrated throughout the section on prosecutions which provides valuable information about where and how early homosexuals met, what they did, and who they were. As a number of critics and historians have shown, the rise of the city increasingly provided a network large enough for secret sex to become organized. G.S. Rousseau (1985: 143) has pointed to this expansion within the city, concluding that 'Earlier the outcry had been directed at the stage as a spawning ground for this detestable breed, but in the 1720s, the fields for breeding had diversified.' The fear of increased occurrences of sodomy (among other vices) led to the creation of societies for the reformation of manners and the Society for the Promotion of Christian Knowledge. These were to play an active role in bringing sodomy to light in a range of prosecutions at the beginning of the eighteenth century. They published manuals for the collection of information and the presentation of it to magistrates in such a way as to guarantee prosecutions (Norton 1992; Bristow 1977).

Sexuality was increasingly constructed not on the basis of sex but on the grounds of self-legitimation and the pluralizing of desire. William Brown, for example, charged with sodomy, was not ashamed to answer, '*I think there is no crime in making what use I please of my own body.*' When such first-person accounts are available they are especially valuable for they challenge the politics of the third-person constructions of many of the pamphlets I have analysed; importantly they allow us to strip back the role of satire, fancy and moral paranoia. As Sedgwick concludes, 'The safer proceeding would seem to be to give as much credence as one finds it conceivable to give to self reports of sexual difference' (26).

The Fall and Great Vices of Sir Francis Bacon

Sir Francis Bacon was a great lawyer, scholar and writer. He served as Solicitor General, Attorney General and Lord High Chancellor (1618). He became Viscount St Albans in 1621. In the same year he was found guilty of having taken bribes (Norton 1992: 22–4). The text is from *Sir Simonds D'Ewes Life, written by himself* (3 May 1621), reprinted in the Appendix *Historia Vitae et Regni Ricardi II . . .* (1729).

For though he were an eminent scholar, and a reasonable good lawyer (both of which he much adorned with his elegant expression of himself and his graceful delivery) yet his vices were so stupendious and great as they utterly obscured and outpoised his virtues, for he was immoderately ambitious and excessively proud, to maintain which he was necessitated to injustice and bribery, taking sometimes most basely of both sides. To this later wickedness the favour he had with the beloved Marquess of Buckingham emboldened him, as I learned in discourse from a gentleman of his bedchamber, who told me he was sure his Lord should never fall, as long as the said Marquess continued in favour. His most abominable and darling sin I should rather bury in silence than mention it, were it not a most admirable instance how men are enslaved by wickedness and held captive by the devil. For whereas presently upon his censure at this time his ambition was moderated, his pride humbled, and the means of his former injustice and corruption removed; yet would he not relinquish the practice of this most horrible and secret sin of sodomy, keeping still one Godrick, a very effeminate-faced youth, to be his catamite and bedfellow, although he had discharged the most of his other household servants: which was the more to be admired, because men generally after his fall began to discourse of that his unnatural crime, which he had practised many years, deserting the bed of his Lady, which he accounted, as the Italians and the Turks do, a poor and mean pleasure in respect of the other; and it was thought by some, that he should have been tried at the bar of justice for it, and have satisfied the law most severe against that horrible villainy with the price of his blood; which caused some bold and forward man to write these verses following in a whole sheet of paper, and to cast it down in some part of York House in the Strand, where Viscount St Alban yet lay:

> Within this sty a hog* doth lie,
> That must be hang'd for Sodomy

But he never came to any public trial for this crime; nor did ever, that I could hear, forbear his old custom of making his servants his bedfellows, so to avoid the scandal was raised of him, though he lived many years after his fall in his lodgings in Gray's Inn in Holborn, in great want and penury.

*Alluding both to his first name of Bacon, and to that swinish abominable sin.

Mervin, Lord Audley, Earl of Castlehaven

The sensational trial of the Earl of Castlehaven began in April 1631. The allegations include rape as well as sodomy. The trial provides details of the recruitment of men for sexual purposes, commencing on the first night of Castlehaven's marriage to his second wife, Lady Anne Stanley. The trial was reprinted in 1699 and in 1708 as *The Case of Sodomy in the Tryal of Mervin, Lord Audley, Earl of Castlehaven, for committing a RAPE, and SODOMY with two of his Servants, viz. Laurence Fitz Patrick and Thomas Broadway.* The trial, condemnation and execution blended the sordid details with ceremonial pomp and splendour, as befitted an upper-class show trial. Castlehaven's Roman Catholicism did not assist his case. Cynthia Herrup (1996) has recently argued that the case was primarily concerned with a threat to patriarchy rather than an offence against sexual normality. See Bingham (1971); Burg (1980); Breasted (1971); Marcus (1983); Feroli (1994); Herrup (1996).

The Lord High Steward's speech

The King hath understood, both by the report and the verdict of divers gentlemen of quality in your own country, that you stand impeached of sundry crimes of a most high and heinous nature; and to try whether they be true or not, and that justice may be done accordingly, his majesty brings you this day to your trial . . .

May it please your Grace

I have been a close prisoner these six months without friends, without council or advice, I am ignorant of advantages and disadvantages of the law, and am but weak of speech at best, and therefore I desire to have the liberty of having counsel to speak for me.

Lord High Steward

For your so long imprisonment, it hath been to you a special favour; for you have had time enough to bethink your self, and more than ever any man had that hath been committed for such an offence, and more favour than ever any had that came to this bar. And you shall demand nothing which the law can allow, but you shall have it . . .

Mr Attorney General's speech to my Lord High Steward

May it please your Grace there are three indictments against Mervin Lord Audley. The first for a rape, and the other two for sodomy.

The person is honourable, the crimes of which he is indicted dishonourable, which if it fall out to be true (which is to be left to trial) I dare be bold to say never poet invented nor historian writ of any so foul: and although Suetonius hath curiously set out the vices of some of the emperors who had absolute power, which might make them fearless of all manner of punishments, and besides were heathens and knew not God, yet none of these came near this lord's crimes. The one is a crime that I may speak it to honour of our nation, is of such variety that we seldom or never knew the like, and for the other we scarce heard of the like, but they are of such pestilential nature, that if they be not punished they will draw from heaven a heavy judgement upon this kingdom.

For the *Crimen Sodomitcum* our Law had no knowledge of it till the 25 H. 8,[1] by which *Statute* it was made *Felony*, and in this there is no more question but only whether it be *Crimen Sodomiticum sine Penetratione*,[2] and the Law 15 Eliz. sets it down in general words, and where the law doth not distinguish neither must we. And I know you will be curious how you will give the least mitigation to so abominable Sin, which brought such Plagues after it as we may see ...[3] But my Lord it seemed to me strange at the first, how a nobleman of his quality should fall to such abominable sins, but ... he had given himself over to lust ... he was constant to no religion, but in the morning he would be a Papist and go to Mass, and in the afternoon a Protestant and go to a sermon ... He believed not God, he had no fear of God before his eyes. He left God, and God left him to his own wickedness, and then what may not a man run into? What sin so foul? What thing so odious, which he dares not adventure. But I find him in things beyond all imagination ...

Walter Bigg deposed that Amptil was a Page to Sir H. Smith, and had no more means when he came to my Lord Audley but the mare he rode on. He entertained him as his page eight years, and afterwards let him keep horses in my Lord's grounds, by which I think he enriched himself £2000 but he never sat at table with my Lord till he had married his daughter, and then he gave him to the value of £7000. That Skipwith was sent from Ireland to be my Lady's page, and that his father and mother were very poor folks there. He spent of my Lord's purse per annum £500 and he gave him at one time £1000 and hath made diverse deeds of land unto him.

My Lord was at first a Protestant, but after by buying Founthill he turned his religion.

That Henry Skipwith had no means when he came to him, and that he had given him £1000 and that Skipwith lay with him ... and that he gave a farm of £100 per annum to Amptil that married his daughter, and at other times to the value of £7000 and that there was one Blandina in his house fourteen days, and bestowed an ill disease there, and therefore he sent her away.

The Lord Steward's advice to my Lord Audley

I would advise you not to deny the things which are clearly proved, for then the Lords will less credit to the rest you say.

The Countess of Castlehaven's examination

That shortly after the Earl married her, *viz.* the first or second night, *Amptil came unto the bed's-side whilst she and her husband were in bed, and the Lord Audley spake lasciviously to her, and told her that now her body was his, and that if she lov'd him she must love Amptil and that if she lay with any other man with his consent, it was not her fault but his, and that if it was his will to have it so, she must obey and do it.*

That he attempted to draw her to lie with his servant Skipwith, and that Skipwith made him believe he did it, but he did not.

That he would make Skipwith come naked into his chamber, and delighted in calling up his servants to show their privities, and would make her look on, and commended those that had the largest.

That one night being abed with her at Founthill, he called for his man Broadway, and commanded him to lie at his bed's-feet, and about midnight (she being asleep) called him to light a pipe of tobacco, Broadway rose in his shirt, and my Lord pulled him into bed to him and her, and made him lie next to her, and Broadway lay with her carnally, whilst she made resistance, and the Lord held both her hands, and one of her legs the while, and that as soon as she was free, she would have killed herself with a knife, but that Broadway forcibly took the knife from her and broke it, and before that act of Broadway she had never done it.

That he delighted to see the act done, and made Skipwith to come into bed with them, and lie with her whilst he might see it, and she cried out to have saved herself.

Then Laurence Fitz Patrick was produced, but before his examination was read, the Earl desired that neither he nor any other might be allowed witnesses against him, until he had taken the Oath of Allegiance.[4] This was referred to the Lords the Judges. The Judges resolved against him, that they might be witnesses unless they were convicted Recusants.[5]

The Examination of Fitz Patrick was then read, the truth of which he then again confirmed upon oath. That the Earl had committed sodomy twice upon his person, that Henry Skipwith was the special favourite of my Lord Audley, and that he usually lay with him, and that Skipwith said that the Lord Audley made him lie with his own Lady, and that he usually made him lie with the young Lady, and that he saw Skipwith in his sight do it, my Lord being present, and that he lay with Blandina in his sight, and four more of the servants, and afterwards the Earl himself lay with her in their sights.

Then Skipwith was produced and sworn, and his examination read, which he again confirmed upon oath, and deposeth:

That the Earl often sollicited him to lie with the young Lady, and persuaded her to love him; and that to draw her thereunto he urged that his son loved her not, and that in the end he usually lay with the young Lady, and that there was Love between them both before and after; and that my Lord said, he would rather have a boy of his begetting than any others; and that she was but twelve years of age when he first lay with her; and that he could not enter her body without art, and that Lord Audley fetched oil to open her body, but she cried out and he could not enter, and then the Earl appointed oil the second time, and then Skipwith entered her body and knew her carnally; and that my Lord made him lie with his own Lady, but he knew her not, but told his Lord he did. That he spent £500 per annum of the Lord's purse, and for the most part he lay with the said Earl. That the Earl gave him his house at Salisbury, and a manor of £600 per annum. That Blandina lay in the Earl's house half a year, and was a common whore.

Fitz Patrick's second examination

That the Lord Audley made him lie at Founthill, and at Salisbury, and once in the bed, and emitted between his thighs, but he did not penetrate his body; and that he heard he did so with others. That Skipwith lay with the young Lady often, and ordinarily, and that the Earl knew it, and encouraged him in it, and wished to have a boy by him and the young Lady. That Blandina lived half a year in my Lords house, and was a common whore.

Edmund Scott's examination

He deposeth that Skipwith frequently knew the young Lady, and that the Earl knew it, and encouraged him therein.

Fry's examination

That Henry Skipwith and the young Lady lay often together, and the Earl in company, and that then the Earl protested, that he would fain have a boy of his begetting.

Then was read the young Lady Audley's examination

That she was married to her husband by a Romish priest in the morning, and at night by a prebend at Kilkenny; that she was first tempted to lie with Skipwith by the Earl's allurements, and that she had no means but what she had from Skipwith; but she would not lie with Pawlet; he sollicited her also to lie with one Green. That the Earl himself saw her and Skipwith lie together divers times, and nine servants of the house had also seen it.

When the Earl sollicited her first, he said that upon his knowledge her husband loved her not, and threatened that he would turn her out of doors, if she did not lie with Skipwith; and that if she did not, he would tell her husband she did.

That she being very young, he used oil to enter her body first, and afterwards he usually lay with her; that it was with the Earl's privity and consent.

Then the Earl entered into his own defence. But the Lord Steward advised him to speak pertinently; whereupon he alleged that he was a weak man, and of ill memory, and therefore desired that he might not be interrupted.

Then he began his defence with exceptions against his wife, urging that she was naught and dishonest with Broadway by her own confession.

Whereunto the Lord Steward answered, *that this made against his Lordship, therefore he ought not to allege for his defence that fact, as an imputation to his wife, which he forced her unto by compulsion and violence.*

Then he objected against the incompetency of the witnesses; as the one his wife, the other his servants, and they drawn to this by his son's practice, who fought his life; and he desired to know if there were not a statute against the incompetency of witnesses. *The Judges resolved him that there was none touching witnesses, but in cases of High Treason there was a statute concerning accusers.*

Then he desired to be resolved whether, because Broadway doth not despose any penetration, but only that he emitted upon her belly while the Earl held her, that should be judged felony as for a rape? *The Judges resolved it to be a rape, and so consequently to be a felony.*

When he desired to be resolved whether his wife is to be allowed a competent witness against him, or not *the Judges resolve that in civil cases the wife may not, but in criminal cause of this nature, where the wife is the party grieved, and on whom the crime is committed, she is to be admitted a witness against her husband.*

Then the Lord High Steward desired the Lords the Judges to resolve the questions which Mr Attorney in his charge submitted and referred to their judgements.

1. Whether it were to be accounted buggery within the statute, without penetration? *The Judges resolve, that it was, and that the use of the body so far as to emit thereupon, makes it so.*

2. Whether, it being proved that the party ravished were of evil fame, and of an unchaste life, it will amount to a rape? *The Judges resolve it to be a rape, though committed on the body of a common strumpet; for it is the enforcing against the will which makes the rape, and a common whore may be ravished against her will, and it is felony to do it.*

3. Whether it is adjudged a rape when the woman complaineth not presently? And whether there be a necessity of accusation within a convenient time, as within 24 hours? *The Judges resolve that in as much as she was forced against her will, and then showed her dislike, she was not limited to any time for her complaint; and that in an indictment there is no limitation of time, but in an appeal there is.*

4. Whether men of no worth shall be allowed sufficient proofs against a Baron, or not? *The Judges resolve, that any man is a sufficient witness in a case of felony.*

The Lord Steward's address to the Earl

My Lord, you have been graciously dealt with in this proceeding, for it is not an unusual thing in so capital and heinous causes as this, to bring the party and witnesses face to face before trial; but you have ... heard their examinations, and questioned and opposed them face to face, and are thereby the better enabled to make your defence; and his Majesty is still graciously pleased to continue his goodness towards you, and hath commanded that you should be heard at full: if therefore you have anything else to say for your self, speak it.

Whereupon the Earl answered

(Having first made a solemn protestation of his innocency, but nevertheless implored the mercy of God and the King),

That he had nothing more to say, but left himself to God and his Peers and then presented to their three considerations three woes.

1 *Woe to that man, whose wife should be a witness against him!*

2 *Woe to that man, whose son should persecute him and conspire his death!*

3   *Woe* to that man, whose servants should be allowed witnesses, to take away his life!

And he willed the Lords to take this into their consideration, for it might be some of their cases, or the case of any gentleman of worth that keeps a footman; or other, whose wife is weary of her husband, or his son arrived to full age, that would draw his servants to conspire his father's death. He said further, his wife had been naught in his absence, and had had a child which he concealed to save her honour. That his son was now become 21 years old, and he himself old and decayed, and the one would have his lands, and the other a young husband; and therefore by the testimony of them, and their servants, added to their own, they had plotted and conspired his destruction and death. And then (being thereunto required by the Lord Steward) he withdrew himself from the bar.

Then the Peers withdrew themselves, and after two hours' debate, and several advices and conferences ... at last they returned to their places, and then the Lord Steward asked them one by one, beginning at the lowest and so ascending,

1   Whether the Earl of Castlehaven was guilty of the rape whereof he stood indicted, or no? And they all gave him guilty.
2   Whether the said Earl of Castlehaven was guilty of the sodomy with which he was charged or not? And fifteen of the Lords condemned him, and the other eleven freed him.

When the Verdict was thus given, the Lieutenant of the Tower was again commanded to bring the prisoner to the bar to hear his sentence, and after he was brought the Lord Steward said unto him,

Thou must go from hence to the prison from whence thou camest, and from thence to the place of execution, and there to be hanged by the neck till thou be dead, and the Lord have mercy on thy soul.

Oh think upon your offences! which are so heinous and so horrible that a Christian man ought scarce to name them, and such as the depraved nature of man (which of itself carries a man to all sin) abhorreth! And you have not only offended against nature, but the rage of a man's jealousy! And although you die not for that, that you have abused your own daughter. And having both honour and fortune to leave behind you, you would have had the impious and spurious offspring of a harlot to inherit! Both of these horrid crimes. But, my Lord, it grieves me to see you stand out against the truth so apparent, and therefore I will conclude with this admonition, that God might have taken you away when you were blinded in your sins, and therefore I hope he hath reserved you as a subject of his mercy; and as he sends you to see this day of shame that you may return unto him, so thereby in a manner he lovingly draws you to him, therefore spend the remainder of your time in tears and repentance, and this day's work I hope will be a correction from many crimes and corruptions.

Whereupon at last the Earl descended to a low petition to the Lords, and very humbly besought them to intercede with his Majesty that he might not die, but be banished, or at least that his Majesty would not suddenly cut him off, but give him time of repentance. And then he desired their Lordships' pardon, in that he had been so great a stain to honour and nobility.

Then a proclamation being made by a serjeant, declaring that the Lord High Steward's pleasure was that all such as had attended this day's service might depart, and then the Lieutenant of the Tower carried the Earl away, and so the court broke up.

Thursday the 14th of May 1631 was appointed for the Earl's execution, who (although sentenced to be hanged, yet by reason of his noble extraction and the King's favour, was permitted to be beheaded) about 9 of the clock in the morning, attended by the Lieutenant of the Tower, Dr Winniss Bean of St Paul's, and Dr Wickham the King's chaplain, the warders of the Tower, and twelve of his own men carrying a black velvet coffin before him, he ascended the scaffold at Tower Hill, and there tarried half an hour in private conference with the doctors, and after pulling off his hat and bowing himself to the people, he said: I know that . . . all here present do expect me that I should say something, but in regard of my age and the weakness of my memory, caused by this my long affliction of imprisonment, I hope you will excuse me from making any long speech; therefore what I shall speak shall be but in brief. And then with a bold courage and loud voice he said:

I do confess that God Almighty have been a most Gracious God unto me . . . The King's Majesty, my sovereign, hath likewise showed very much and great favour towards me, in giving me an honourable trial by my peers, in giving me a long and large time of repentance, in which time I hope, by my true humiliation and sorrow for my sins, I have made my reconciliation with God . . . I do confess that my sins have been many and great, and such as have deserved death, but for these two great crimes laid to my charge among the rest, I call God to witness (in whose presence I now stand) I am innocent from them, and not guilty of them. Yet nevertheless, I confess, I have deserved death, and to that end I am brought hither, which God in his mercy enable me to undergo. And whereas at my trial there was some question made of my religion, I do confess that herein I have been too negligent, and too much externally favoured Popery and superstition, but in my judgement and opinion I have always held the Protestant religion and the tenets of the Church of England . . .

Then he held out a piece of paper and said: I have here with my own hand set down the articles which I have always believed, and will now die in, which by reason of the weakness of my sight I am not able to read myself, therefore I desire that they may be read with a loud voice ... After which he said, I have nothing more to say, but to entreat all these good people here, and all the world to forgive me, for I do forgive all the world, and as for those who were the cause of my bringing hither, I do as heartily forgive them as I do desire God to forgive me.

Then he bowed himself, and went to the middle of the scaffold, kneeling down and lifting up his hands and eyes to the heaven (each doctor kneeling on either side of him), he prayed to God; which prayer being ended (after some conference with the doctors, and with divers on the scaffold) with a smiling countenance he took his leave of all men, and desired their prayers to Almighty God for him; and then he prepared himself to die, pulling off his hat, band and doublet; and then tying a handkerchief about his face, most willingly and patiently laid down his body, submitting himself to the power of the executioner, who with one small blow severed his head from his body, which was received by his servants in a scarlet cloth, and put into a red silk bag, and with his body put into his coffin, and so carried into the Tower, where it was buried in a grave which he himself saw made for him in the morning.

The Case of John Atherton

Bishop Atherton was hanged for buggery in Dublin on 5 December 1640. The case was reprinted in 1710, 'the whole written by Nicolas Barnard, Dean of Ardagh, at the command of Archbishop Usher, and to him dedicated'. The text below is taken from *The Case of John Atherton, Bishop of Waterford in Ireland: Fairly Represented. Against a late partial edition of Dr Barnard's Relation, and Sermon at his Funeral ...* (1710). It provides a unique insight into the uses and abuses of such publications; the manner in which they were priced; how they were advertised and defended; their likely readership.

The reprinting of the case of this unfortunate Bishop near seventy years after he is dead and gone, and when the matter ought to have been buried in oblivion, and quite forgotten, is not a little surprising ...

The author of the *Additional Preface* to this edition, to avoid any umbrage, or suspicion of his having any ill design therein, pretends to remove the prejudice, which at first sight occurs, and would not have the reader think, that the *Revival of this sad relation is levelled to asperse the Episcopal Order*.

I cannot say he had such a design, and I wish with all my heart he had not; but however, he must give me leave to say it looks a little suspicious to set forth this story (which ought to be forgotten) anew, to dress it in the worst colours, and make some uncharitable additions, and reflecting inferences, which were not in the former editions thereof.

But all this slight varnish will scarce induce any thinking man to adjudge that the editor had any due regard to the *Order* in printing this story. If he will ingeniously confess that the sole motive, which engaged him thereunto in these bad times of trade, was to get money by the edition, we will believe him. That probably might be his aim, he well knowing that so scandalous and reflecting story, right or wrong, would not fail of meeting with a gainful account in this evil age, wherein many are so ready to embrace all aspersions on the Ministers of Christ, as well as on the Christian Religion.

The Prefacer intimates, 'That he having printed the Trial of Mervin, Lord Audley, Earl of Castlehaven, two years ago, his reason of reprinting at this time the sheets, which made up the lamentable narrative of Bishop Atherton, were not other than this, *viz.* that the Cases being somewhat parallel, and the only ones, which were ever proved criminal in this part of the world, might by their examples being known, deter such persons, as are unnaturally vicious, from commiting the like offences.'

I desire to know, whether it were not better to have let both these stories have lain asleep; and whether it is not a greater offence to morality and virtue, to raise up such a horrid parcel of proofs, and obscene testimonies, as are in my Lord Audley's trial, or to have let them die, and been buried with him. I pray God defend virtue, religion, and all Christian Ministers from such treacherous advocates. It looks like an odd way of reformation to bring such unnatural crimes to light, and expose them to the knowledge of thousands who would never have so much as dreamed they had been committed in a Christian country by persons of such high degree, and quality, had not the story been reprinted, to refresh the remembrance of them, and acquaint the naughty world with them, a new way of reclaiming the age, too prone by report to unnatural vices, without encouragement from reading such evil examples.

The publisher had better have told us that the profit of the edition was the true reason for the publication. And that the reader may infer so much from the bottom of the title page, where he tells us the price is one shilling, which is very high for a pamphlet of about four sheets. The novelty of so rare a subject and scandalous story (he thought) would not fail of alluring buyers at any rate; and gain is the chief design, those little mercenary writers have in their undertakings ...

The title page runs thus:
THE PENITENT DEATH OF A WOEFUL
SINNER, OR, THE PENITENT DEATH OF
JOHN ATHERTON, Executed at *Dublin*, the
5th of *December*, 1640

The title page of this edition is altered thus,
THE CASE OF JOHN ATHERTON, BISHOP
of *Waterford* in *Ireland*.
WHO
Was Convicted of the Sin of Uncleaness with
a COW, and other Creatures, for which he
was Hanged at *Dublin, Decem*. 5, 1640.

Which last scandalous words or any like them are not inserted in the title pages of those [earlier] editions: but here they are, and some of the most offensive in capitals, to render the most *remarkable and odious thing* more observable. And as if that were not enough to make it sufficiently known, the public papers must be filled with this *Modest Title Page* to carry it far, and near on the wings of an advertisment.

The Trial and Conviction of Several Reputed Sodomites

From *The Tryal and Conviction of several reputed sodomites, before the right honourable the Lord Mayor, and recorder of London, at Guild-hall, the 20th day of October, 1707*. The pamphlet provides evidence for the kinds of men involved in sexual acts, and their favoured meeting places or 'cruising grounds'.

Thomas Lane, a foot soldier, was indicted for assaulting of Mr Richard Hemmings and Mr Samuel Baker on the 15th of September last. The evidence declared, that Lane was standing upon London Bridge, and that he came to Mr Hemmings, and, pulling out his nakedness, offered to put it into his hand, and withal unbuttoned the evidence's breeches, and put his hand in there, but Mr Hemmings put his hand away: he the rather bore with the filthiness of the action, because Mr Baker, the other evidence, had told Mr Hemmings that Lane the prisoner was such a kind of person, and therefore designed to apprehend him, which they did. He said in his defence, that he had been at St Thomas's hospital and, coming over the bridge, he went to make water, and that the evidence's hand slipped upon his nakedness, and such like frivolous stuff; and withal endeavoured to say that the evidence assaulted him. But the matter appeared plain against him; and he had little else to say but that he had been so many years in King William's, and the present Queen's service, and never used to do such things. After which the Recorder gave his charge to the Jury; the verdict being omitted, till the rest of these obscene trials were over.

John Williams was indicted for assaulting Thomas Jones and John Jones, in September last. The Prosecutors each severally declared that the prisoner upon the Exchange put his hand into their breeches, and likewise had his nakedness out, which he offered to put into their hands: he was a youth, and being carried before Sir Richard Levet, he confessed he had been seduced to that practice, by one Fish, in Mayfair; and that he had done it about four times. He endeavoured to deny on his trial, all he had said before the Justice, and said the Prosecutors threatened him if he did not own it, but all appeared frivolous and he had no evidence to call.

William Huggins was indicted for assaulting Richard Hemmings and Thomas Jones, upon the Exchange, the 9th of September last; the Prosecutors declared that, walking upon Change, with design to detect such wicked persons, they were sat upon one of the benches, and the prisoner came to them severally, and offered to put his hand into their breeches, pulling out his nakedness at the same time; upon which they apprehended him, and said, at that time, that he had heard there were such sorts of persons in the world, and he had a mind to try. He had counsel of his side, and called several to his reputation, who all said he was a very honest man as to his course of life; otherwise, that he was employed as a porter. He said that he had been carrying 6 pound of coffee into Leaden Hall Street; that he had been married about a year to a young wife, who was big with child; and that he always seemed very fond of her. He denied the fact, and said he never used any such practices; but none of the evidence speaking as to what he was indicted for, the matter was then left to the Jury.

Charles Marriot was indicted for assaulting of Robert Bokins, Richard Hemmings and two others upon London Bridge. They declared he came to them severally, and pulled out his nakedness, and unbuttoned their breeches, and after they had apprehended him, he confessed that day seven-night, he was picked up by a gentleman in black, with whom he committed an indecent action, and said the gentleman offered to commit sodomy with him; but he refused that. He confessed the same before Sir Richard Beachcroft, but denied all upon his trial, and said he was coming that way, and had no such design, but it was very plain against him.

Paul Booth was indicted on the same account, for assaulting Robert Bokins, John Butterman and one tailer upon the Exchange. The evidence was much the same; all which appeared plain against him.

Benjamin Butler was indicted for assaulting Thomas Grantford and another in the same manner upon the exchange: he confessed the fact when taken, but denied it upon his trial, making very lame and trivial excuses, which all availed him nothing.

John Blithe was indicted on the like action for assaulting Robert Bokins and Thomas Grantford; the evidence was much the same as the former, he confessed it when taken, and had very little to say for himself.

James Brooke pleaded guilty to his indictment, which was much the same with the rest.

The trials being over, the jury found them all guilty of the said indictments.

A Notorious Gang of Sodomites

From A Full and true Account of the discovery and apprehending A notorious gang of Sodomites in St James's: with the examinations and commitment of two of them to Newgate, by Sir Henry Dutton Colt (1709). Rictor Norton has argued that the Society for the Reformation of Manners played an important part in bringing a number of sodomites to prosecution (1992: 49–53).

Notwithstanding the example made of several of these kind of people, called sodomites, who in a beastly way themselves with one another to the dishonour of God, and the lessening of mankind; yet, several knots, and gangs of them still associate themselves together; and 'tis confidently said that Skelthorp the soldier, who was executed last sessions, gave a private intimation of some of them, and the houses they met at. He affirming after his death, and with his last dying words, that he knew many of them, and had thought in his lifetime to have discovered them, some now say that this gang has been discovered by his means, others that a foot-boy belonging to his Grace the Duke of O———[6] gave notice of their meeting, and had them apprehended.

So that last night officers were ordered in search of them, and, according to the account given, they apprehended nine of them, some at a brandy shop near Germane Street, the person that kept the said shop being himself one of the gang, who was also apprehended, as likewise the footboy belonging to the Duke of O———, and some of them at other places.

Being brought before Sir Henry Dutton-Colt, at St James's, they were examined, and upon many instances of the beastly fact of sodomy alleged against them they were this day, being Thursday the 7th instant, committed two of them, *viz.* the foot-boy, and the brandy man and some to the Gatehouse.

It is also discoursed that a discovery is made of many more of them, for whom officers are out in search; so that 'tis hoped the whole knot of them will be now detected, to the great satisfaction of all honest people.

The trial of George Duffus for Sodomy

Trial dated December 1721, from *Select Trials* (1742). This case and the one that follows are unusual insofar as they deal with accusations of violence and rape. The punishment may appear moderate, but it is worth noting that prisoners could be killed in the pillory, if the crowd was sufficiently hostile to their crime. See Norton (1992: 112–14).

George Duffus was indicted for assaulting and committing in and upon the body of Nicholas Leader the unnatural Sin of *Sodomy*, on the 9th of October last.

Nicholas Leader

The first time of my seeing the prisoner was at a meeting-house in Old Gravel Lane. When service was ended, he came to me and, appearing very devout, began some discourse in commendation of the minister, by which means, for three or four Sundays successively, he endeavoured to insinuate himself into my good opinion, and indeed I took him to be a religious young man. He invited me to drink with him at Mr Powel's in the Minories; I complied; and, at parting, he asked me where he might hear of me another time; I told him, at the Three Merry Potters, at the Hermitage. He promised to come and see me in a few days, and was as good as his word; we sat together drinking and talking 'till it was pretty late, when he told me that he lived a great way off, and therefore should be glad if I'd let him live with me that night. As I mistrusted nothing, I made no objection to it; but as soon as we were got into bed, he began to hug me and kiss me, and call me his dear. I asked him what he meant by it? He answered, No harm, nothing but love, and presently got upon me, and thrust his tongue into my mouth. I threw him off. He got on again three or four times, and I as often served him as before, and told him if he would not lie still, I would kick him out of bed. With that he suddenly seized me by the throat, so that he had almost strangled me, turned me upon my face, and forcibly entered my body about an inch, as near as I can guess; but in struggling, I threw him off once more, before he had made an emission, and having thus forced him to withdraw, he emitted in his own hand, and clapping it on the tail of my shirt, said, Now you have it! I had then turned him out of door, but for fear of disturbing my ancient grandmother, who lay sick in the next room. Next morning he told me that I need not be so concerned at what he had done to me, for he had done the same to several others, and named in particular, a cabin-boy. In a few days after, I acquainted some of my friends with it, and they advised me to prosecute him. Upon which, I procured a warrant from Justice Tiller, and, taking a constable with me, went on Sunday morning to the same meeting as before, where we found the prisoner. The constable whispering to me and then sitting down by him, he suspected, I suppose, that we had some design against him, and so took his hat and went out, and we followed him, and he perceiving it, began to run; but we pursued, and soon overtook him. He cried for mercy, and begged that we would not expose him to public shame, adding that we were all sinners, and it was hard for a man to suffer for the first fault.

Mr Powell

The first time I saw the prisoner was at a lecture. He followed me out, and began to tell me what an excellent discourse we had had, how affecting it was and what comfort and refreshment his soul had felt under the precious teachings of such a heavenly man. This occasioned a pretty deal of religious conference between us, at the end of which he said he should be glad to drink with me at any other time; but, it being the Lord's Day, he did not care to go into a public house then. So we made an agreement to meet at my father's in the Minories, on the 12th of October last. We met accordingly, and spent the evening in religious discourse. When it grew late, he told me his wife was out of town, and he had a pretty way home, and therefore wished I would let him lie with me for one night. I readily consented, as I not at all suspecting his design; but we had not been long in bed before he began to kiss me and take hold of my privities. *How lean you be!* says he, *Do but feel how fat I am!* and so he endeavoured to convey my hand to his privities. I turned from him, and lay upon my back; he got upon me, kept me down, and thrust his yard[7] betwixt my thighs, and emitted. He told me, that I need not be troubled, or wonder at what he had done, for it was what was very common, and he had practised it with others. At the same time, he desired me to act the same with him; but I refused, and told him I was a stranger to all such practices, and if I had known what sort of a man he had been, I would never have lain in the same bed with him.

The spermatic injection not being proved, the court directed the jury to bring in their verdict *Special.*

The judges meeting afterwards to consider of this verdict, they agreed in their opinion, that the prisoner had not completed the felony of which he stood indicted. But that he might not escape the hands of justice entirely, a bill of indictment against him for attempting to commit sodomy with Nicholas Leader, was laid before the Grand Jury of Middlesex, who finding it *billa vera*,[8] he was brought to his trial at the sessions in March following, when Nicholas Leader deposed that, being in bed with the prisoner, the prisoner seized him by the throat, forcibly turned him on his face, and endeavoured to commit sodomy with him.

The jury found him guilty, and he was sentenced to pay a fine of twenty marks, to suffer two months' imprisonment, and to stand upon the pillory near Old Gravel Lane.

Thomas Rodin, Alias Reading, for Attempting Sodomy

The trial took place in October 1722 and was reprinted in *Select Trials* ... (1742). The case demonstrates that the jury was from time to time reluctant to bring in a verdict of guilty.

Thomas Rodin, was indicted for a misdemeanour, in assaulting a person unknown, with an intent to commit the unnatural and detestable sin of *Sodomy*.

Henry Clayton: I and the prisoner lodged in one room, at Peter Wright's, a shoemaker, at the Three Shoes next door to the Harrow in Long Alley in Moorfields. My landlady keeps a bawdy-house, and lets out lodgings. Some time in March last – I forget the day – there accidentally comes in a stranger to lodge; the prisoner drank with him, and at half an hour past ten they went up to bed together; and I saw the prisoner lying with him in the nature of carnal copulation, as a man lies with a woman.

Court: How could you be sure of that?

Clayton: I did put my hand between them; but it was a moon-light night, and I was a-bed in the same room, and could see what they did plain enough.

Court: Were they in bed?

Clayton: No, they were upon it. The stranger at first said he would not do it then, for he was too drunk. The prisoner bid him pull his

	breeches off, which the stranger not doing readily, the prisoner struck him several times. I believe he might give him fifteen blows, and then the stranger let down his breeches, and the prisoner turned him on his face, and fell on him.
Court:	It's very surprising that a man should make such an abominable attempt upon a stranger; and that a stranger should so soon comply; and that they should both do this before witness.
Clayton:	Why, the stranger was drunk, and the prisoner was so far from being ashamed of such a thing that he gloried in it; for I heard him say afterwards that he took more pleasure in lying with a man, than with the finest woman in the world; and that he had not touched his wife these nine months.
Court:	How long was it before you spoke of this?
Clayton:	I spoke on't the next day.
Court:	And why did not you prosecute sooner?
Clayton:	Because I had lodged there seven months, and was got £13 in my landlady's debt for gin, and other matters; and I was afraid to proceed till I had cleared that account . . .
Prisoner:	I and my wife keep stocks-market: I sell fruit, and she sells greens. I was one day at the Green Dragon alehouse in Moorfields, when Clayton came in and quarrelled with me, and called me Molly and Sodomite. Whereupon I indicted him at Hick's Hall; and he met me next day, and said, *I'll do your business for you, and spoil your going to* Hick's Hall.
Wright:	This Clayton is scandalous villain. He and Angelica Latham (one of his whores, who has got several husbands) abused the prisoner, and called him pick-pocket and sodomite dog; for which the prisoner indicted him at Hick's Hall; and thereupon Clayton charged the prisoner with this fact. But the prisoner is a poor, honest, ignorant man, and he and his wife lodged twelve months in my house, and he always behaved himself well, and kept good hours; for his business at the market requiring him to be up very early in the morning, he commonly went to bed by seven or eight o'clock, and I never knew him to be up so late as ten. And that night, as Clayton charged the prisoner with this fact, my husband was at work by the prisoner's bedside, so that no such thing could be done but he must have seen it.

The Jury acquitted the prisoner.

Trial of William Brown

In July 1726, Brown defended himself by claiming that he was innocently making water. He argues that he has been married, and that he is not a 'woman-hater'. He also makes the radical claim 'I think there is no crime in making what use I please of my own body'. From *Select Trials* (1742).

William Brown was indicted for a misdemeanour, in assaulting Thomas Newton, with an intent to commit sodomy with him.

Thomas Newton, Willis and Stevenson the constables, having a warrant to apprehend sodomites, I went along with them to an alehouse in Moorfields, where we agreed that I should go and pick up one, and, that they should wait at a convenient distance. There's a walk in the Upper Moorfields, by the side of the wall that parts the Upper Field from the Middle Field. I knew that this walk was frequented by sodomites, and was no stranger to the methods they used in picking one another up. So I takes a turn that way, and leans over the wall. In a little time the prisoner passes by, and looks hard at me, and, at a small distance from me, stands up against the wall, as if he was going to make water. Then by degrees he fiddles nearer and nearer to where I stood, 'till at last he comes close to me. *'Tis a very fine Night*, says he; *Ay*, says I, *and so it is*. Then he takes me by the hand, and after squeezing and playing with it a little (to which he showed no dislike) he conveys it to his breeches, and puts —— into it. I took a fast hold, and called to Willis and Stephenson, who coming up to my assistance, we carried him to the watch-house. I had seen the prisoner before, at the house of Thomas Wright, who was hanged for sodomy.

Willis: We have asked the prisoner why he took such indecent liberties with Newton, and he was not ashamed to answer, *I did it because I thought I knew him, and I think there is no crime in making what use I please of my own body.*

Prisoner: As I was going across the fields, I stood up to make water, and with no other design, at which time Newton coming along, took hold of me, and then called out to the two informing constables.

Several of both sexes appeared to his reputation. They deposed that he had been married twelve or thirteen years; that he bore the character of an honest, sober man, a kind husband, and one who loved the conversation of women better than that of his own sex.

The jury found him guilty. His sentence was, to stand in the pillory in Moorfields; to pay a fine of ten marks, and to suffer twelve months' imprisonment.

The Trial of Mother Clap for Keeping a Sodomitical House

The house kept by Mother Clap was raided on a Sunday night in February 1725/6. The prosecutions were assisted by an informant known as P—, who was a molly himself, and appears to have been betrayed by his associate, one Mr Harrington (see *The Trial of Thomas Wright*). Evidence is first offered by Constable Stevens. (See Norton 1992: 54–69). The evidence presented may be compared with Ned Ward's account of the mollie's club (1709).

Margaret Clap was indicted for keeping a disorderly house, in which she procured and encouraged persons to commit Sodomy, December 10, 1725, and before and after.

Samuel Stevens

On Sunday night, the 14th of November last, I went to the prisoner's house in Field Lane, in Holborn, where I found between forty and fifty men making love to one another, as they called it. Sometimes they would sit in one another's laps, kissing in a lewd manner and using their hands indecently. Then they would get up, dance and make curtsies, and mimic the voices of women, *O, Fie, Sir! – Pray, Sir – Dear, Sir – Lord, how can you serve me so? – I swear I'll cry out. – You're a wicked Devil – and you're a bold face – Eh! ye little dear Toad! Come, buss!* – Then they'd hug, and play, and toy, and go out by couples into another room on the same floor, to be married, as they called it. The door of that room was kept by —— Eccleston, who used to stand pimp for them, to prevent anybody from disturbing them in their diversions. When they came out, they used to brag, in plain terms, of what they had been doing. As for the prisoner, she was present all the time, except when she went to fetch liquors. There was among them Will Griffin, who has been since hanged for sodomy; and —— Derwin, who had been carried before Sir George Mertins, for sodomitical practices with a link-boy.[9] Derwin bragged how he had baffled the link-boy's evidence; and the prisoner at the same time boasted, that what she had sworn before Sir George in Derwin's behalf, was a great means of bringing him off. I went to the same house on two or three Sunday nights following, and found much the same practices as before. The company talked all manner of gross and vile obscenity in the prisoner's hearing, and she appeared to be wonderfully pleased with it.

Joseph Sellers deposed to the same effect, that he believed there were above forty sodomites taken from that house and committed to prison in one night.

Prisoner

As for Derwin's being carried before Sir George Derwin's, it was only for a quarrel. I hope it will be considered that I am a woman, and therefore it cannot be thought that I would ever be concerned in such practices.

The evidence being full and positive, and nobody appearing to her character, the jury found her guilty. Her sentence was to stand in the pillory in Smithfield, to pay a fine of twenty marks, and suffer two years' imprisonment.

The trial of Gabriel Lawrence for Sodomy

The trial began in April 1726. Lawrence argues that he did not know that Mother Clap's was a molly house. He did not offer a confession, and asserted that Newton had committed perjury. From *Select Trials* (1742).

Gabriel Lawrence was indicted for committing, with Thomas Newton, aged 30 years, the heinous and detestable Sin of Sodomy, not to be named among Christians, July 20, 1725.

Thomas Newton: About the end of June, or the beginning of July, one Peter Bavidge, who is not yet taken, and ——— Eccleston, who died last week in Newgate, carried me to the house of Margaret Clap, who is now the compter,[10] and there I first became acquainted with the prisoner. Mother Clap's house bore the public character of a place of rendezvous for Sodomites. For the more convenient entertainment of her customers, she had provided beds in every room in the house. She had commonly thirty or forty of such kind of chaps every night, but more especially on Sunday nights. I was conducted to a bed up one pair of stairs, where, by the persuasion of Bavidge, who was present all the while, I suffered the prisoner to ———. He, and one Daniel, having attempted the same since that time, but I refused, though they bussed[11] me, and stroked me over the face, and said I was a very pretty fellow. When Mother Clap was taken up in February last, I went to put in bail for her; at which time Mr Williams and Mr Willis told me they believed I could give information; which I promised to do; but at the end of the same month I was taken up myself.

Willis:	In March, Newton was set at liberty, but he came the next day, and made a voluntary information.
Williams:	He informed against several of the Sodomites at that time, but did not discover the prisoner till the 2nd of this month, and then I took his information at Sir John Fryer's.
Samuel Stevens:	Mother Clap's House was in Field Lane, in Holborn, it was next to the Bunch of Grapes on one side, and joined to an arch on the other side. It was notorious for being a molly house. I have been there several times, in order to detect those who frequented it: I have seen twenty or thirty of them together, kissing and hugging, and making love (as they called it) in a very indecent manner. Then they used to go out by couples into another room, and, when they came back, they would tell what they had been doing, which, in their dialect, they called *marrying*.
Joseph Sellers:	I have been twice at that house, and seen the same practices.

The prisoner's defence

Prisoner:	I own I have been several times at Mrs Clap's house to drink, as any other person might do; but I never knew that it was a resort for people that followed such sort of practices.
Henry Yoxan:	I am a cow-keeper, and the prisoner is a milkman. I have kept him company, and served him with milk these eighteen years. I have been with him at the *Oxfordshire-Feast*, where we have both got drunk, and then come home together in a coach, and yet he never offered any such indecencies to me.
Samuel Pullen:	I am a cow-keeper too, and have served him with milk several years, but never heard any such thing of him before.
Margaret Clap:	I have known him seven years. He has often been at my house, and, if I had suspected any such stories of him, he should never have darkened my doors, I'll assure ye.
William Preston:	I know him to be a very *sober* man, and have been in his company when he was *drunk*, but never found any ill by him.
Thomas Fuller:	Nor I neither. He married my daughter eighteen years ago: she has been dead seven years. He had a child by her, which is now living, and 13 years old.
Charles Bell:	He married my wife's sister. I never heard the like before of the prisoner; but, as for the evidence, Newton, I know that he bears a vile character.

The Jury found him guilty. *Death*.

He was a second time indicted for committing sodomy with P—, November 10. But, being convicted of the former, he was not tried for this.

The Ordinary's[12] account of Gabriel Lawrence

'Gabriel Lawrence, aged 43 years, was a Papist, and did not make any particular confessions to me. He kept the chapel with the rest for the most part; was always very grave, and made frequent responses with the rest, and said the Lord's Prayer and Creed after me. He owned himself of the *Romish* Communion; but said, that he had *a great liking to the Church of* England, *and could communicate with them*; but this I would not allow, unless he renounced his error. He said Newton had perjured himself, and that in all his life he had never been guilty of that detestable sin; but that he had lived many years with a wife who had born several children, and kept a good sober house.

At the place of execution he said, that a certain person had injured him when he took him before a Justice of the Peace, who committed him, in swearing or affirming, that fifteen years ago he had been taken up for that unnatural sin, and, that it cost him £20 to get himself free, which, he said, was utterly false; for, 'till this time, he was never suspected.

He was hanged at Tyburn, on Monday, May 9, 1726.

The Trial of William Griffin for Sodomy

From *Select Trials* (1742). Griffin failed to produce character references. He states that he had no money and was therefore obliged to seek shelter wherever possible. He also asserts that he was married with two children.

William Griffin, alias Griffith, was indicted for committing sodomy with Thomas Newton, May 20, 1725.

Thomas Newton:	The Prisoner and Thomas Phillips, who is since absconded, were both lodgers, near two years, in Clap's house. I went upstairs while the prisoner was a'bed, and there he——.
Sam Stevens:	On Sunday 4th November, I went to Clap's house and found

about a dozen mollies there; but, before I came away, the number increased to near forty. Several of them went out by pairs into another room, and, when they came back, they said they had been married together. I went again the next Sunday night, and then, among others, I found the prisoner there. He kissed all the company round, and me among the rest. He threw his arms about my neck, and hugged and squeezed me, and would have put his hands into my breeches. And, afterwards, he went out with one of the company to be married. Every night, when I came from thence, I took memorandums of what I had observed, that I might not be mistaken in the dates.

Prisoner: I lodged at Clap's a year and three-quarters, but I know nothing of what these fellows have sworn against me. As for Newton, it's well known he's a rogue, and a tool to those informers, Willis and Williams.

The Jury found the prisoner guilty. Death.

The Ordinary's account of William Griffin

'William Griffin, aged forty-three years, an upholsterer by trade, in Southwark, had, as he said, been a man of good business, but, having squandered away or lost his memory, was fallen into poverty. He denied the fact for which he died, calling Newton, the evidence, perjured; and saying, that that abominable sin was always the aversion of his soul; for he had lived many years with a good virtuous wife, who had several children, two of which, a boy and a girl, are living. And he said both of them behave mighty well, and to the satisfaction of all concerned with them. And he hoped that the world would not be so unjust as to upbraid his poor children with his unfortunate death.'

At the place of execution, Griffin would not own the commission of that detestable sin.

He was hanged at Tyburn, on Monday, May 9 1726.

The Trial of George Kedger for Sodomy

From *Select Trials* (1742). The trial indicates that Tom Orme kept a molly house. Kedger states that he had been at school with Orme.

George Kedger, alias Keger, was indicted for committing sodomy with Edward Courtney aged 18 years, July 15.

Edward Courtney:	I have known the prisoner about a year. I first became acquainted with him when I lived a servant at the Yorkshire Grey, in Bloomsbury market. I went from thence to live at a cook's shop in St Martin's Lane, and there the prisoner followed me. One day, in July last, he came there to dine, and sat in a back room in the yard. When I went to fetch away the foul plates, he squeezed my hand, and kissed me, and took me in his arms, and asked me to let him ———, to which I consented, and he put ——— and ———.

I went afterwards to live with Thomas Orme, a silk-dyer, at the Red Lyon, in Crown Court, in Knaves-Acre. He kept a molly house and sold drink in private back rooms to such sort of company; and there the prisoner often came after me upon the same account.

Prisoner:	Ned Courtney asked me to do it, when he lived at the cooks, but I told him I could not, *What*, says he, *am not I handsome enough for ye? That's not the case*, says I, *but I have got an injury. That's only a pretence*, says he, *but, if you don't like me, I have got a pretty young brother, and I'll fetch him to oblige ye.* As for my going to *Tom Orme's*, he was my school-fellow, and sold a pot of good drink; and there likewise Ned solicited me to do the story, and fain would have had me to have gone into the necessary-house with him, for he said, he could not rest till he had enjoyed me. And afterwards, when he was turned out of his place, I met him by chance, in a very poor and ragged condition, and he told me, that he had nothing to subsist upon, but what he got by such things. I advised him to leave off that wicked course of life; but he said, he wanted money, and money he would have, by hook or by crook; and, if I would not help him to some, he would swear my life away.
Frances Crouch:	I always found the prisoner to be a very civil man, and I

> believe he loved a girl too well to be concerned in other affairs.

Another woman deposed to the same purpose.

The jury found him guilty, and he received sentence of death, but was afterwards reprieved.

The Trial of Thomas Wright for Sodomy

Wright maintained a busy molly house and confessed that he was a sodomite. The report omits certain details, but they may be inferred readily from the foregoing accounts. From *Select Trials* (1742).

Thomas Wright was indicted for committing buggery with Thomas Newton, 10 January 1724/5.

Thomas Wright:	Will you swear that I ——— in ———?
Newton:	Yes. The prisoner is a woolcomber by trade, but sold ale to the mollies, though it was privately, for he did not keep an alehouse, but fetched the drink from other houses, and we allowed him a profit out of it. He removed to Beech Lane, where he likewise kept rooms for entertainment of the molly-culls, and sold ale as he did at his other house. He has often fetched me to oblige company that way, and especially to one Gregory Turner,[13] who commonly chose me for his sweetheart.
Joseph Sellers:	On Wednesday the 17th of November last, I went to the prisoner's house in Beech Lane, and there I found a company of men fiddling and dancing and singing bawdy songs, kissing and using their hands in a very unseemly manner. I was introduced by P— who was one of their members; but it seems they were jealous he had made some discovery, for they called him, a *treacherous, blowing-up, mollying bitch,* and swore they'd massacre any body that should betray them. But the prisoner taking P—'s part, the matter was made up. At going away, the prisoner kissed me with open mouth.
William Davison:	The discovery of the molly houses was chiefly owing to a quarrel betwixt P— and ——— Harrington; for upon this

78

quarrel, P—, to be revenged on Harrington, had blabbed something of the secret, and afterwards gave a large information. The mollies had heard a little of the first discovery, but did not imagine how far he had proceeded, and what farther designs he had upon them. By his means, I and Davison were introduced to the company, at the prisoner's lodgings. In a large room there we found one a-fiddling, and eight more a-dancing country dances, making vile motions, and singing, *Come let us ——— finely*. Then they sat in one another's lap, talked bawdy and practised a great many indecencies. There was a door in the great room, which opened into a little room, where there was a bed, and into this little room several of the company went; sometimes they shut the door after them, but sometimes they left it open, and then we could see part of their actions. The prisoner was very fond of us, and kissed us all at parting in a very lewd manner.

The prisoner's defence

Edward Sanders: I have known him several years, he was born and bred at Newberry, and I never heard any such report of him before this time.

Mary Cranton, and Mary Boulton deposed that they lived in the same house with the prisoner; that his apartment was below, and theirs above; that indeed they had sometimes heard music and merry-making; but knew nothing of any such practices as had been sworn against him, and that he behaved himself like a sober man, and was *a very good Churchman*.

The jury found him guilty. Death.

The Ordinary's Account of Thomas Wright

'Thomas Wright, born in Newberry, aged 32 years, was instructed in his younger years in the principles of Christianity, and inclined to the *Anabaptist* way. He said also that Newton swore falsely against him; but could not deny his following these abominable courses, only he refused to make particular confessions. Although he had been unused to go to separate meetings, yet he said that he loved and esteemed the Church of England, and was willing to communicate with the Church, as soon as with Dissenters; that he always lived soberly, following his employment, which was that of woolcombing. That he died in the Christian faith, a Protestant, and believing to be saved only through the merits of Jesus Christ.

At the place of execution Wright could not deny his guilt; but reflected on Newton the evidence, as perjured in some particulars.'

He was hanged at Tyburn, on Monday, May 9 1726.

The Trial of George Whittle for Sodomy

Riggs gave evidence that Whittle's Royal Oak tavern had a poor reputation and was judged to be another molly house. He claimed that his back room was used by surgeons for the treatment of clients suffering from venereal disease; he produced a variety of witnesses for his good character. Norton affirms that Whittle 'was certainly the most resourceful of the mollies, and he proceeded to mount a brilliant defence' (62–3). Text from *Select Trials* (1742).

George Whitle, alias Whittle, was indicted for committing sodomy with Edward Courtney, December 1, 1725.

Edward Courtney: The prisoner kept an alehouse, the Royal-Oak, at the corner of St James's Square, in Pall Mall. He had a back room for the mollies to drink in, and a private room betwixt that and the kitchen. There is a bed in that middle room, for the use of the company when they have a mind to go there in couples, and *be married*; and for that reason they call that room, *the chapel*. He has helped me to two or three husbands there. One time indeed, he put the bite upon me; for, *Ned*, says he, *there's a country gentleman of my acquaintance, just come to town, and if you'll give him a wedding night, he'll pay you very handsomely.* So I stayed until midnight, but no gentleman came, and then it being too late for me to go home, the prisoner said I should lie with him, which I did. He put his hand upon —— and promised me a great deal of money, if I would let him —— which I agreed to, and he did. But in the morning he gave me no more than sixpence.

Mr Rigs:	For two or three years past it was commonly reported, that the prisoner kept a molly house, and therefore the neighbours did not care to go and drink there.
Drake Stoneman:	I have known the prisoner's house for two or three years. I have seen men in his back room behave themselves sodomitically, by exposing to each other's sight what they ought to have concealed. I have heard some of them say, *Mine is best. Yours has been Battersea'd.*[14] I don't know what they mean by that expression. There is a little private room between back room and the kitchen; they call it the *chapel*, to which they sometimes retired, but I can't say for what purpose.

The prisoner's defence

Prisoner:	This Ned Courtney is such a scandalous fellow that he deserves no credit. He has been thrice in *Bridewell*.[15]
Courtney:	'Tis very true, I have been three times in *Bridewell*, but it was for no harm, as you shall hear. First, when I was a servant in the Cardigan's Head at Charing Cross, I went to see the prisoner, and he made me drunk in his *chapel*, and when I came home, I abused my master's mother, for which I was sent to *Bridewell*, and my master would not take me in again. Then, sir, I went to live at a molly house; but my master breaking, and I helping him to carry off his goods by night, a constable stopped me, and I being saucy, and refusing to tell him where the rest of the goods were, I was carried before a Justice, and sent to *Bridewell* a second time. And the third time was only for raising a disturbance about a mollying-cull in Covent Garden.
Prisoner:	As to the report of my being a Sodomite, it was raised out of spite; for I unfortunately let a barber's shop to one Johnson, whose wife was a cursed bitch, and had been in Newgate for perjury. Johnson owed me half a year's rent, and I arrested him, for which his wife, whenever she got drunk, used to call me a sodomite dog, and so the scandal begun, and was spread among my neighbours. I had a wife, but she has been dead these two years. I had two children by her, one of them is dead likewise, but the other is here in court, a girl of 13 years old. I was going to marry another woman, a widow, just before

this misfortune broke out. As for what Drake Stoneman says about some things that he has seen in my back room, there is nothing in it but this: I was acquainted with several young surgeons, who used to leave their injections and syringes at my house, and to bring their patients, who were clapped, in order to examine their distempers, and apply proper remedies. I have had them there on that account eight or ten times a week.

Peter Grenaway: Ned Courtney was bound to my master. He told me a quarter of a year ago that one butler, a chairman, was the first man that he had had to do with; and, he has told me since that the occasion of his quarrelling with the prisoner was because the prisoner refused to let him have a pint of beer when it was late. The prisoner was a peacemaker, he kept a creditable house, and always advised his customers to go home betimes to their wives.

Will. Baylis and Nicholas Croward: they had lain with the prisoner several times when his wife was living, and never found anything in his behaviour that might give them the least ground to suspect him inclinable to sodomitical practices.

Steward and Eliz. Steward: the first news they heard of such a thing was from the wife of Johnson, to whom the prisoner had let a shop.

Alexander Hunter and William Brocket: such a report was indeed whispered in the neighbourhood a little before the prisoner was taken up, but they knew not what foundation there was for it.

Others of the prisoner's neighbours deposed that they never heard anything like it.

Ann White: I was the prisoner's servant. I know of no room that was called the *chapel.* The middle room and back room were public for any company, and there was neither locks nor bolts to the doors.

Ann Cadle: I have been the prisoner's servant ever since the 13th of October last. I lay in the house every night. I don't so much as know this Ned Courtney. I never saw him at our house: and I think I should have seen him if he had lain there all night with my master.

The jury acquitted the prisoner.

Proposals for Castrating Criminals

Text from a pamphlet published in Ireland, *Gentlemen's Magazine* (December 1731).

1. If the following reasons be approved, a law may be made for a short term by way of trial.

2. We do not find by the scriptures that *castration of mankind* was forbidden; but, on the contrary, that *eunuchs* have been in great esteem, and ministers of state.

3. It appears from the confessions of dying criminals, that they were brought to shame by indulging their lusts with lewd women.

4. Since the pleasure of love, and hopes of issue, are almost universal, no punishment can have a deeper impression on the mind. Mothers and nurses (for certain reasons) will be always plying their children with good advice, and a smart whipping for every little pilfering trick. The planters in America are weary of our transported felons; the pains of hanging are soon over; the death and name of the party forgotten; whereas the circumstance of *castration* will remain as a living monument of shame and disgrace. Such a law cannot be justly taxed with cruelty, since other civilized nations use severer punishments.

5. In Barbadoes was an insurrection among the Moorish slaves. The planters considered they should be losers by their deaths, therefore punished them with *castration*, and have not had a rebellion since.

6. It has been observed that *rapine* and *theft* often run in the blood. Such a law will disable a set of vile people from leaving their pernicious breed behind them. Hector Boethius[16] affirms, that the most ancient Scots gelded such as laboured under madness, or infectious distempers, which they thought might be communicated to their offspring.

7. Criminals will afterwards become dull, and timorous; and, if cut when young, the shrillness of voice and want of beard will discover them. They may become useful to the public as musicians and fine singers, and save the money which is given to Italians and other foreigners, and may be trusted with the care of our wives and daughters.

8. As to the female felons, it will be a severe mortification to think that their husbands, &c. may come under this punishment.

9. This will cool the heat of those that are guilty of *rape* and *sodomy*.

10. It is computed that 5000 examples of this kind will have such an influence upon the wicked, that our judges and juries will have much less business on their hands.

A Dissertation upon Flogging

Text from *Gentlemen's Magazine* January 1735.

I have often wondered, that among all the learned dissertators of this and the last age none have treated professedly of flogging. That it is an art, I think, most people agree, and I hope to show that it is one which deserves our particular cultivation. This lucubration then shall explain wherein the art consists, enumerate the wonderful uses of it, and give some account of the most remarkable professors. To begin with the distinction: *flogging* is an art which teaches us to draw blood from a person's posteriors in such a manner as may twinge him most severely without the danger of a mortification. To proceed methodically, I shall consider this art under its four causes. The material cause is a rump which rises with a noble projection. I have seen a professor foam with ecstasy at the sight of a jolly pair of buttocks. The efficient cause is a grim pedant in his nightgown, with a big, dull look, whisking a *birch fascis*.[17] The formal cause is the nice administering the rod in an angle of about 45 degrees. For it is a maxim that this does the business far more effectually than the most violent perpendicular impression. The final cause, or the advantage, of flogging may be considered either in regard to the patient or agent in the operation. As to the former, it has been observed that there is a great sympathy between the bum and the head; and that a proper application made to the posteriors draws the stupefying humours from the *cranium*,[18] thoroughly purges the brain, and quickens the fancy wonderfully. Besides, the operation reduces the buttock into a decent size and form, effectually hindering that immoderate tumour which though so convenient and lovely in the fair sex, is yet, I think universally condemned in a man. But not only the patient, but also the professor receives great benefit from flogging. As these gentlemen's lives are generally sedentary, flogging is a very necessary exercise, putting the body into a kindly agitation, and sometimes a gentle sweat. Besides, here a man has an opportunity of venting his spleen and ill-nature, and so qualifying himself for the company of his friends. Moreover, as every man has some ambition, what a vast satisfaction must it be to him to lord it so absolutely over a school full of his fellow creatures? *Bumbalio* has owned to me that (though he has an admirable stomach) he had rather cut up the buttock of a country squire than the finest loin of beef. I shall now proceed to give a short account of some eminent professors. This art does not seem to have flourished much amongst the ancients, and I wonder that the great writer Mr Wotton has not so much as hinted the mighty superiority of the Moderns[19] in this respect, which would have afforded him as just and copious matter of triumph, as our excellency in the statute-laws and divinity above Plato and Tully ... I cannot help adding for the honour of my country that this art is practised as much now as ever, there being hardly a great town in this island but has a worthy professor in it. To all such I most humbly dedicate this painful dissertation, being very sensible in how great need it stands of their protection, heartily begging their pardon if there should be found grain of wit in it, which I hardly believe, since I have been at great pains to make it as dull and heavy as possible, in order to give it the better title to their patronage; and if any of 'em are displeased, my modesty has not suffered me to celebrate them by name, I here promise to do 'em all possible justice in the second edition of this work upon their directing their requests to me at my booksellers. Worthy sirs, yours, to command, THYRSIS.

Mr Swinton Accused of Sodomitical Practices

Text from *A Faithful Narrative of the Proceedings in a late Affair between the Rev. Mr John Swinton, and Mr George Baker, both of Wadham College, Oxford: wherein the Reasons, that induced Mr Baker to accuse Mr Swinton of sodomitical Practices, and the Terms, upon which he signed the recantation ... To which is prefix'd a Particular Account of the Proceedings against Robert Thistlethwayte, Late Doctor of Divinity, and Warden of Wadham College, For a Sodomitical Attempt upon Mr W. French, Commoner*[20] *of the same College* (1739). The text provides a detailed and reasoned analysis of a series of events at Wadham College, Oxford. The account was later used as source material for a burlesque poem.

On Saturday, Feb. 3. 1739. Robert Thistlethwayte, late Doctor of Divinity, Warden of Wadham College, immediately after divine service in the afternoon sent his servant the Manciple[21] to Mr W. French, Commoner of the said College, a young gentleman of about two years standing, as he was talking with some fellow collegiates in the gateway; upon which he went directly to the Warden's lodgings, and was not seen afterwards by any of his friends till supper-time six o'clock. Whilst he was sitting with them at the same table, they observed that he was very much disordered and uneasy at something or other that had happened; and as they knew he had been with the Warden, they asked him whether the Warden had given him a *Jobation*,[22] &c. to which he would give no answer. When supper was over, Mr French, with two or three more, adjourned to a gentleman's room in the College to spend the evening, where Mr French was taken very sick and vomited, to the surprise of the company. He afterwards sat down, and behaved during the rest of the night as if he had been distracted, calling the Warden the worst of scoundrels and villains. Such uncommon behaviour amazed the company, who begged to know what was the matter. *The matter*, he said, *the murder of one's father, or whole family is nothing to it; you can't conceive anything bad enough*: but he would not tell them what it was. When they found that, they waved the discourse: Mr French, however, could not sit in peace during the whole night; but seemed full of horror and amazement. All Sunday he continued in the same condition, sometimes shedding tears, and sometimes calling the Warden the worst of names in the most public manner; often saying, that it was in his power to expel him. During all this time his acquaintance did not suspect the real cause, but imagined it something very bad. On the Monday Mr French invited Mr George Baker and some few more of his acquaintance to breakfast with him, when the gentlemen, who had been with Mr French before, told Mr George Baker in what an unaccountable manner Mr French had behaved ever since he came from the Warden's lodgings; repeating the names he called him; in what manner he threatened him; and that he said it was in his power to expel him. Upon hearing these things, Mr Baker advised Mr French to be more cautious in what he said of the Warden; for, if it came to his ears he would certainly expel him. Mr French answered very warmly, that he could make good everything he said, and insisted, that he could have the Warden expelled whenever he pleased. Mr Baker then told him, if the Warden had acted to him in a manner so villainous as to exceed parricide, &c. and he was well assured of the sufficiency of his evidence, that he ought to apply to some magistrate, and not talk of it publicly in all companies; for that was the way to put the Warden upon beginning with him first. After some farther conversation, in which Mr French was advised not to talk so freely as he had done; Mr Baker, and all the company, except one gentleman, went away. Mr Baker dined with the gentleman, who stayed behind with Mr French, the same day, who gave him an account of everything Mr French had said; and from his expressions, and the manner in which he behaved, they both concluded that it must be some iniquity of a very deep dye. Whilst they were guessing what it was most likely to be, Mr Baker recollected, that, about a fortnight before, it had been suggested to him, that *the Warden did not love women*. As the person who told him this had been just complaining of the Warden's ill usage of him in respect to his business, and might therefore say such a thing of him out of ill-will (though the man is of a fair character, and behaved well after), he took no notice of it at that time; and the rather, because it was generally believed, that the Warden was over-familiar with a certain woman in Oxford. This, however, coming in to his thoughts on the present occasion, upon comparing circumstances, the other gentleman and himself concluded it most probable that the Warden had made a sodomitical attempt upon Mr French. In consequence, as Mr Baker had always been very intimate with Mr French, his neighbour in the country, and his professed friend, he resolved to go to him, to enquire into the matter, and advise him how to proceed, in case it was as he imagined. Accordingly, when he returned to College, he went to Mr French's room, where he found him walking by himself in a very melancholy and disconsolate condition. Mr Baker told him he was very sorry that anything should give him so much trouble and anxiety; that he was come as a friend, to offer him all the service in his power, and insisted that he should tell him what it was that afflicted him. Mr French answered, that he must tell it one time or other, but that he chose rather to defer it till he had taken his Bachelor's degree; being apprehensive that if he should attack so powerful an adversary as the Warden before, and should miscarry by any means, that he should be expelled, and consequently ruined. Mr Baker then told him that by all the circumstances he had heard from him, and from what he remembered to have been suggested to himself some little time before, concerning the Warden, the thing could be nothing but sodomy; and that, if the Warden had made any such attempt upon him, he was indispensably obliged to divulge it, and bring him to Justice. Mr French upon this seemed very desirous to prosecute the Warden, if he could do it with safety to himself, and Mr Baker insisting upon the obligation he was under to make it known, for the good of the College, university, &c. and assuring him, that he should not want friends to assist him, he replied that if there was any other fellow in the town besides Mr Swinton, he would disclose it to him; but that he did not care to let Mr Swinton into it, though his tutor, lest he should do his utmost to quash it. Mr Baker then told him: that should be no obstacle; for he would dispatch a special messenger for one of the Fellows the next morning. After this Mr Baker and Mr French spent the evening together, and Mr French disclosed the whole matter to him. The next day the gentleman Mr Baker had sent for (the Rev. Mr Stone) came to Oxford, and after having heard the affair, he thought it of such consequence as made it proper to call in more advice. On Wednesday morning therefore a second messenger was dispatched for another of the Fellows (the Rev. Mr Watkins) who came to College the same night, when a letter was sent to London for the advice of council. On Thursday morning the Fellows sent for Mr French; and, for better Security, thought proper, that Mr French should give an account of the whole affair under his hand. Accordingly, in the presence of the aforesaid Fellows, James Birt, Bachelor of Arts, and Mr George Baker, he signed a declaration at large, of which the particulars are judged too gross and obscene to be repeated, and such as amounted to the most notorious sodomitcal attempt conceivable.

Nothing more was done till the advice of council come down by the post on Friday. This was, that Mr French should apply to a Justice of Peace, particularly the Vice-Chancellor, and make an affidavit of the whole affair. As Mr French had no positive evidence besides himself, and the Warden's influence and fortune, gave reason to apprehend that he might find means, and prostitutes, that would swear anything to bring him off, which could not happen without involving Mr French in great difficulties and misfortunes; his friends in College advised him not to open the matter to a magistrate, till he had first communicated it to his father. Hereupon, Mr French set out on the Saturday for his father's house, with a pressing letter to him from Mr Baker, who was well acquainted with him; and both came to Oxford the Thursday following. The old gentleman on his arrival expressed very great concern for what had happened, and was inexorably determined upon justice. One of the Fellows of the College (George Wyndham, Esq., barrister at law) being expected in Oxford on Friday night, the opening of the affair to the Vice-Chancellor was put off till Saturday morning. That gentleman came at the time, and advised old Mr French and his son to lay the thing before the Vice-Chancellor on Saturday morning. Accordingly, Mr Baker went with the old Gentleman and his son to the Vice-Chancellor, to whom he opened the occasion of their coming. The Vice-Chancellor was engaged at that time, and desired young Mr French to get a testimonium from his College, and come to him again between eleven and twelve. All this while, neither the Warden nor anybody else, except seven or eight of Mr French's friends, knew anything of what was transacting. Mr French, his son, with Mr Baker returned to College, and Mr Baker drew up a form of a testimonium, which young Mr French carried to the Warden's lodgings, in order to have it signed and sealed. The Warden, according to custom, sent it round to all the fellows in the College, to know their opinions; who all approved it. After this the Warden found fault with the form of the testimonium, and desired it might be drawn up in another. Having pointed out the passages he did not approve, Mr Baker wrote another with the Warden's emendations. Mr French went back with the new form; at which time the Warden began to smell what he was about; and addressed himself to him in the following Terms. Mr French, *I am sorry to find the firm friendship, which has subsisted so long between you and me, is about to be broken off. In what manner?* says Mr French. *Why, I hear,* says the Warden, *that you are going to make known to the world my behaviour to you some time ago in my parlour. Yes, Sir,* says Mr French, *I have been with the Vice-Chancellor already, and am come to you with this testimonium, to know whether you will sign it. Tell me whether you will or not. Have you any objection to my character or behaviour in College? No indeed, Sir,* says the Warden, *I always thought you the most regular man in my College. – Why then don't you sign my testimonium? – So I will, with all my Heart: But pray, my dear Mr French for God's sake, do conceal it; for we shall both be ruined; if you should make this known to the world.* Mr French still insisted upon his signing the testimonium directly; or that he would tell him plainly he would not do it: upon which the Warden signed it. He then earnestly intreated Mr French to conceal what had passed, and said, *My dear, I'll give you anything; nay, all that*

I am worth in the world, if you will not expose me; and continued for some time praying, and making him the most tempting offers to the same purpose. Mr French told him, as his final answer, that he was the worst of men; that if he could propose the most valuable consideration in the world, he would not put it up, but would make his behaviour known to the public; that he would prosecute him to the utmost rigour, and desired no other satisfaction than the justice the law would afford him. Mr French then came out of the Warden's lodgings in a great passion, and cried out *Bribery, Bribery*, in the College quadrangle, where ten or twelve young gentlemen were standing, to whom he declared the overtures the Warden had been making to him. The testimonium was immediately after signed by all the Fellows in the College.

Old Mr French, and his son, with Mr Baker, waited again upon the Vice-Chancellor, who appointed them to meet the Warden at his lodgings at six in the evening. Old Mr French, and his son, Mr J. Birt, Mr George and Nicholas Baker, who were witnesses in the affair, attended at the time, where they found the Vice-Chancellor, Dr Pardo, Principal of Jesus College, Counsellor Wright, Justices of the Peace, and the Warden of Wadham. Old Mr French and his son were first called in to the Justices, in order to the latter's giving his depositions; previously to which, Dr Pardo, in a speech of almost an hour long, represented in the strongest terms, the difficulties and dangers Mr French was about to engage in, and the irrecoverable misfortunes that would attend his not making good his allegations. As Mr French was conscious of his just grounds for the accusation, and the sufficiency of his evidence, those remonstrances did not intimidate him, and he insisted that his depositions should be taken, which was granted. What he deposed was the same in substance with the above-mentioned declaration signed before the Fellows of Wadham, with the addition only of the Warden's offers to induce him to conceal the fact. The depositions of the other persons, who were afterwards called in, were only to prove Mr French's sickness and disorder of mind, before he divulged the affair; and that they saw him come from the Warden's lodgings, and cry out *Bribery*, &c. in the quadrangle. After the witnesses had continued at the Vice-Chancellor's till half an hour after ten at night; the farther examination was adjourned till the Monday morning following, at half an hour after seven.

The next day, Sunday, between eleven and twelve in the forenoon, Mr French and his son went to the Rev. Mr Swinton, who, as is said before, was tutor to the latter. The whole discourse turned upon this business: and upon Mr Swinton's expressing his concern that such a thing should happen, and much resentment against the Warden, young Mr French said to him; Sir, I presume, you very well remember, that you came to the Warden's lodgings yesterday fortnight in the afternoon; that you found the parlour door bolted; that you waited some time before the Warden opened it; and that, when you came in, you found him and me together. Mr Swinton replied, Yes, Sir, I very well remember it; and it was as you say. Mr French then added, that circumstance was the most material evidence to corroborate his own, and that therefore he hoped Mr Swinton would be so good as to be at the Vice-Chancellor's the next morning, at half an hour after seven, in order to give it in. Mr Swinton promised the father and son faithfully that he would not fail. They then parted. Young Mr French saw Mr Swinton again the same night, when he told him, that he had and his father were with him in the morning, and that he had confessed all that Mr French accused him of to be true. Several times the same evening Mr Swinton called old Mr French out of our company, and very earnestly entreated him to put off the farther examination before the Vice-Chancellor for two or three days, which he refused. Next morning, being Monday, by five o'clock, before it was light, Mr Swinton's bed-maker came and called old Mr French, who lay in the College, out of his bed, and told him the Warden and Mr Swinton desired to speak with him. After some persuasions the old gentleman dressed himself, and went down into the quadrangle where he found Mr Swinton waiting for him, who conducted him to the Warden's lodgings. The Warden was in his parlour with a good fire, burnt wine, chocolate and coffee. As soon as they were set down, after some words had passed, the Warden and Mr Swinton joined in entreating Mr French in the most earnest terms to take his son into the country, telling him that the Warden would provide handsomely for him. When the old gentleman could not be prevailed on to consent to that; Mr Swinton desired him to put off the farther examination before the Vice-Chancellor for two or three days, and offered him a paper to sign, of which he does not know the contents; and this he also refused. After this discourse had continued about half an hour, Mr French was carried privately from the Warden's lodgings through the garden of the Warden and Fellows.

Between six and seven the same morning, the Warden's servant was sent to the Vice-Chancellor, to tell him that Mr French and his son had agreed to put off the farther examination, till the Wednesday following. Upon receiving that unexpected message, the Vice-Chancellor sent his servant to Wadham College, to desire Mr French and his father to come to him immediately. When they came, the Vice-Chancellor told them the message he had received by the Warden's servant; and asked them if they had agreed to put off the examination. Young Mr French, in a very great surprise, made answer that no such proposal had been made to him; that it was an imposition; and that he insisted upon the affair's being brought on immediately. The Vice-Chancellor then asked Mr French senior, whether any such thing had been proposed to him? He answered, that Mr Swinton had asked him to put off the hearing for two or three days, which he had refused. The Vice-Chancellor upon that appointed nine o'clock for attending before him; when another gentleman (Peter Maurice, Scholar of the said College) deposed concerning young Mr French's behaviour after the attempt had been made upon him.

Mr Swinton, though he had promised young Mr French his pupil, and old Mr French, so faithfully to be at the Vice-Chancellor's, and to give his evidence concerning what he knew, and though he had expressed himself so much against the Warden, was so far from coming, that though he was diligently sought after in most parts of the town, he could not be found.

Mr French was bound over to prosecute the Warden at the following Assizes, as the Warden and his bail were in a bond of two hundred pounds for his appearance: soon after which the Warden left Oxford.

Not long after the Warden disappeared, about a fortnight before Assizes, William Boxley, a young fellow, who was known to be very much in the Warden's Lodgings, and had been heard to drop some ambiguous expressions, happened to be in a gentleman's rooms, where five or six more were together. The hints that had escaped him made them so curious as to ask some questions; and he confessed such things in respect to himself and the Warden, as occasioned so much laughter that he was ashamed, and would go on no farther. However, he told Mr Baker, who was one of the company, that if he would go downstairs with him, he would tell him all in private. Accordingly, he declared [though not] in express terms, to him, and a third person, Mr J. Birt, whom Mr Baker thought proper to call in, that the Warden had committed sodomy upon him; describing the act in other words. Mr Birt and Mr Baker waited upon the Vice-Chancellor, and informed him of what they had heard, and from whom; but were told, that he had no power to compel the fellow: so the affair dropped.

This Boxley had waited upon Mr Swinton about two years; and though what he reported of the late Warden had been told to Mr Swinton, he continued to serve him, till the present Warden came down; who, upon hearing the story, immediately turned the fellow out of College.

Before the Assizes came on, Mr French and his friends had intelligence given them that there were other persons, on whom the Warden had made sodomitical attempts. There were Robert Langford, butler of Wadham College, and William Hodges a barber; both of whom were served with subpoenas to give evidence at the Assizes.

Mr French's evidence before the Grand Jury was exactly the same in substance, as his declaration to the Fellows. Mr Swinton who was served with a subpoena, proved that he found the Warden's door bolted, and Mr French and him together. Richard Harris attested, that he went, by the Warden's order, on the Saturday before mentioned, to tell Mr French that the Warden wanted to speak with him; and that he came into the parlour with the Warden's wig, whilst Mr French and he were together. Mr J. Birt, Mr P. Maurice, and Mr Geo. and Nich. Baker, deposed the manner of Mr French's behaviour after the attempt, as above.

The evidence of Robert Langford the butler, was to the following effect: 'That about five or six years ago the Warden invited him to supper: That the Warden and he set down (nobody else being present) and drank a bottle of wine together, when the Warden began to talk and act in a beastly manner; endeavouring to kiss and tongue him, and to put his hand into his breeches; that he soon understood him, and desired him to be quiet; for he did not like such usage: that the Warden, notwithstanding, persisted then, and at several other times, and once in particular in a very violent manner; upon which he expressed great resentment, and quitted the room; resolving never to go into the Warden's company again alone. He farther deposed, that the Warden had very frequently sent his servant the Manciple to tell him he wanted to speak with him, and that the servant added, the Warden was angry at his not coming, when he had been so often sent for: that he told the Manciple his reason; and bid him tell the Warden, that though he was assured he would turn him out of his place in College, he would never come to him again; and that if he thought fit to inflict that punishment upon him for not coming, the world should know his reasons for it: that the Warden himself came once to his house; and that he was so far from treating him with respect, that he took his hat, and ran out of his house directly: that he used commonly to go out of the College the back way, to avoid being seen by the Warden from his study window, lest he should be obliged to go to him; that about two years ago that happened to be the case; for going home from the buttery through the quadrangle, the Warden was looking out of his study window, and called him: that as there were several gentlemen in the quadrangle, he did not know what to do, and thought it would appear very odd if he refused to go to the governor of the College, when he called him: That therefore he went, and as soon as he came into the room the Warden began his caresses, trying to kiss him, &c. as before: that he begged him to desist, adding, he would expose him if he did not: that upon the Warden's continuing his addresses, he told him, that he wondered gentlemen of his fortune did not provide themselves with women, or wives, and not act in so vile and beastly a manner: That the Warden made answer, that he would not give a farthing for the finest woman in the world; and that he loved a man as he did his soul; at which, having expressed his just resentments, he left him, and never went to him after.'

Mr Langford, during the prosecution, was solicited to be silent, but absolutely refused all proposals upon that head.

William Hodges, the barber, deposed: 'That about a year and a half ago he went to shave the Warden, about eleven in the forenoon: That the Warden being dressed in his gown and cassock, he put his nightgown over him, to avoid dawbing him: that whilst he was shaving him, he found something tickling his breeches, but thought at first that it might be the effect of the gown's not sitting right upon the Warden, wherefore he altered the position of it, and went on: That immediately after he found the Warden trying to introduce his hand into his breeches: That thereupon he asked him what he meant: that the Warden answered, there is no harm in this, my dear; and talked to the same effect so long, that the barber swore he would never shave him again, for he knew what he wanted, and that he was the wrong person for his purpose: That when he went home he told his Master the Warden's behaviour, and that he would not shave him no more: that his Master desired, though he did not continue to shave him, that he would go, however, for two or three days; for if he did not go, that the Warden would suspect he had told him (his Master) and it would be to his prejudice: That accordingly he went again one day, and as soon as he came into the room, the Warden said to him, How dost do, my dear barber. How dost thy cock do, my dear barber? Let me feel it; and then went to kiss him: that upon this, he said to the Warden, Damn you, you son of a bitch, what do you mean? And knocked him backwards in his chair: That Thistlethwayte got up and attacked him again, as lewdly as before and that he again knocked him down, ran away, and never went near him afterwards.'

The Grand Jury found the Bill *nemine contradicente*: the Warden was called upon to appear in Court at the Assizes, as were his bail to bring forth his body: but neither the one nor the other appeared.

We come now to the more immediate concern of this publication, the recantation of Mr Geo. Baker; and as we have avoided reflections in the foregoing account, and confined ourselves strictly to fact, we shall observe the same simplicity in the following relation ...

In March last, Mr Baker received a letter from a gentleman in the country, a Master of Arts, of Wadham College. He had heard of the Warden's behaviour to Mr French, and in what manner Mr Swinton had acted during the prosecution; and he knew how remarkably intimate Mr Swinton had been with the Warden, ever since the return of the former from Italy. These things gave him some suspicion; and he imagined, that something might be discovered, by enquiring into a circumstance, that he recollected to have passed whilst he was in College. Francis Smith and his wife, who waited upon this gentleman when at Oxford, had a boy that served them, who at that time told his master and mistress that he had lain with Mr Swinton. Nobody then suspected anything of Mr Swinton, but it was a matter of wonder, that he would take a boy to bed to him, who was very lousy, and so ragged and filthy, that the gentleman whom Smith served in College would not suffer him to come into their rooms.

After the breaking out of the sodomitical affair at Wadham, he thought fit to impart this circumstance for the sake of other discoveries. Soon after Mr Baker had received this letter, he went to Smith, who is since gone from Wadham to New College, where he is under-porter, and told him what his *quondam*²³ Master had suggested concerning Mr Swinton, and the boy that lived with him, when he belonged to Wadham. Smith made answer that Robert Trustin, his servant at that time, not coming home to bed for two or three nights, and neglecting his business in the College in the day, he suspected that he either idled away his time, or spent it in some roguery; that wherefore, when he came home, he examined him, where he had been, and why he did not assist him in College as usual? That the boy told him, he had been with Mr Swinton in his chamber, during that time, to wait on him: that believing he lied, as Mr Swinton had a bed-maker of his own, who had a wife and servants under him, and that he only said so to avoid punishment, he beat him: That his wife, hearing the boy still persist in the same story, asked him where he lay, while he was with Mr Swinton in his chamber; and told him that the boy said that sometimes he sat up in the great chair, sometimes lay down before the fire, and that Mr Swinton sometimes bid him lie down on the bed, which he accordingly did: That upon her telling him so, he was very angry with the boy, and said he would break his bones, if ever he knew that he went near Mr Swinton's bed again, for he would fill him full of lice, and he should have a fine noise about it: that soon after, the boy going to Mr Swinton, told him that he (Smith) had beat him, and on what account; and that Mr Swinton sent for him, and told him he should not have beat the boy Bob; for that he had kept him, being out of order, to give him medicines, and desired that he would let the boy continue to do so: That he consented, not thinking of any harm of Mr Swinton, who found the boy in victuals during the time he was with him. Mr Baker told Smith, in answer that he wished there was not something more in this than was quite right, for Mr Swinton's late behaviour in the Warden's affair had given most of the College strong suspicions of him. He then asked Smith whether the boy had ever dropped any thing since, tending to confirm such suspicions; to which he answered, No. However, Mr Baker concluded, that as the thing seemed very suspicious, it would not be amiss to question the boy about it. A day or two after, Smith brought the Boy to the King's Head tavern in Oxford, where Mr Baker, and three or four more gentlemen were then in company, who then all went into a room with Smith and the boy. At the sight of so many strangers the boy was confounded, and would say nothing: upon which every body left the room except Mr Baker, Smith and the boy, to whom one of the gentlemen, that went out, gave a penny, which was afterwards alleged to be given by Mr Baker, by way of bribe; how falsely will soon appear. The boy then affirmed to Mr Baker and Smith, that he used to lie in the bed with Mr Swinton; that Mr Swinton used to tickle and play with him in the morning; that he used to play with Mr Swinton's cock, which used to stand; that Mr Swinton used to kiss him. Mr Baker asked him whether Mr Swinton used to put his tongue in his mouth, to which the boy answered, No. And then being asked whether Mr Swinton did not use to get upon his back, he answered, No; but said, that he used to get upon his belly, between his thighs, and that he used to put his cock into his a— h—, and that he felt something warm come from him, and that he sometimes made him wet between his thighs. He was then asked, whether he ever gave Mr Swinton physick,[24] to which he answered, No. Mr Baker then gave Smith a gill of wine (as he frequently did, on account of his being an old servant), of which Smith gave part to the boy. After the boy had said these things, in a manner, that by no means argued him an idiot, as he was afterwards judged to be, Mr Baker went out of the room, and said to Smith: Frank, it would be very improper for me to give the boy any halfpence, because, as it is probable, that this affair will be farther enquired into, if it should ever be said, that I had given the boy money, it might be thought that I had bribed him, to say what he does of Mr Swinton. After this, Mr Baker saw the boy no more, till he was sent for by the Vice-Chancellor; but Smith was with the boy some time after, and asked him, Bob, are you sure that what you have told Mr Baker and me is true? Yes, the boy answered, it is all very true. Smith added, Be sure to say nothing of Mr Swinton, but what you are well assured to be true: the boy said he had not. Then Smith left the boy for that night. The boy went almost every night afterwards to Smith's house, where he several times repeated what he had told Mr Baker and Smith at the King's Head, to Smith's wife, and once, accidentally, to Smith's brother-in-law. The boy added a circumstance he did not mention to Mr Baker, which was this. Upon their asking him whether Mr Swinton did not hurt him but put his cock, &c. as above. Yes, said the boy. And did not you cry out? Yes, and Mr Swinton bid me be quiet, and be a good boy. The boy was particularly cautioned by those persons, every time he spoke of the affair, to be sure to tell the truth, and to say no more than what he knew to be true. After the boy had in this manner confirmed Mr Baker in his suspicion, he thought it incumbent on him to acquaint the Fellows of the College with the whole, and accordingly invited the sub-warden, and one of the senior Fellows to spend the evening with him at his room. He there told them all that had passed from his receiving the letter, in which the affair was first suggested to him, till then. The sub-warden and the other gentlemen thought proper, that Mr Bowditch, another of the Fellows, should be acquainted with the thing the next morning at breakfast; at which time he was desired to tell Mr Swinton what was alleged against him. This he did that morning, being Friday. The same evening Smith and his wife saw the boy again, who told them, that he had been before the Vice-Chancellor. Upon which Smith asked him who Mr Swinton sent for him. The boy answered, John Kimber. This Kimber, as was said above, is Mr Swinton's bed-maker. Well, says Smith, and what did Mr Kimber say to you? The boy answered, in Friar's Entry he bid me deny everything I had told you and Mr Baker, and he would give me something next Sunday. Well, says Smith, and did you deny before the Vice-Chancellor what you told me and Mr Baker? Yes, says the boy. And why did you, you dog? Because, answered the boy, they said I should do so. He then said to Smith, Master, shall I be hanged? It was the morning Kimber went for the boy, but he was not carried before the Vice-Chancellor till the evening, when, as Mr Baker afterwards found, he had denied everything he had said to him and Smith; and had said that Mr Baker had given him money, &c. to say as above of Mr Swinton. The next morning, being Saturday, Mr Baker was sent for, as were Smith and his wife, to come before the Vice-Chancellor, with whom he found Dr Pardo and Mr Wright, Justices of the Peace, one of the senior Proctors,[25] Mr Swinton, and the boy. The Vice-Chancellor told Mr Baker that Mr Swinton was come to complain of him, for having spread a report about the town, that he had been guilty of sodomy with the boy there present. Mr Baker replied he never had reported that Mr Swinton had positively committed sodomy upon the boy; but that he had told some friends what the boy had said to him and Francis Smith. Mr Baker then went on to inform the Vice-Chancellor in what manner the thing had been suggested to him in a letter from a gentleman of Wadham College, who remembered that Smith and his wife, who had waited upon him as a nurse in College, had told him, that Mr Swinton had borrowed the boy of him to give him physick, and that the boy, upon being asked where he lay, had said, with Mr Swinton. Smith and his wife were then questioned upon that head, who both declared that Mr Swinton did borrow the boy of them, at the time when that gentleman was in College, to give him physick, as he said, because he was out of order, and wanted some body to wait on him: that after the boy had been two or three days with Mr Swinton, they asked him where he lay, and that the boy answered, with Mr Swinton; they added, that the boy was with Mr Swinton a fortnight or three weeks. The Vice-Chancellor then told Mr Baker, that the boy and Mr Swinton had been with him the night before; and that the boy affirmed that Mr Baker had extorted what he said of Mr Swinton from him; and that Mr Baker had given him money. Mr Baker then told him all that had passed; in what manner he had used the boy; and what the boy had told him and Smith, in respect to giving the boy money, on leaving the room; which both Mr Baker and Smith offered to swear. The Vice-Chancellor then said to the boy, *Did Mr Swinton* ever put his cock into your a— h—? Yes, sometimes, says the boy: after which the boy both affirmed and denied almost all the questions that were asked him. Mr Baker then told the Vice-Chancellor what the boy had said the night before to Smith and his wife; *viz.* that Mr Swinton's bed-maker had bid him deny everything he had told him and Smith. The Vice-Chancellor asked the boy whether Mr Swinton's bed-maker had said so to him: to which the boy answered,

Yes. But upon being asked the same question again, he denied it. Smith and his wife then offered to take their oaths that the boy had said so to them but the night before. Mr Swinton's bed-maker was then called in; and he offered to swear that he had said nothing more to the boy than that he should be sure to speak the truth; and that he never knew the boy lay in bed with Mr Swinton; but that when he came into Mr Swinton's room in the morning, he found the boy either in a great armchair, or lying on the hearth: but as to this witness, the magistrates did not put him to his oath. Mr Swinton said that he was in a very high fever, and that wanting somebody to wait on him, he borrowed the boy to give him physick; that the boy was next to an idiot; that he never lay in his bed, but that he lay before the fire upon the hearth, or in a great chair. It was then urged that the boy might more probably speak truth to such people as Smith and his wife, with whom he was familiar, than before the Vice-Chancellor and their company, whose presence might confound and awe him so much as to make him prevaricate in the manner he did. The Vice-Chancellor then told Mr Baker that there was no stress to be laid on such an evidence; that he was much to be blamed for taking away a clergyman's character with no better foundation, &c., and added, that the least Mr Baker could do would be to ask Mr Swinton's pardon publicly, and acknowledge that he was very sorry for what he had done; and that he had done wrong, &c. Mr Baker answered, Mr Vice-Chancellor, if I make such an acknowledgment, I shall say what I don't believe to be true; and therefore I do not care to do it. He added that his only motives for what he had done were for the good of his College, and the public in general; and the persuasion that after the affair had been made known to him in so clear a manner, it was his duty, as well as every man's in the University, as they had all suffered in their characters upon Thistlethwayte's account, to have their eyes about them, and not to suffer even the suspicion of so great a crime to escape them. Mr Baker soon after left the Vice-Chancellor, and in two or three days went to him again; when the Vice-Chancellor made Mr Baker sensible of the great power he had over him by the statute of the University concerning defamation, by which he could oblige him to recant, imprison, or expel him. At the same time, he showed Mr Baker the form of the recantation, which Mr Swinton insisted upon. Mr Baker answered that it is very hard, a man should be obliged to submit in such a manner for his good intentions of bringing the most pernicious crimes to light: that the recantation was worded in such terms as could not but imply in the strictest manner that he had intentionally, and without any grounds whatsoever, endeavoured to ruin the character of Mr Swinton. The Vice-Chancellor himself said then that the terms were too strong, and that he had drawn up another in milder words to the following effect. *That Mr Baker had CONDUCED to the spreading of such a report; and that he had not had a PROPER FOUNDATION for it.* This Mr Baker approved much more than the first, though persisted to think it very hard that he should be obliged to stoop to a person he still believed undoubtedly guilty. When the Vice-Chancellor showed Mr Swinton the milder form of his own drawing up, he objected to it, and insisted that the first should be signed. The Vice-Chancellor upon that sent again for Mr Baker, and told him Mr Swinton would not be satisfied with his mild form, but insisted on the other. Mr Baker replied, that if he recanted in those words, he should be guilty of saying a great falsehood; and hoped he should not be obliged to sign what he believed far from true. He added, that he had a very great opinion of the Vice-Chancellor's candour and integrity, and that he would entirely submit to what he should think most achievable and prudent for him to do. The Vice-Chancellor answered, Really, Mr Baker, I think you had better do it, and then it will all be over. Mr Baker then asked for a copy of the recantation, in order to show it to his friends, and consult them about it; which the Vice-Chancellor gave him: he also desired, that the signing of the recantation might be deferred for a day, till his friends came to town; but that was absolutely refused. About a quarter of an hour before the time fixed for his signing this recantation, his friends, who were just come from London, sent for him, and as soon as they had heard as much of the matter, as the shortness of time would admit, they all not only advised, but enjoined him, not to sign it in that form; for it would be much better to be expelled, than to sign a thing so injurious to his reputation, and so contrary to truth, and his real sentiments. The hour fixed for his appearance before the Heads of Houses being come, he left his friends, fully determined not to recant in the manner proposed, and went into the schools. He there sent one of the beadles[26] for the Vice-Chancellor. Mr Baker said, that he was come from some friends, who were just returned to Oxford, and they advised him not to sign the recantation upon any account; and that he would not sign it in the form proposed. Mr Baker continued: Mr Vice-Chancellor, you must be very sensible, that everything contained in this recantation is directly the reverse of my real sentiments; and that it is expressed in such terms, as will admit of no construction, but that I have designedly, and without any grounds whatsoever, endeavoured to ruin Mr Swinton's character. The Vice-Chancellor replied that such strong expressions were only *matter of form*, as in the case of indictments, in which the words were used of much stronger signification, literally accepted, than what was really true: and then he repeated several forms of law of that kind. Mr Baker answered, that as *mere matter of form* he would sign it, but not otherwise. He then said to the Vice-Chancellor, Sir, I put myself into your hands; do you think I can do this with prudence or safety? To which the Vice-Chancellor replied that he might do it very safely, and that it was his best way to do it. Some little time after, Mr Swinton and Mr Baker were called into *Golgotha*,[27] before the Heads of Houses, and Mr Baker signed the recantation. The Vice-Chancellor asked Mr Swinton whether he was satisfied, to which he replied, Yes; and that he required nothing farther from Mr Baker. The Dean of Christ Church (the Rev. Dr Conybeare) then said to the Vice-Chancellor that he had something to move, if Mr Baker would retire. Accordingly, Mr Baker withdrew, and when he came in again, he found, they had agreed, that he should give a bond for his good behaviour to Mr Swinton: with which Mr Baker made no difficulty to comply.

About four or five days after, Mr Baker, to his great amazement heard, that the form he had signed was to be inserted in the newspapers. Upon that information he went to the Vice-Chancellor, under pretext of knowing, upon what day he should wait on him to give the above-mentioned bond, and at the same time took occasion to tell him, that he was told Mr Swinton intended to publish the recantation, which he had signed, in the newspapers; and that if he should be suffered to do so, his character, and himself, in consequence, would entirely be ruined; for the world, not knowing the conditions on which he signed it, would take the words in their literal sense, and conclude him the vilest and most abandoned wretch in nature; and he was infinitely afflicted, that he had been guilty of so great a weakness. The Vice-Chancellor answered that some of the Heads of Houses, were scarce satisfied with that only; and were for having the statutes put farther in force against him. Mr Baker replied that if what was expressed in the recantation was true, and his real sentiments, and if he had accused a clergyman of so horrid a crime without any foundation, as it specifies, he not only deserved to be expelled from the University but the world; for that a person capable of so notorious a wickedness was not worth continuing a member of any society whatsoever. He added that himself (the Vice-Chancellor) would be much censured for suffering such a person, as he should appear to be from that publication, to continue a member of the University. After some few more words had passed to this purpose, the Vice-Chancellor appointed Mr Baker to attend at the Professor's of law, where Mr Baker gave a bond of one hundred pounds for his future good behaviour to Mr Swinton, and Mr Swinton gave Mr Baker a general release.

The reader has here the whole circumstances of this affair, from first to last, without the least falsification, and as they were conceived to be the best apology that could be made for Mr Baker, it was thought proper to give them to the public in the simple dress in which they were collected. If there be any objection made to the truth of any one of them, the next relation of it, to prove its veracity, will be by depositions upon oath, which are ready.

The Wadhamites: A Burlesque Poem[28]

A version of the preceding text. The poet stresses the danger of a learned (or artificial) sexuality replacing the natural orientation to heterosexuality. Text from *College Wit Sharpen'd: Or, The Head of a House, with, A Sting in the Tail: Being, A New English Amour, of the Epicene*[29] *Gender, done into the Burlesque Metre, from the Italian. Adress'd to the Two Famous Universities of S-d-m and G-m-rr-h* (1739).

At length the *Quarere*[30] is decided;
And disputants, long since divided,
Must now in one opinion join,
OXFORD does CAMBRIDGE far out-
    shine.
There reigns, and thrives, an ancient
    ART,
T'improve the health, and cheer the
    heart ...

ATTEND, I'll paint you out a case,
Which happen'd, in that learned place.
Not Pembroke's Warden; no, 'tis
    W-dh-m-,
The word, i'faith, sounds much like
    Sodom:
Deeply in this rare ART acquainted;
Virtuous; no Vice his Soul e-er tainted:
Nay, more, abhors a pretty wench.
Pleas'd with the sprightly air of Fr–ch,
Kindly determines to impart
To him, the secrets of his ART.
Straightway the Manciple he sends,
That Dr Th-stle-th-e intends,
The choicest favours to bestow
On pretty Fr–ch, that he must go
Directly to the Warden's chamber,
The truth can never be a slander.
AWAY comes Fr–ch, the Warden
    meets him,
And with the greatest friendship, treats

him;
But sad neglect, ne'er asks his mind,
If he was to the ART inclin'd:
But *Nolens Volens*,[31] learn he must,
And at him makes a potent thrust,

Fr–ch, tho' a Youth of solid parts,
Well read in many useful arts.
Could not the W-rd-n's science relish;
But basely, often call'd it hellish.
This must be owned, no disgrace is,
Since gifts are various as faces.
Some are for one thing, some another;
This a divine, a lawyer t'other:
What one esteems a useful ART,
Another values not a fart.
Thus W-dh-m's W-rd-n, learned, wise,
Extols this ART above the skies.

The worth Dr kindly try'd,
T'instruct the youth, (who still deny'd)
With all the symptoms of affection;
And promises of his protection:
To which he adds, an ardent kiss,
As earnest of that future bliss
He might expect, would he but once
Submit to learn; yet still a dunce.
Hard Fate. O! Th-stle-th-te, is thine,
To cast thy pearls, before such swine,
L–gf–d, and H-dg-s, are the next,
The Warden preach'd to, from that
    text;

Lab'ring with more than human skill,
His wholsome doctrine to instill;
Describ'd it in its proper light,
As yielding profit with delight:
And to eradicate each doubt,
That might subsist, he straight pull'd
  out,
An instrument, most finely fram'd,
(I cannot say I heard it nam'd:)
To give a demonstration plain,
He taught them not, in hopes of gain.
Then eagerly he went to work.
I'm told, there hardly is a Turk,
In that most spacious tract of land,
But what this ART does understand.

THAT by the bye. This man of W-d-h-m,
Whose ART existed first in Sodom,
Began to show his skill most truly,
Hard Fate! The wretches prov'd
  unruly.
H-dg-s bowl'd out, forbear, be civil:
L—gf—d cries, fury, hell, the devil.

This stopped a while his
  demonstration,
And fill'd his soul with great vexation.
Then both in one petition join'd,
Dear Mr W-rd-n, pray be kind,
We cannot learn: O pray give o'er,
And we'll provide you with a wh-re.
The W-rd-n says, I pray don't hollow:
Your inference, can never follow;
My ART may seem most strange to
  you,
Your ign'rance, that's the cause; 'tis
  true.
But you are not too old to learn;
Will riches do you any harm?

THEN took he L—gf—d in his arms,

My dear, you are all over charms.
Oh! Why so coy, my pretty jade;
Why, of my sacred ART afraid?
Discard your doubts, disperse your
  fears,
Joy shall attend your future years;
You I'll secure, from ev'ry woe,
Then change for yes, the dreadful No.
View but how Sw-nt-n spends his time;
Pleasure and profit, both combine,
To make his days one single scene,
Of perfect bliss; then what d'ye mean?
Embrace the present happy time;
Int'rest can never be a crime.

THIS said, he made a fresh attack,
His skill to prove, upon his back.
What shall we say, this base ingrate,
With stick of oak, he broke his pate;
Leaving the W-rd-n on the floor,
To rowl and wallow in his gore:
Rend'ring for good, the greatest evil,
Sure, their some kin unto the devil.

BUT let me crave your close attention,
To what I farther have to mention.
After they had this fact committed,
For which they should have been De
  Witted,
Conscience disturb'd, for the
  transgression,
Fear of their spirits took possession.
What might be done, with speed, to
  screen 'em,
Was often argued between 'em.

SCHEMES are advanc'd, again
  rejected,
For fear they both should be detected.
At last, as fortune often smiles,
On knaves, and honest men beguiles,

They heard by chance, Oh happy day!
That Fr—ch as stupid was, as they;
That after all the W-rd-n's pains,
He curs'd the ART, and call'd him
    names.

WITH joy they speedily repair,
T'acquaint him with the whole affair;
Tell him their case, and what they
    fear'd,
The which, when Fr—ch had fully
    heard,
Courage (says he) keep all quiet,
We'll ruin him, they both cried *fiat*.[32]

THIS is the Scheme, (and we'll declare
    it,
Nay, more than that, we'll roundly
    swear it,
Before the jury-men with speed,
Which if by you, 'tis but agreed,
My life for't, when they've heard the
    case,
They'll soon expel him from this
    place;)
That being void of holy fear,
An ev'ry grace, to Christians dear,
Holds conversation with the devil;
Deals in black ARTS, and ev'ry evil;
Raises up spirits, horrid, frightful:
In short, that he is grown so spiteful,
As to destroy the health and ease,
Of all, who dare him to displease.

THIS scheme contriv'd, with hellish
    ART,
They to the Jury-Grand impart,
Back'd with an oath, to bind it
    stronger;
The jury could contain no longer,
But send immediately a Proctor,

To cite before them, W-dh-m's doctor.

BUT he withdrew; for having heard,
Their base designs, he wisely fear'd,
That right, or wrong, he might be cast;
Thus they were conquerors at last.

THIS you well know, sometime's the
    case,
Virtue and learning meet disgrace;
Yet very often gets the best
Of vice and falshood: hear the rest.

Sw-nt-n, a man, to most super'our,
To none in W-dh-m is infer'our,
In the same ART the W-rd-n taught;
Bless'd with a happy turn of thought,
To screen himself secure from spite:
In that he certainly is right;
For tho' as harmless as a dove,
Yet surely it does well behove,
For to assume the serpent's wit.
Least like the W-rd-n he is bit.

Sw-nt-n's success in S-d-m's ART,
Should animate each fearful heart,
To cultivate, and spread the science,
And bid each en'vous dunce defiance.
If their dull souls cannot attain
This ART, promoting health and gain;
Why should they envy brighter mind?
This was the case, as you will find,

Sw-nt-n desiring for to spread
The skill, in which he's deeply read,
To all around, both rich and poor;
No indication can be truer,
Of a diffusive public spirit,
Which few are born to inherit;
After his ART with great success
He'd taught to twenty, more or less,
Some rich, some poor, as he could find

Their genius was thereto inclin'd;
Beheld with sympathy a youth
Poor, yet unprejudic'd to truth;
Of soft behaviour, pregnant wit:
This lad he instantly thought fit,
To well instruct in ev'ry part,
Of this late revived ART.
Then took him home to board and bed,
And daily lectures him to read,
That by degrees he might prepare him,
For fear the first attempt might scare
   him;
And between whiles, he strok'd his
   face,
And felt him over in each place,
And closely hugg'd him in his arms,
Swore none alive possess'd such
   charms.

IN short Sir, Sw-nt-n by degrees,
Taught him the MYSTERY with ease.

BUT as it often is the Fate
Of virtuous, fortunate, and great,
To be by envious tongues defam'd:
This was the case of him just nam'd.
A man there was of genius mean,
Crafty and base, as will be seen;
Not born to taste such ARTS as these,
Him Nature had not form'd to please;
With hellish malice views the boy,
Caress'd by Sw-nt-n; call'd his joy:
Forms a most base and vile design,
To swear on Sw-nt-n the same crime,
Charg'd on the W-rd-n by his foes:
This done, away the traitor goes;
Prevails on Bob the fact to charge,
Before the C——-ll-r at large,
Upon the very best of masters,
Virtue will not prevent disasters.
This wicked boy, of grace devoid;

All sense of gratitude destroy'd,
Affirms, and aggravates the case,
With mimic probity in's face;
Declares, that should the human race,
His wicked master's ART embrace,
Mankind would soon become no more,
Things would be just as heretofore.
Thus far the scheme did well succeed,
And Sw-nt-n would have been decreed
At least, to leave that famous place,
With detestation and disgrace,
Had he not plainly made appear
His innocence: once more give ear.
What is't that promises won't do?
He sends to Bob, I vow 'tis true,
Upbraids him with his base designs;
Bob's conscience pricks him for his
   crimes:
What can he do to make amends,
His injur'd master, best of friends?
No more's required on this score,
Unsay what you have said before;
Declare that B-k-r mov'd you to't,
By cash and promises to boot.
Bob acts his part, the tables change,
(My friend, there's nothing new or
   strange;)
B-k-r before the C——-ll-r's cited,
Who tells him that he is indicted,
Upon the defamation act,
And press'd him warmly to retract;
And own, that malice was the cause,
Against all justice, truth and laws
That moved him to forge this story,
To blast forever Sw-nt-n's glory:
And adds with domineering note,
That he must sign, what they had
   wrote,
Or he'd commit him, and expel him:
Thus Sir, you see, what has befell him.

WHAT could he do, who dare withstand,
The stroke of his vindictive hand?
He sign'd the scowl; own'd truth a lie,
My tale is told: dear Sir, good-bye.

THUS thrives an ART, none dare oppose,
Unless he'll forfeit food and clothes.

A Court Martial

Text from *Gentleman's Magazine* (February 1745).

A court martial was held on board the Dutch admiral's ship at Spithead for the trial of the 1st lieutenant of one of their ships for committing sodomy on the boatswain's son. He was found guilty, and ordered to be tied up in a sack, with a large weight fastened to it, and flung overboard at high water (which is the usual punishment inflicted by the Dutch for crimes of that nature committed at sea) but his life was spared upon the intercession of some English gentlemen, and his sentence changed into a whipping, after which he was stripped of his clothes, and set ashore at Gosport, in an old jacket and trousers, to shift* for himself. The admiral immediately dispatched to Holland, an account of his proceedings to the States General, in order for the confiscating of the delinquent's estate and effects, worth £500 per annum sterling.

*In Smith's voyages we read of an African prince who destroyed a whole city, lest one sodomite should escape, to infect the rest of his people.

The King versus Wiseman

The author discusses how and when sodomy could be punished, and attempts to define terms in use, together with past usages and practices. Legalities begin to seem as unstable as sexualities. Text from 'The King versus Wiseman' at Rochester Assizes in Kent, in John Fortescue's, *Reports of Select Cases* (1748).

This was an indictment for committing of sodomy in the *Ano*, with a girl of eleven years of age, which was tried before Mr Justice Probyn, at Rochester in Kent; the fact was committed by the master of a workhouse at Maidstone in Kent, with one of the girls then there with him. The defendant was tried and convicted on this indictment at the Assizes held for Kent . . .

This being a particular case, though as most thought, not a very difficult one, the Judge reprieved the prisoner, in order to have the opinion of all the judges, on this offence, whether it was buggery within statute or not.

The judges met once or twice on this occasion, and the case was argued by them, and a few were of the opinion that this was not express buggery within our law; though, as Justice Fortescue A. remembered, there was a great majority that were of the opinion it was plain buggery by our law; but yet, because two or three judges held out, there was no further meeting, and consequently no unanimous opinion given.

But Justice Fortescue A. was exceeding sorry, that such a gross offence should escape without any punishment in England; when it is a crime punishable with death and burning at a stake, all over the world besides.

It being so horrid and great a crime, and so that no colour should be given to such an offence, Justice Fortescue A. wrote to the Earl of Macclesfield, then Chancellor of Great Britain, concerning this matter; and his answer was by way of letter, that he wondered at the variety of opinions; that he had not the least hesitation in agreeing it to be plain sodomy, that he could not think of one objection to which he should be able to give the appearance of an argument; that it is a crime exactly of the same nature, as well as the same action, as if committed upon a male, the difference of the subject only makes it more inexcusable, and it is within the letter of the Act of Parliament, as well as within the meaning, that it seems little to the purpose to say that possibly the law-makers might not think of this crime; whether they did or not, appears not; the words reach it, and the reason of the law reaches it; and when a crime is forbid in general, it is not necessary that every species of it should be under consideration, unless such species should be less criminal.

The word *Buggery* made use of, is not a term of art appropriated to the Common Law, but the punishment is provided, because of its being a vice so detestable and abominable, and against Nature. Buggery with the most filthy, or the most dreadful Creature, is Buggery, though never so unlikely to be committed, and though the lawgivers had thought it impossible it ever should be committed. Besides, the unnatural abuse of a woman seems worse than that of a man or a beast; for it seems a more direct affront to the Author of Nature, and a more insolent expression of comtempt of his wisdom, condemning the provision made by him, and defying both it and him. His Lordship cited two or three Cases in the Civil Law, which are very much to the Purpose . . .

The Case is within the Words as well as the Meaning of the Statute 25 H. 8 *cap*. 6 . . . because there is not a sufficient Punishment for the detestable Sin of Buggery, committed with Mankind or Beast, and then it takes away Clergy from this Offence.

It is called . . . *une Peche mortelle encontre le Roy de Ciel*, and said to be worse than ravishing a Mother; and the Punishment in the Time of the Saxons was burying them alive ...

In Cowel's *Interpreter*,[33] buggery is defined to be *carnalis Copulatio contra Naturam*. Sodomy is a carnal copulation against nature, *viz*. of a man or woman, in the same sex, or of either of them with beasts. *Amor Puerorum* is a species of buggery, and they are not men strictly speaking.

Justice Fortescue A. had the curiosity to write to Dr Strahan, one of the most learned Doctors of the civil law, the author of *The Civil Law*;[34] and he gave his opinion in writing in these words, 'I take it to be sodomy in our law, as well as where the act is committed by a man upon a woman, as where it is committed by a male upon a male; the crime is looked upon to be equally unnatural in both cases, and the actors in both cases are subject to the same punishment. This I take to be the received opinion in our law.'

And Justice Fortescue A. said he would appeal to all the lawyers in England whether the woman in this case is not as much Pathick, and has done the selfsame thing *in Ano*, as in the case of a man; and whether the woman in one case is not indictable as well as the man in the other, being the same crime and same fact, but rather the greater offence, because it has greater aggravations, as there is no temptation nor sollicitation from nature, and a woman at hand.

A Full and Genuine Narrative of the Confederacy

Edward Walpole, brother of Horace Walpole, was indicted for buggering John Cather. Following a verdict of not guilty, Walpole prosecuted three of the men involved in a blackmail plot against him; successful prosecutions led to a range of punishments (including the pillory, whipping, imprisonment and hanging). The selected text explores the criminal uses of sodomy in the hands of an 'unnatural' agent. From *A Full and Genuine Narrative of the Confederacy Carried on By Cather, Cane, Alexander, Nixon, Paterson, Falconer, and Smith, which last was executed by Tyburn with McLeane, Against The Hon. Edward Walpole, Esq. Charging him with the detestable Crime of Sodomy, in Order to extort a large Sum of Money from him; together with an Account of their remarkable Trial and Conviction* (1751). For more on blackmail see Norton (1992: 139–45).

John Cather, at present a prisoner in the Kings Bench, is the son of a labourer who lived in the County Dunnegall in the kingdom of Ireland; he was bred to no employment or handicraft, but gained his bread as his father had done; and upon some disgust at his mother, who hindered his marriage with a young woman, who was passionately fond of him, and he of her, he became very rude and insolent, and frequently has been found exercising his aged parent with a discipline that the most abandoned can scarce be judged capable of; the neighbours who were witnesses of his behaviour reproved him, but observing his deafness to remonstrance, they gave him up to himself, while the poor woman was a daily sufferer by his brutal hands: one day an aged matron who had been acquainted with Mrs Cather came into the house at the time he was treading her under his feet, and bending her breast with the patella of his knee; and dragging him off her with expostulations and invectives, he became stunned and all at once seemed as one sunk in melancholy and despair; but recovering his consternation she thus addressed him, 'O John what a vile and detestable crime it is in you to abuse and beat your aged parent; a person who can be barbarous to a parent, can never be kind to a spouse, you seem to be a Woman Hater and I am much mistaken if you will not turn out a sodomite.' The phrase struck him! He became exceeding anxious to know its import; she expressed herself in modest enough expressions, but such as easily conveyed an idea of the thing, which according to my information he afterward did or at least endeavoured to practise; the beating his mother rendered him odious in the place, a mere spectacle to the town, and a byword to the children; that having no peace there, he withdrew to Barncrannah a little village in the same county where he continued for some time, and where my informer knew him; it was here that the report spread of his attempting the crime of which he accused Mr Walpole, and for screening himself from infamy he thought proper to leave the Kingdom and come to this metropolis, where he perpetuated the villainy I am now to relate.

He had been in Dublin during the time of the Parliament and observing the intimacy between Mr Walpole, Secretary to the Duke of Devonshire, Lord Lieutenant of that kingdom, and Lord Boyne, he thought proper to give himself out as a tenant's son of his lordship, and to make application under that fictitious name to Mr Walpole, who reckoned his lordship's regard to any man an ample recommendation, they having travelled through France, Germany and Italy together, and had afterwards continued united by mutual good offices: for by Mr Walpole's interest, Lord Boyne obtained a seat in the House of Commons, two of his relations the Office of Collectors, and several of his friends were provided for, as Cather might, being a tall young fellow, five foot ten inches high, very fair and well skinned, if he had been capable of discharging the functions of any employment: being disappointed in his expectations from Mr Walpole, he began to seek as he pretended for business elsewhere, though in reality he employed himself with Walter Paterson, Patrick Cane, and some others of the like character: it was by means of this correspondence that he got some of the fine laced clothes in which he was dressed, when he sent for Mr Walpole's servant William Collier, to a tavern where they stayed sometime, but as parting he enjoined him secrecy and begged he would not discover the circumstance of his dress to his master, but as the enjoining of secrecy is the very way to disclose it, so in this case, the servant considered the honour and interest of his patron, acquainted him with what he had seen, and what had been enjoined; the gentleman rightly judging that such precautions are never used except from design, wisely gave over to countenance him, or give him either by himself or his servants, encouragement, directly or indirectly, to come to his house; this raised his resentment, and kindled that anger, which was the result of his disappointment into the most violent hatred, that in time burned throughout, and grew into an intense and deliberate revenge; notwithstanding for some time, he was by secret considerations hindered from perpetrating anything against him; whether this restraint proceeded from fear, the constant attendant of a dishonest heart, and a vicious inclination, or that his genius was not adequate to his keenness, I leave with others to determine; however at last getting acquainted with a number of adventurers, like himself, among whom William Smith, a Presbyterian parson's son in Ireland, who made his fatal exit October 3rd 1750, along with James McLean, he soon contrived a scheme for ruining Mr Walpole's character, and for disencumbering him of his purse: and that was, by swearing to the design of committing one of the most atrocious crimes that a man can be supposed guilty of; a crime not only horrid in the sight of the law, but contrary to nature, and an open violation of everything sacred and humane; it seems the gang, so I must call them, stood in need of a little money; to procure which they fell upon the following villainous, though artful contrivance; and none other conditions were required, but secrecy in the transactions, and an equal division of what might be obtained.

The gang had been informed of Mr Walpole's character, and bethought themselves of laying something to his charge, of which he could not fail to be ashamed, and to smother which, he would not scruple any expense: big with the hopes of success, they fix upon Cather as the proper person to swear to his laying hold of him, dealing with him, and earnestly solliciting his compliance to the commission of the horrid, abominable, shocking and odious crime of sodomy, at one time, and buggery at another; allured with the mighty prospect of gain, blind to the fatal consequences and deaf to the dictates of generosity and conscience, the creature went to Hicks Hall 26 of March 1750 and there swore as narrated above; and the jury going upon the examination of the bills, soon found an indictment against Mr Walpole; which news the conspirators were not wanting to propagate; for this purpose they went into two or three coffee houses where they published the matter, and laid it down with all the skill that design and long meditation could suggest, or craft and artifice could inspire, and that they might reap as soon as sow, they soon sent for one Alexander to whom they imparted the scheme ...

The Trial of Richard Branson

Sodomy was increasingly seen as a threat to young men: it must be punished harshly otherwise it will spread like the plague and infect a whole generation of young men. Text from *The Trial of Richard Branson, for an Attempt to commit Sodomy, on the Body of James Fassett, one of the Scholars belonging to God's-Gift-College, in Dulwich. Tried at the General Quarter Session of the Peace, held at St Margaret's-Hill, in the Borough of Southwark* (1760).

The Jurors for our Lord the King, upon their oath, present that Richard Branson, late of the parish of Camberwell, in the county of Surrey, labourer, on the first day of August, in the thirty-third year of the reign of our Sovereign Lord GEORGE the Second, king of Great Britain, &c. not having the fear of God before his eyes, but being moved and seduced by the instigation of the devil, with force and arms, at the parish aforesaid, in the County aforesaid, in and upon James Fassett ... then and there being, did make an assault, and him the said James Fassett, then and there, did beat, wound, and ill treat, so that his life was greatly despaired of, with an intent that most horrid, detestable, and sodomitical crime (not among Christians named) called Buggery, with the said James Fassett, against the order of Nature, then and there, feloniously, wickedly, and devilishly, to commit and do, to the great displeasure of Almighty God, to the great damage of the said James Fassett, and against the Peace of our said Lord the king, his Crown, and dignity.

James Fassett, one of the youths of poor scholars of God's Gift College in Dulwich, the Prosecutor, being sworn, deposed as fellows: I knew the defendant, and first saw him on the first of August last, about nine o'clock in the evening; that as I was sitting at the Back Gate of the College, Edward Bailey, another of the poor scholars about twelve years old, came to me with a message from the defendant (who was then sitting on the bench belonging to the public house across the way called the bell) to desire me to drink a glass of wine, which I refusing, Bailey returned to the defendant; and delivering it to him, he immediately came to the place where I sat, and desired me to go over and drink a glass of porter with him, which I accepting, we went over together to the bench, where were present only myself, the defendant, said Bailey, and one William Cotton, another of the poor scholars; and after having drunk one glass of porter, the defendant observing to the master of the house (who came to the door and went in directly) that it was a fine evening for a walk, he asked me to take a walk with him; before we got to the grove, the defendant asked me my name and age. A little before we got to the Grove Gates, he asked me, if I never got any girls, or if I never f—ed 'em; I answered no; I was not old enough, and had no such thoughts. He said I was old enough. We then walked arm in arm, till we came to a private place in the grove; this was about half an hour past nine o'clock, he then kissed me, put his left hand round my neck, and kissed my lips only; he asked the name of the place, I said it was called the grove, he answered 'twas Love's Grove; then he kissed me again, putting his tongue into my mouth; and sucking my lips, tried to thrust his right hand into my breeches: I can't say where his left hand was, but he tickled me here (pointing to his groin) with his right hand, and endeavoured to put it into my breeches, which I avoided by forcing myself from him; and keeping my hands a top of the waistband of my breeches, he laughed at me.

Upon seeing two horses at a distance, he said they were two men; he let me go and seemed very much frightened; and asking me if I was not, I answered, No.

We then went out of the grove on the right hand towards the College; and going about as far as from one post to another, he said it was lonesome, that he would go back into the grove, for he liked to see the trees, and desired me to go back with him. He attempted nothing in going back, till after we got into the grove he pulled me towards the hedge, kissed me, put his tongue into my mouth, sucked my lips, and asked me if I never fr-gged[35] myself; to which I answered, No. His left hand being round my neck, he tried to thrust t'other into my breeches, which I prevented by keeping my hands at the waistband; he then asked where the road led to; and opening the gate which leads to the College the fore way,and stopping me at the gate kissed me, put his tongue in my mouth, and sucking lips, said my hands were soft and warm, but my heart was very cold.

When he came out of the grove, he asked me a second time if I never fr-gged myself; I said I did not know what it meant; he said if I would go back he would learn me; but I did not go back. He asked no more questions then; but going towards the summer house, he asked me if I had my maidenhead, if I had he should be very glad to take it from me, but supposed I saved it for a young woman; he said no more then, but kissed me several times as we were walking down, put his tongue in my mouth, and sucking my lips. When we were got some way further he asked me, if he should ravish me? I answered, No. He said, he would not against my will. We then went towards the College, and 'twas almost ten before we got there; the College gates were not shut. I walked some little distance behind him; after he said he should be glad of my company another time; he then crossed the road to the Bell, and I was going into College; but seeing the gardener at the bench went over to him, that I might tell him as soon as possible, and go in with him, having stayed out longer than usual. I said nothing while we stayed at the bench which was about five minutes; I did not tell the gardener at the bench, because as I had been out later than I ought, I was afraid it would make a disturbance, and when the gardener and I got into the College, I told him the whole; and he would have gone back to thrash him, but I desired he would not for fear of anger from the Master, and the rest of the gentlemen, for staying out too late.

On Saturday morning one of the boys came to me, and told me to go to the Master; when I came to him he examined me; I gave him an account, but not of everything, being ashamed to speak some parts; but, by the Master's order, I went away and wrote down everything that I was ashamed to speak. I went before the Justice on Tuesday, and was sworn: Mr Branson was there when the information was read.

William Cotton sworn

I am near fourteen; I know the prisoner; saw him at the Bell, and was there between seven and eight with Bailey; Mr Branson was at the Bell; I saw Bailey go to Fassett, and come back again; then I saw Mr Branson go over, and Fassett and he came over together, and drank one glass of porter each; Mr Branson said it was a fine evening for a walk, and heard him ask Fassett to take a walk; they then went away together, and Bailey and I sat out to go with them; but Mr Branson said, 'twas not fit for such children to go: we then returned to the Bell, but went to bed before they came back. When Fassett came to bed, he told the Boys, who all lie in a room, how he had been served.

Samuel Maton sworn

I am the gardener, and as such 'tis my duty to shut the College-gates; and going out for that purpose, just before ten, I saw Cotton and two more boys sit at the bench before the Bull, with a bottle of porter before them; I told them 'twas time to go to bed; and asking whose beer it was, they said it was a gentleman's who was gone to take a walk with Fassett: the boys then went into the College, and the maid came out of the Bell at the same time: I saw them both return in about two minutes from their walk; Fassett was some distance behind t'other, who came to the bench, and Fassett came and stood by me; nothing material to this matter happened: I stayed 'till the clock struck ten; and, going in, Fassett begun telling me how he had been used before I could bar the gate, and seemed to be in so much pain and agony; and in a very great fright, said he would never go with Mr Branson again: finding him so uneasy, I offered to go over, and said I would thrash him or he should me; but Fassett objected to this, and desired I would defer it 'till next morning, when he was willing to go with me; I went over about eight o'clock, but he was gone to London.

Dr Allen sworn

I am the Master of God's Gift College, in Dulwich, and am by my oath of office not to see the poor scholars abused. Mr Baker came to me, and told me one Branson had abused Fassett; I asked how; Mr Baker said in a criminal way; it being Chapel-time, we put it off 'till the service was over; then Mr Baker telling me further, I sent for the boy, and charged him to tell me the truth; he then told me the whole, except some indecencies his modesty would not let him pronounce. I thought it my duty to prosecute him, and sent my coachman to direct Fassett to commit the whole to writing. Next morning my coachman brought me a paper in Fassett's writing, containing in substance what he has now sworn: accordingly, on the Tuesday morning, he was sworn before Mr Hammond. He is the most sober, quiet, orderly boy in the College.

The Reverend Mr George Baker sworn

I am a Fellow of the College; was informed of this affair by Ann Carpenter, a poor woman of the College; and enquiring further into the particulars, took the first opportunity to ask Fassett himself, but his modesty stopped his mouth: I am also one of the schoolmasters. [I] then reported it to the Master, who postponed it 'till after Chapel; and the boy being sent for, related the circumstances of the treatment, except what he was ashamed to speak. All his accounts agree in substance, and material facts. He has been in the College six or seven years; I always observed great regularity, decency, and modesty in his behaviour; and never caught him in a lie.

Prisoner's defence

The Council, upon opening the defence, applied to the court and jury for mercy; hinted that he was in liquor, and that there was a house within an hundred yards of the grove; but that the prosecutor never cried out.

Susannah Wells sworn

I am a Servant at the Bell; remember Mr Branson being there on the first of August, and believe me he was in liquor: about nine o'clock Fassett and he went for a walk; I was with him after his return, when he kissed me, and seemed very fond of me; he had three bottles of porter, two before and one after the walk.

Cross-examined

I have lived at the Bell nine months; don't believe he was in liquor before the walk; often saw him before that night, but never since. This witness behaved in so rude a manner, laughing, and making a joke of her testimony, that she received a very severe rebuke from the chairman.

Richard Miller sworn

I am a servant of the Bell; saw him before the walk; he came down on horseback in the even; had one bottle of porter before the walk; some people, and the two boys, drank part of it; I did not observe him in liquor 'till after the walk, when he seemed very fuddled, and they all drank together except the gardener; the boy was not frightened, but very merry, and I heard him drink Mr Branson's health.

Cross-examined

He was not in liquor when he got off his horse.

Henry Mackrill sworn

I live at Dulwich; did not see Mr Branson 'till between nine and ten, when he was sitting on the bench, and much in liquor. To this the Council for the Crown replied that as the defendant had not called any witnesses to disprove the fact, to destroy the boy's character, or support his own, but merely attempted to show the defendant was drunk, though they failed even in that; which, had they proved, would have been an aggravation; therefore, he hoped the jury would find him guilty: and then addressing himself to the court, demonstrated the fatal consequence of this wicked attempt; for had he prevailed with this lad, now sixteen years old, to commit this horrid and most detestable crime, he would have infected all others; and, as in course of years they grew big enough, they would leave the College to go into the world and spread this cursed poison, while those left behind would be training the children to the same vicious practices; for which reason (if the jury found the defendant guilty) he humbly hoped the court would order a most exemplary punishment.

The jury applied to the court, and, declaring themselves satisfied with the evidence, desired the chairman would save himself the trouble of summing it up, for that they were already agreed in their verdict, and accordingly brought him in guilty; upon which he was committed to the custody of the Keeper of the common gaol, and then received the judgement of the court; to be fined one hundred pounds, and committed to close custody in the New Gaol, Southwark, for one year, and until the fine be paid.

Short Extracts

The following short extracts are taken from the *Gentleman's Magazine.*

11 January 1745

At a court martial held on board the Dutch admiral's ship at *Spithead* two sailors were ordered to be keel-hauled; and a captain that was found guilty of sodomy was whipped, and discarded.

30 May 1752

We hear from Dublin, that a personage of great distinction in the British nation has lately suffered an amputation of both his ears by a gentleman on whom he had the impudence, as well as the enormous baseness to attempt the commission of sodomy. *Daily Gaz.*

The Cities of Sodom and Gomorrah, says a writer in the *D.G.* suffered the vengeance of eternal fire as an example to deter mankind from this detestable sin. Asa, a king of Judah, in his reformation of the people, *took away the Sodomites out of the land*: And truly, *such casting out of Sodomites* is demanded by the voice of reason and nature; for they counteract the foundation laws of all human society; they disgrace and degrade the very make of man. No monstrous births are equally hateful and offensive to the contemplative human eye.

Our own laws thus define the enormity, *Carnalis copula contra naturam, & hoc vel per confusionem specierum.* It is a sin against God, nature, and the law; in ancient times was punishable with burning or burying alive: it is felony without the benefit of clergy. In 12 Geo. I *three sodomites* were put to death; so atrocious is this crime, that it is excepted out of our acts of general pardon.

Every man, who is a man, and knows any thing that belongs to decency or order, will utterly detest the horrid, the impudent attempt, and the abandoned, the vile miscreant ought to be exposed to universal indignation. No rank, no condition, no consideration whatsoever should tempt any man to conceal such a design, such an outrage intended against God, nature and law. With as much reason may any man conceal an attempt to murder, as an attempt of Buggery. A love of our species, and the preservation of it; a love of our country, and the preventing of the most dreadful plagues which this sin threatens, should determine all Britons to do their utmost to expose and bring to condign punishment the Sodomite. This is the work of the Lord, *to take away the Sodomites out of the land.* Let no eye *pity*, let no hand *spare* these pests of society, this brood of vipers!

3 April 1763

A man stood in the pillory at Stratford for sodomy, and was killed by the populace. The coroner's jury brought in their verdict *wilful* murder, against some persons now in custody.

28 January 1771

A person known by the name of Charles Waddall, of the *Orford* man-of-war, lying at Chatham, was ordered to receive two dozen lashes for desertion, but when tied up to the gangway the culprit was discovered to be a woman. She declares that she had travelled from Hull to London after a man with whom she was in love; and hearing he was on board the *Orford* at Chatham, she entered the rendezvous in London, for the same ship, the 9th instant. On the 17th of this month she came on board; but finding that her sweetheart was run away, in consequence thereof she deserted yesterday. She was immediately carried before Admiral Dennis, who made her a present of half a guinea; Commissioner Hanway, and most of the officers of the Yard made her presents also.

8 August 1772

Four persons were tried at York for smothering a boy, that had been bitten by a mad dog, and was raving mad himself, between blankets. They are said to have been acquitted for want of evidence. At the same assizes, a clergyman was convicted of an attempt to commit an unnatural crime, fined £20 to be imprisoned for two years, and find sureties for his good behaviour for two years more.

10 April 1780

One Read, a coachman, and one Smith, a plasterer, stood in the pillory, St Margaret's Hill, for unnatural practices; the former of whom perishing before the time expired, owing to the severity of the mob, the same was taken notice of in the House of Commons. The Attorney General was desired to prosecute the officer whose business it was to see the sentence of the law executed, and a hint thrown out for a new law to alter the mode of punishment.

February 1785

A gentleman, with one servant, having called at the Angel Inn at Tunbridge, in his way to Lewes, where he was going to take a survey of part of an estate of which he lately came possessed in right of his wife, was observed to be particularly attentive to a young lad, the nephew of the landlord, who he enticed, when he went to bed, to sleep with him. This being discovered by the family, they suddenly rushed into the room, and rescued the boy from a situation which justified their taking the gentleman into custody. After a short examination before two of his Majesty's justices of peace, he was by them bound over to appear at the next assizes, himself in £100 and his two sureties in £500 each.

3 REPRESENTATIONS

Introduction

In the course of the eighteenth century it was possible to discern an increasing consciousness of the need to define gender differences and sexual subdivisions. A dominant feature of the early eighteenth century was the emergence of the 'effeminate' man who was not definable merely by his foppishness. The 'molly' or homosexual represented an aberrant personality, a lifestyle. As a group, their constitution hinged on mimicry of women, affectation and same-sex relationships; such representations placed them beyond natural essentialist categories; they could not be included in the 'system of nature'. Sodomitical practices were, above all, unnatural and artificial. Before proceeding to discuss in detail how mollies and sodomites were constructed, it is worth noting that sexual behaviour was increasingly observed and regimented according to increasingly specific and normative archetypes. Moving beyond anatomical differences (hermaphrodites as lesbians, for example) transgression of sexual roles was increasingly reflected in specific affectations of behaviour, mannerisms and dress which 'properly' belonged to the other sex. The need for strict enforcement of boundaries can be seen in the diatribes against groups of men who constructed themselves as both misogynistic and effeminate. As *The Levellers* noted, men were losing their solid virtues such as 'Honour, Courage, Learning, and Judgement'. In *The Modern world Disrob'd*, Ned Ward portrayed a figure called 'Sir Narcissus Foplin ... the Self-Admirer,' which clearly went further than mere foppishness. The sketch followed Aristotle's line on the grotesque, that monsters were produced when the sexual motions of the female (in the womb) were not mastered by those of the male; it outlined also a behavioural pattern clearly conditioned by the manner of one's upbringing, especially the failure to follow in one's father's footsteps. Inevitably the portrait pivots on the deviancy of sexual *practice*, although it strangely mixes these with a traditional outrage at foppish ostentation; the duplicity, however, was not so much hypocrisy; rather it was a form of cheating on what the fop naturally had available to him: his manhood, which he maintained only for the sake of respectability. In large part the description still worked through anatomy and sex, with the emphasis on peg (pego/penis) and the comparison with the capon, a castrated cock or eunuch. Yet the portrait moves towards an *ars erotica*, beginning to serve as a manual of homosexual roles and typologies. More seriously, however, desire is self-constituting and autonomous, it subverts the power structures that govern and order society. The underlying concern here is with transgressive categories and the abuse of power. This third-person description of the fop most interestingly shows an outrage at a subversion and deflation of power and male authority, reconstituting and defining it along different lines. Desire and power are inseparable in many such accounts. As Foucault stated in his *History of Sexuality*, 'Where there is desire, the power relation is already present ... there is no escaping from power ... it is always-already present, constituting that very thing which one attempts to counter it with' (81–2). In this instance, the proto-fop-sodomite was a paradox of power: wealth without virility.

In seventeenth-century terms the fop's social vices were chiefly affectation, excessive sensitivity to his health and exotic (i.e. imported) dress. Moreover, the behaviour of the fop contributed importantly to the typological *identity* of the molly. In line with the process of sexual novelization at work in texts such as *Hell upon Earth* (1729), it was essential for the fop-sodomite to cultivate his novelty, writing himself in the very moment of his self-exhibition; the fop melted everything down into a single, self-made shape, just as the novel collapsed a variety of earlier texts and genres: 'His wit is like his habit, of the newest fashion ... he affects unintelligible terms of speech, and, like an apothecary, will reduce a whole sentence into a monosyllable.' Language was collapsed (along with the primacy of the nation-state) into the great undifferentiated; the fop can only therefore display himself 'in a compound of French, Italian, and broken Latin, to adorn his peacock's feathers with a little pedantry'. This figure does not strictly speaking belong to male company, for 'Men of sense withdraw from him as from a pestilential infection.' Finally there was a degree of ambivalence in the conclusion of the diatribe, for the fop ultimately commits the final act of self-erasure 'Thus a supercilious life brings an ignominious death, and for want of reason to guide his passions, Sir Foppington falls into despair, and dies in suicide'. Nonetheless, molly suicides were fairly uncommon (Norton, 1992: 116). *Sir Narcissus Foplin* is a good example of the desire to explore a wider framework for the definition of sodomy. Such representations increasingly move beyond behaviour and imposed moral categories to other concerns. This description explores, for instance, the effects of the parents' lack of sexual energy; the danger of being influenced excessively by the mother; and concludes with a sense of social outrage at the blurring and slippage of categories scandalously exhibited to a wider social world. Remarkably, some of these generalizations are still in force today.

Nonetheless, the category of the 'molly' sometimes avoided the censure of sodomy as a diabolical act; its grotesqueness was modernized by building on neo-classical anxieties about mixture, formlessness and the metamorphic. The new crime of the sodomite, like that of the arsonist, called for different responses, but they still demanded exemplary prosecutions. In this light, G.S. Rousseau and Roy Porter have argued that 'official attitudes to homo-eroticism hardened, turning the occasional sin of buggery into the more terrifying stereotype of the sodomite' (1987: 3). How could this shifting category be described in such a way as to identify, control and prohibit it? A grotesque mixture of male and female attributes, it was basically hybrid. Nonetheless, the homosexual as bestial or diabolical sodomite belonged to a model of the grotesque that was outdated and outmoded, but which persisted throughout the period. In the older sense, sodomy surpassed all other crimes; in its sinfulness it also included all of them: from blasphemy, sedition, and witchcraft, to the demonic. It was, as many extracts declare, the crime without a name; language was incapable of sufficiently expressing the horror of it. The category was a repository for many items, yet in the eighteenth century a highly specific portrait of an individual, and of a group, was increasingly displacing an undiscriminating, demonic generalization.

The early eighteenth-century homosexual subculture drew together a number of characteristics that typified the grotesque's relation of heterogeneity to the main or 'official' culture; the grotesque and ridiculous dress of dance and pantomime; the definition of marginal spaces and subsequent encroachments upon them. In addition, 'molly houses' threatened traditional sexual *mores*, patriarchy and the family. The city, itself often characterized as a grotesque, provided a site for these exchanges. Yet the 'molly' can in many respects be considered the product of an inevitable mutation within the prevailing culture. If identity and behaviour could be artificially fashioned or constructed and then naturalized (as in *homo economicus*) then it followed that other reconstructions, at the fringes, might also seek to naturalize themselves.

There were different kinds of response to secret sexual activity. The author of *A Short treatise on these Heads, viz. of the Sins of Sodom* (1689) deployed his own confession as a model for others who might have fallen into similar sins. Yet to publicize what had been secret has the side-effect of establishing recognizable characteristics for the signification and production of sodomy. These discourses operated within a moral programme that castigated riot, luxury, idleness and fornication. Yet these were in themselves unsteady categories and tended to collapse wider notions of excess or superfluity.

Ned Ward's *Of the Mollies Club* was significant for its outsider's insights into the world of secret sexuality. He depicted the mollies' mimicry of women (particularly speech and dress) as a degeneration from masculinity. One of the important trends at the close of the seventeenth century was a desire to reassert masculinity against the fashion for effeminacy. In the past, the fop had simply represented the exotic and affectation; he was devoid of sexuality. By the end of the seventeenth century the fop had been reconstructed to include the hatred of women and the smear of same-sex desire. Moreover, Ward's attack on the mollies reverted to the charge of undertaking 'beastly obscenities' and 'devilism' thereby deploying terminologies from the previous century.

Many of the stereotypes that have governed the construction of modern homosexuality were embryonic in a variety of early publications. Above all, sodomy was artificial, like society itself. *Reasons for the Growth of Sodomy* (1749) notes the manner of educating children, the dangerous effects of indulgence, of a lack of exercise, and a tendency to indolence. We also learn about styles of dress, the dangers of same-sex kissing and effeminacy. It is also noted that trivial entertainments fail to provide the young with the heroic values that will make them men. The sodomites prefer Italian opera, and mixed entertainment of a lower order: drolls, puppet-shows and pantomimes. Such entertainments represented a movement down the social scale that mirrored a slippage down the scale of being: as sodomites, men became beasts. Moreover, the heterogenous nature of such entertainments was symptomatic of a more general disruption of categories, and of gender as a simple binary opposition.

Hell upon Earth expands our knowledge of early secret sexual life. The curious reader learns of the places where sodomites meet (bog-houses), their characteristic manner of speech, their desire for converts and proselytes, and their unhappy end – suicide. Such material was soon finding its way into mainstream literature. Often, other discourses were welded to it, in order to multiply the grotesque effect. Alexander Pope, for instance, famously represented Lord Hervey as 'Sporus' making explicit uses of his ambiguity. Pope's composite portrait leaves us unsure of Hervey's status; he is finally shapeless, a grotesque mixture: sodomite, hermaphrodite and eunuch.

Moving into the *public* sphere of sexuality, the available literature indicates that a diversity of sexual practices was available. Yet the mutation of new sexual identities was central to the grotesque sexual dynamic that playfully subverted categories, confronting the completeness of taxonomy with the exciting hybrid. In Alan Bray's analysis of homosexuality at the beginning of the eighteenth century, 'There was now a continuing culture to be fixed on and an extension of the area in which homosexuality could be expressed and therefore recognised; clothes, gestures, language, particular buildings and particular public places (92).

Many texts which appear to be primarily concerned with one vice lose themselves in a rainbow alliance of others. This tendency was nowhere more clear than in *Hell upon Earth* (1729). The long preamble consists of a seemingly inexhaustible list that includes items such as *Of the Encrease of the Hempen Manufactory and the Decrease of the Woollen Manufactory*. The list begins again on the first page, with forty-one fashionable 'crimes' beginning with the letter A, from *Absurdities* and *Abuses* to *Audacities* and *Aversions*. We are then taken through a typical Sabbath, listing a variety of sins hour by hour; a detailed proposal for a system of fines; an inventory of the goods to be seen near the opera house in the Hay Market. There is a tirade against the fantastical manner of eating; there is even a diagram of a meal consisting of 'Viper Soup, Stew'd Snails, Couple of Roast Hedge Hogs, Fricasee of Frogs and Badger's Ham and Colliflowers'. It would be difficult to find a text that was more playful in its exercise of grotesque heterogeneity. Insofar as homosexuality was 'invented' by such commentators, it was patched together and was subversively parasitic upon other material. As art, or artifice, it was against Nature.

Exotic terms such as 'fribble', 'macaroni' and 'pretty gentleman' came into fashion to designate different varieties of sodomite from the middle of the eighteenth century. In his study of the stage at this time, Laurence Senelick has explored the different usages of these words, and their repercussions in sexual practices. He concludes that 'The capital crime which in 1700 could not harm an actor's reputation had by 1770 become so damaging that a popular performer might be debilitated by a false accusation . . . By the end of the century the fop had dwindled into a mere clothes-horse' (1990: 67). New terminologies had clearly had the ability to define sexual orientation but they were also the precondition of its simultaneous exclusion. The anus, it could be argued, was a grotesque vanishing point, the end and the denial of vision. Ned Ward unmasked the mollies, just as Giles Jacob, Charles Ancillon and James Parsons lifted the petticoats of eunuchs and hermaphrodites, delighting in the invasion of their secrecy; yet when they have stripped all away, it is clear that there was a profound sense that sexuality was no longer capable of being fixed. As a 'molly', the early eighteenth-century homosexual rendered himself monstrous. He erased his productive sexual organ; he made it redundant to accepted preferences; gave up his manhood; turned to foppish effeminacy. Alternatively, in using his orifice 'improperly' he became more monstrous still, a sodomite, and a forerunner of the homosexual.

Sins of Sodom

The extract from *A Short Treatise on these Heads, viz. of the Sins of Sodom* (1689) is an example of how a confessional mode both condemned and constructed sodomy as crime and sin. See Foucault (1990); Cohen (1989); Katz (1994).

The author of this small book has concealed himself, not that he is afraid to own anything he has here writ, but only because he has observed few names so happy to beget prejudices; from which, if possible, he would have all who read this, free.

I have searched and tried *my own ways*, and have turned unto thee with all my heart, O Lord, thou knowest it.

I acknowledge I have contributed very highly, by my private guilt, to fill up the measure of the public sin; but thou hast graciously touched my heart with a sense of my share therein, and I *have mourned*, and, by the grace, will *go mourning in secret* for it *to my grave*.

Though I understand not all my errors, yet thou knowest my foolishness; and my sins are not hid from thee. I am very far, O God, from exempting myself, or pretending to have been guiltless, as to many of these wickednesses which I shall enumerate: but as I have been partner with, and occasion to, others to sin, so give me leave thus to provoke others, at least all of the same Communion with myself to join in repentance with me.

I will judge here the same judgement, which I use towards myself: I will censure and bewail, not only what is *notorious*, but what is *suspicious* and carries with it appearance of evil: and do thou Lord be merciful unto our sin for it is great.

Behold this was the Iniquity of *Sodom*, Pride, Fullness of Bread, and abundance of Idleness, was in her and her daughters, neither did she strengthen the hands of the poor and needy: and have not *these nations* committed like abominable things, and justified her and her daughters.

WHERE is there, O God, a country throughout the known world, in which thou hast more abundantly provided for all the ranks and degrees of men, all things appertaining to life and Godliness? And where is there any people that have more generally grown wanton against thee the donor of all?

Pride in apparel

What kind of *Pride* is not notorious amongst us? In that of *luxurious apparel* have we not outdone *Sodom* herself? How many expend more in clothes and garniture in one year, than they bestow in alms deeds in seven, nay perhaps in their own lives? We may daily see some single persons purchasing a fantastic sort of nets or cobwebs (for they cannot be called clothes,) through which they may be seen a great part naked, at far greater sums than would suffice wholesomely to clothe, or cover the nakedness of some poor, industrious families? Thus has the *vainest* sort of *Pride supplanted* the *greatest* of all *Christian Virtues* (thy darling, O Lord, and Image) *Charity*.

And these practices might be esteemed more tolerable, were people guilty thereof only in the years of folly or were the vain and giddy multitude the only offenders herein? Or were they to be found only in such Persons, to whom for distinction sake something of pomp may be allowed? But O Lord the *plague* is *epidemical*, and the several ranks and degrees of people among us are even confounded, & ordinarily not to be known one from another, by this means.

YET amongst all, none are more inexcusable either before thee or before the world, than such persons of the Order peculiar to thee, who are guilty herein. To see these every day go clad in rich and choicest silks, whom for their own and the people's sins it might become rather to be clothed in sackcloth; to see families, that ought to be, from the eldest to the least, patterns of modesty, humility and self-denial, maintained in the pomps and vanities of this wicked world, living in all the gaudery, superfluity and height almost that they can invent, and that upon those very revenues, which were originally designed for services of charity and piety, O God, what shall we say? Shalt not thou take vengeance on a race of such unjust stewards?

Riot and luxury

Thou has otherwise, O most bountiful God, fed, and that with plenty of the choicest outward goods, and with these we have only otherwise waxen fat and kicked against thee. What is the effect of our plenty, but most *excessive luxury* and *riot*? Even almost to the moving the ancient bounds of virtue and vice in this respect. That, which is with us reputed temperance at present, would have been some ages ago, and perhaps in some countries would be still adjudged gluttony and drunkenness. We oppress our tables first, and then ourselves: few meals with us which are not feasts: and in those which are professedly feasts, how seldom do the generality of people put an end to them, till they have by drinking, raised in themselves a kind of thirst, and then downright added drunkenness by their thirst.

Idleness

BUT we have more of our elder sister *Sodom*: indeed scarce is there any kind of sensuality assignable which may not be observed in the generality of most sorts of men and particularly many of us even *labour under Idleness*: How great is the multitude of those that dwell at ease, and rather suffer their days to pass over them, than live; being every way unprofitable. Nay to that height of allowance of themselves herein are the most men grown, that they look upon sloth, and a general lazy unconcernment, as a felicity and special blessedness above others, indulged them by God, rather than any sin: yea they esteem it a kind of curse and misery of life, for men to have employments or work to do; at least whether they esteem it so or no, ye how many thousands are there throughout the three nations, whose life it is to sit down to eat and drink and rise up to play. And a pitch of leisure, with accommodations for some such circle of sensuality as this, most people who can hope to attain it, seem to make the end at which all their endeavours aim. So that it is most plain, besides the vast number every where that are idle, more would be so, did their circumstances permit them.

Fornication &c.

HENCE all that *Whoredom, Fornication, Adultery, Incest* and other *horrid impurities*, some not to be named, which are daily, if not hourly committed in these kingdoms. Men will not find themselves honest business, and then it must needs come to pass that the devil and their own lusts must employ them. Thus O Lord is this good Land polluted before thee, according to the abominations wrought by the vilest of heathen nations.

Mundus Foppensis

The poem plunders from classical and recent history for relevant evidence of the dangers of effeminate and unnatural behaviour. A fop finally mutates into a sodomite. Text from *Mundus Foppensis: or, the Fop Display'd* (1691).

What dunces are our tonsors[1]
grown,
Where's their gold filings in an amber
box,
To strew upon their master's locks,
And make 'em glitter in the sun?
Sure English *Beaus* may out-view
Venus,
As well as *Commodus*, or *Gallienus*.
'Twas Goldilocks, my lovely boy,
Made *Agamemnon* ruin *Troy*.

I could produce ye Emperours
That sate in women's dress whole hours,
Expos'd upon the public stage
Their catamites, wives by marr'age.
Your old trunk-hose are laid aside,
For what-d'-ye-call-em's tail to hide;
So straight and close upon the skin,
As onely made for lady's eyne;
To see the shape of thighs and groin:
Hard case Priapus should be so
restrain'd,

That had whole orchards at command.
. . .
   Bless us! what's there? 'tis
   something walks,
A piece of painting, and yet speaks:
Hard case to blame the ladies washes,
When men are come to mend their
   faces.
Yet some there are such women
   grown,
They can't be by their faces known:
Some would be like fair *Adonis*;
Some would be *Hyacinthus* cronies;
And then they study wanton use
Of Spanish red, and white ceruse;
The only painters to the life,
That seem with nature's self at strife;
As if she only the dead colours laid,
But they the picture perfect made.
What *Zeuxis*² dare provoke these elves,
That to out-do him paint themselves?
For tho' the birds his painted grapes
   did crave,
These paint and all mankind deceive.
This sure must spend a world of
   morning,
More than the ladies quick adoring;
They have found out a shorter way,
Not as before, to wast the day;
They only comb, wash hands and face,
And streightway, with a comely grace,
On the admired *Helmet* goes,
As ready rigg'd as their lac'd shoes.
Far much more time men trifling
   waste,
E'er their bodies can be drest;
The looking-glass hangs just before,
And each o'th' legs requires an hour:
Now thereby, ladies, hangs a tale,
A story for your cakes and ale.

A certain *Beau* was lately dressing,
But sure, e'er he had crav'd heavens
   blessing;
When in comes friend, and finds him
   laid
In mournful plight, upon his bed.
Dear *Tom*, quoth he, such a mischance
As ne'er befell the foes of *France*;
Nay, I must tell thee, *Fleury* battle
Was ne'er to *Europe* half so fatal;
For by I know not what ill luck,
My glass this morn fell down and
   broke
Upon my shin, just in my rolling;
Now is not this worth thy condoling?
See stocking cut, and bloody shin,
Besides the charge of healing skin.
'Twas the only kindness of my fate,
It mist the solid piece, my pate.
   Ladies, this was ill luck, but you
Have much the worser of the two;
The World is chang'd I know not how,
For men kiss men, not women now;
And your neglected lips in vain,
Of smugling *Jack*, and *Tom* complain:
A most unmanly nasty trick;
One man to lick the other's cheek;
And only what renews the shame
Of *J.* the first, and *Buckingham*:³
He, true it is, his wives embraces fled
To slabber his lov'd *Ganimede*;
But to employ, those lips were made
For women in *Gommorrha*'s trade;
Bespeaks the reason ill-design'd,
Of railing thus 'gainst woman-kind:
For who that loves as nature teaches,
That had not rather kiss the breeches
Of twenty women, than to lick
The bristles of one male dear *Dick*.

The Levellers

The extract takes the form of a dialogue in which effeminate men and bachelors are attacked. Some brutal and inventive penalties are proposed for men who refuse to marry. Text from *The Levellers: A Dialogue between two young Ladies, concerning Matrimony, proposing an Act for enforcing Marriage, for the Equality of Matches, and Taxing single Persons. With the danger of Celibacy to a Nation. Dedicated to a member of Parliament* (1703). Text from *Harleian Miscellany* (1745).

Politica: Every creature desires to propagate its species, and nature dictates to every part of the creation the manner of doing it. The brute beasts are subservient to this law, and wholly answer the end of their creation: now is the same desire in mankind; but we, who are endowed with noble faculties, and who have countenances erected to behold the wonders of God in the firmament of heaven, look so far into the earth, that we sink beneath the dignity of beasts. In being averse to generation, we offer violence to the laws of God and Nature imprinted on our minds ...

Sophia: The men, they are grown full as effeminate as the women; we are rivalled by them even in the fooleries peculiar to our sex: they dress like anticks and stage-players, and are as ridiculous as monkeys: they sit in monstrous long Perukies, like so many owls in ivy-bushes; and esteem themselves upon the reputation of being a beau, than on the substantial qualifications of honour, courage, learning, and judgement. If you heard them talk, you would think yourself at a gossiping at *Dover*, or that you had heard the learned confabulation of the boys in the piazza of *Christ's-Hospital*. Did you ever see a creature more ridiculous than that stake of human nature which dined the other day at our house, with his great long wig to cover his head and face, which was no bigger than an *Hackney-Turnip*, and much of the same form and shape? Bless me how it looked! just like a great platter of French soup with a little bit of flesh in the middle. Did you mark the beau Tiff of his wig, what a deal of pains he took to toss it back, when the very weight thereof was like to draw him from his seat? Did you not take notice how he replenished his snout with snuff, and what pains he took to let us know that it was *Vigo*? Did you not wonder at his learned discourse of the women's accoutrements, from the top-knot to the laced shoe; and what lectures he read on the fan, masque, and gloves? He understood ribbons and silk as well as a milliner and mercer, and was a perfect chemist in beauty washes and essences: in short, madam, did you ever see a more accomplished coxcomb in all your life ...

Politica: Truly, my dear, our cases are both desperate; we cannot *come up* to good estates, and gentlemen of good estates will not *come down* to us. I have often wondered, that there are no compulsive laws enforcing matrimony, but that, instead thereof, there are laws discouraging of marriage, as is the Act of Births and Burials, especially to the poorer sort of people, who are generally the greatest breeders; for, by this act, when there is a certain charge to a family, there is a certain duty to the Queen. Now, if there was a law enforcing of matrimony, it would more effectually answer the end of her majesty's pious proclamations for the encouragement of virtue, and for the suppressing of all manner of immorality and profaneness. For such a law would put a stop to abundance of whoring; it would make the women virtuous, on purpose to get good husbands, and the men thrifty and diligent in their callings, in order to maintain their families. The ruin both of body, soul, and estate proceeds from this omission in our laws. I am sure, a law of this nature would not only be acceptable in the sight of God, but it would be very advantageous to the kingdom.

Sophia: I am very well satisfied in the truth of what you say, but, at the same time, I do not think a law compulsive of marriage reasonable in all respects; there are a sort of monsters of men, called *Women-haters*; these brutes would be destroyed by this Act. Nature also has excluded, by its deficiencies, some men from the state of matrimony; others are of such monstrous ill humours, that they can match no where but in the nunnery of Billingsgate; therefore, madam, if you get this Act passed, it must contain many provisos and exceptions.

Politica: Not in the least; I would have it a general compulsive Act, after this manner: every bachelor, at the age of twenty-four years, should pay such a tax to the Queen; suppose it twenty shillings per annum for the meanest rank of men, and what the Parliament thinks fit for those of higher degree ... The reasonableness of the Act is plain, for that unmarried people are, as it were, useless to the state; they are, like drones in a hive, reaping the advantage of other people's labours; they have their liberties and freedoms secured by the loss of other men's lives, and do not, from their own loins, repair the native strength of the kingdom; they are not so good as the spider, which hangs in the loom drawn from her own bowels: on the other hand, it is reasonable to ease such taxes, as have numerous families to the advantage of the Commonwealth; for these are at daily charge in breeding up their issue for the defence and safety of the kingdom ... Now, it is an easy matter for the Parliament of England to bring marriages on the same level, as was designed at first by nature. I will propose how: suppose every gentleman of one-thousand pounds *per annum* was obliged to marry gentlewomen of such quality and portion with ourselves, and, if he would not marry at all, his estate should become forfeited to the use of the public.

Politica: That would be hard, to take away all a man has in the world, because he will not marry.

Sophia: We will then find a medium: suppose we build and endow them an alms-house with their own money, where every one of them shall have a convenient apartment, with a bed, and two pair of sheets, one chair, one candlestick, a chamber-pot, and fire-place, and some other cheap necessaries. We will allow them one coat a year, with a yellow badge on the arm, as the mark of a bachelor; and every ten of them shall have one old woman to wait upon them: they shall be chiefly fed with water-gruel, and barley-broth; and, instead of meat, they shall eat potatoes, *Jerusalem* artichokes, turnips, carrots, and parsnips; for you know they come into that hospital, because they do not love the flesh.

Politica: Oh! fye Madam, fye upon you! that would use brisk young gentlemen at such a cruel rate: this is downright tyranny.

Sophia: I am sorry to see you so tender of those, who are so cruel to our sex: but here is no cruelty at all in the case; consider the thing rightly, madam, and you will find it otherwise: We esteem it the highest charity to provide alms-houses for the ancient superannuated poor, who are past their labour; now a man that is not come to his labour of generation, at twenty-five years of age, is certainly past it, and we ought to reckon him as superannuated, and grown an old boy, and not fit to be trusted with what he has, as not knowing the use and benefit of riches.

What I say in this respect, is the common practice of mankind in things of another nature: the husbandman, if he has got a tree in his orchard, that has grown a long time, and has bore no fruit, he cuts him down for fuel, and plants another in his room: why may we not do the same by human *bachelor* trees; especially since they are grafted on good stocks, and are so well watered and pruned? This is a very ill sort of seed that will fructify in no soil. It is the same thing in government; a bachelor is a useless thing in the state, does but cumber the ground, and takes up the room of a generous plant, which would be of great advantage to the Commonwealth. I tell you, madam, according to the Laws of Nature and reason, a bachelor is a minor, and ought to be under the government of the parish in which he lives; for, though he be a housekeeper and for himself, as they call it, yet, having no family, he cannot be reckoned a good commonwealth's-man; and, if he is not a good one, he is a bad one, which ought not to be suffered; nay, he is not a perfect man till such time as he is married, for it is the woman is the perfection of the man.

Politica: Madam, I know you are endowed with true English principles, pray consider, whether the law you mention be not destructive of *Magna Charta*, since, without cause or offence, it deprives a man of his property, and takes him from the estate which legally descended to him from his ancestors.

Sophia: Madam, I find you hold me to hard meat, I must give reasons for the passing of my bill: I argue thus, a person who has broken, and forfeited his right to the *Magna Charta* of nature, ought to have no protection by the *Magna Charta* of Englishmen: I prove my proposition thus, a bachelor of age, as such, has broken the Laws of Nature: increase and multiply is the command of nature, and of the God thereof; now, having broken the Laws of Nature, he ought not to have any protection from the Laws of England, because such, as have protection by those laws, do contribute to the support of those Laws, which an adult bachelor does not do according to the constitution of *Magna Charta*: our forefathers purchased the liberties of *Magna Charta*, with the hazard of life and limb; they sealed that writing with the blood of themselves and their children, and, after the same manner those privileges were procured, must they be supported and maintained; now, a bachelor contributes little or nothing to the support of our freedoms; the money he pays as taxes is inconsiderable to the supplies given by others in children, which are an addition to the native strength of the kingdom: money is like the soft and easy showers, which only cool and moisten the surface of the earth; children are like the soaking rain which goes to the root, and makes trees and vegetables fructify for the use of man: indeed, my dear, a bachelor can, in no sense, be esteemed a good Englishman ...

Politica: But, pray, how do you design to punish such of this sort of bachelors, that will not comply with your Act? I hope you will allow them a separate maintenance; you will build them an alms-house also, will you not?

Sophia: As the others are used like fools and superannuated persons, so we will use these like madmen. We will build them a convenient Bedlam,[4] wherein every one of them shall be chained about the middle to a post, like a monkey; we will feed them with low diet, as the others, and once a month they shall be blooded and shaved. To aggravate their crime, we will make every one of them a *Tantalus*,[5] by bringing every day handsome ladies before them, who shall laugh and jeer at them, and then turn their backs upon them ...

The Women-Hater's Lamentation

A topical satire on effeminate mollies. It notes that one hundred were apprehended for their unnatural lust, and that some committed suicide. Text from *The Women-Hater's Lamentation: or, a New Copy of Verses on the Fatal End of Mr Grant, a Woolen-Draper, and two others that Cut their Throats or Hang'd themselves in the Counter; with the Discovery of near Hundred more that are accused for unnatural dispising the Fair Sex, and intriguing with one another* (1707).

I

Ye injur'd *females* see
   Justice without the laws,
Seeing the injury,
   Has thus reveng'd your cause.

II

For those that are so blind,
   Your beauties to despise,
And slight your charms, will find
   Such Fate will always rise.

III

Of all the crimes that men,
   Through wicked minds do act,
There is not one of them
   Equals this brutal fact.

IV

Nature they lay aside,
   To gratify their lust;
Women they hate beside,
   Therefore their Fate was just.

V

Ye *Women-haters* say,
   What do's your breasts inspire,
That in a brutal way,
   You your own sex admire?

VI

Woman you disapprove,
   (The chief of earthly joys)
You that are deaf to love,
   And all the sex despise.

VII

But see the fatal end
  That do's such crimes pursue;
Unnat'ral deaths attend,
  Unnat'ral lusts in you.

VIII

A crime by men abhor'd,
  Nor Heaven can abide
Of which, when *Sodom* shar'd,
  She justly was destroy'd.

IX

But now, the sum to tell,
  (Tho' they plead innocence)
These by their own hands fell,
  Accused for this offence.

X

A hundred more we hear,
  Did to this club belong,
But now they scatter'd are,
  For this has broke the gang.

XI

Shop-keepers some there were,
  And men of good repute,
Each vow'd a Bachelor,
  Unnat'ral Lust pursu'd.

XII

Ye *Women-Haters* then,
  Take Warning by their Shame,
Your brutal lusts restrain,
  And own a nobler flame.

XIII

Woman the chiefest bliss
  That Heaven e'er bestow'd:
Oh be asham'd of this,
  You're by base lust subdu'd.

XIV

This piece of justice then
  Has well reveng'd their Cause,
And shows unnat'ral lust
  Is curs'd without the laws.

The Mollies' Club

Edward Ward (1667–1731), a prolific and popular writer, was satirized by Pope in *The Dunciad*. His *London Spy* recorded many aspects of ordinary life, often lingering voyeuristically on sordid details. Ward's portrait of the mollies has been discussed widely by Randolph Trumbach and Rictor Norton for the 'evidence' it presents on the role of effeminacy in the construction of homosexuality. Text from *The History of the London Clubs* (1709).

There are a particular Gang of *Sodomitical* Wretches, in this Town, who call themselves the *Mollies*, and are so far degenerated from all masculine deportment, or manly exercises, that they rather fancy themselves women, imitating all the little vanities that custom has reconciled to the female sex, affecting to speak, walk, tattle, cursy, cry, scold, and mimic all manner of effeminacy, that ever has fallen within their several observations; not omitting the indecencies of lewd women, that they may tempt one another by such immodest freedoms to commit those odious bestialities, that ought for ever to be without a name. At a certain tavern in the city, whose sign I shall not mention, because I am unwilling to fix an odium upon the house; where they have settled a constant meeting every evening in the week, that they may have the better opportunity of drawing unwary youth into the like corruption. When they are met together, it is their usual practice to mimic a female gossiping, and fall into all the impertinent tittle tattle, that a merry society of good wives can be subject to, when they have laid aside their modesty for the delights of the bottle. Not long since, upon one of their festival nights, they had cushioned up the belly of one of their *sodomitical* bretheren, or rather sisters, as they commonly called themselves, disguising him in a woman's nightgown, sarsenet-hood,[6] and nightrail,[7] who, when the company were met, was to mimic the wry faces of a groaning woman, to be delivered of a jointed baby they had provided for that purpose, and to undergo all the formalities of a lying-in. The wooden offspring to be afterwards Christened, and the holy Sacrament of Baptism to be impudently Prophaned, for the diversion of the profligates, who, when their infamous society were assembled in a body, put their wicked contrivance accordingly into practice.

One in a high crowned hat, and an old beldam's pinner representing a country midwife, another busy ape, dizened[8] up in a hussifed coif,[9] taking upon himself the duty of a very officious nurse, and the rest, as gossips, applied themselves to the travelling woman, according to the midwife's direction, all being as intent upon the business in hand, as if they had been women, the occasion real, and their attendance necessary. After abundance of bustle and that they had ridiculously counterfeited all the difficulties that they fancied were accustomary in such cases, their buffoonery Mauking[10] was at length disburdened of her little jointed bastard, and then putting their shotten[11] impostor to bed upon a double row of chairs; the baby was dressed by the midwife; the father brought to compliment his new-born son; the parson sent for; the gossips appointed; the child Christened, and then the cloth was spread; the table furnished with cold tongues and chickens; the guests invited to sit down and much joy expressed that my Gammar[12] Molly had brought her honest Gaffer a son and heir to town, so very like him, that as soon as born, had the eyes, nose, and mouth of its own credulous daddy. Now for the further promotion of their unbecoming mirth, every one was to tattle about their husbands and children: and to use no other dialect but what gossips are wont to do upon such loquacitous occasions. One would up with a story of her little Tommy, to show the promising genius of so witty a child, that if he let but a fizzle,[13] would presently cry out, *Mammy how I tink*. Another would be extolling the virtues of her husband, and declare he was a man of that affable, kind, and easy temper, and so aversed to jealousy, that she believed, were he to see another man in bed with her he would be so far from think her an ill woman, that nobody should persuade him they had been naught together. A third would be telling what a forward baggage her daughter *Nancy* was; for though she was but just turned of her seventh year, yet the young jade had the confidence to ask her father *Where girls carried their maidenheads that they were so apt to loose'em?* A fourth would be wishing no woman to marry a drunken husband, for her sake; for all the satisfaction she found in bed with him, was to creep as close to the wall as she could to avoid his tobacco breath and unsavoury belches, swearing that his son Roger was just like him, for that the guzling rogue would drink a pint of strong-ale at a draught before he was three years old, and would cry, *Mam, more ale.* A fifth would sit sighing at her ill-fortune, and wishing her husband would follow the steps of his journeyman;[14] for that was as careful a young fellow as ever came into a family. A sixth would express himself sorrowfully under the character of a widow; saying, *Alas, you have all husbands, and ought to pray heartily that you never know the miss of 'em; for tho' I had but a sorry one, when I was in your condition, yet, God help me, I have cause enough to repent my loss; for I am sure, both day and night, I find the want of him.* Thus every one, in his turn, would make a scoff and a little banter of the little effeminate weaknesses which women are subject to when gossiping, over their cups, on purpose to extinguish that natural affection which is due to the fair sex, and to turn their juvenile desires towards preternatural[15] pollutions. No sooner had they ended their feast, and run through all the ceremonies of their theatrical way of gossiping, but, having washed away, with wine, all fear of shame, as well as the checks of modesty, then they began to enter upon their beastly obscenities, and to take those infamous liberties with one another, that no man, who is not sunk into a state of Devilism, can think on without blushing, or mention without Christian abhorrence of all such heathenish brutalities. Thus, without detection, they continued their odious Society for some years, till their sodomitical practices were happily discovered by the cunning management of some of the under-agents to the *Reforming-Society;*[16] so that several were brought to open shame and punishment; others flying from justice to escape the ignominy, that by this means the diabolical Society were forced to put a period to their filthy scandalous revels.

'Tis strange that in a country where
Our ladies are so kind and fair,
So gay, and lovely, to the sight,
So full of beauty and delight;
That men should on each other doat,
And quit the charming petticoat.

Sure the curs'd father of this race,
That does both sexes thus disgrace,
Must be a monster, mad, or drunk,
Who, bedding some preposterous
    punk,
Mistook the downy Seat of Love,

And got them in the sink[17] above;
So that, at first, a t–d and they
Were born the very self same way,
From whence they draw this cursed itch,
Not to the belly, but the breech;
Else who could woman's charms refuse,
To such a beastly practice use?
'Tis true, that swine on dunghills bred,
Nurs'd up in filth, with offal fed,
Have oft the flow'ry meads forsook,
To wallow belly deep in muck;
But men who choose this backward way,
Are fifty times worse swine than they:
For the less savage four-leg'd creature,
Lives but according to his Nature:
But the *Bug'ranto* two leg'd brute,
Pursues his lust contrary to't;
The brawny boar will love his sow;
The horse his mare; the bull his cow;
But *Sodomites* their wives forsake,
Unmanly liberties to take,
And fall in love with one another,
As if no woman was their mother:
For he that is of woman born,
Will to her arms again return;
And surely never choose to play
His lustful game, the backward way.
But since it has appear'd too plain,
There are such brutes that pass for men;
May he that on the rump so doats,
Be damn'd as deep as doctor *Oates*,[18]
That scandal unto all black coats.

Sir Narcissus Foplin

The role of the fop changed significantly between the seventeenth and eighteenth century. The portrait begins to appear as a version of the 'molly'. Text from 'Sir Narcissus Foplin: or, the Self-Admirer' in *The Modern World Disrob'd* (1708). See Staves (1982); Meyer (1994); Senelick (1990); Trumbach (1990).

He is the spindle-shanked progeny of a half-witted father, who drowsily begot him, betwixt sleeping and waking,[19] to pleasure his lady, much rather than himself; and dying, left the fruits of his nuptial drudgery to the mother's care, who, by effeminate fondness, has made him all woman, except the masculine peg,[20] which is hung on by nature, for the distinction of sexes.

Though he is very conversant with the fair sex, and a mighty man among the fine ladies, he only rivals them in their own vanity; and, as they hope to be admired by him, so the fool fancies they are his admirers; but if they were, they might ease their passions with their own solitary sights; for he has so cool a sense of female favours, that he has less respect for the charms of a petticoat, than for the loathsome condescensions of a fricatizing[21] *Catamite*,[22] who is beast enough to ease his sodomitical desires with anti-venereal exercise. Yet, after all, the squeaking *Homunculus*,[23] with his capon's[24] voice, who, in contempt of the fair sex, can be manual operator of his own lust, can loll in his gilt chariot, and keep his brawny slaves to bow down and worship him, must set himself up, forsooth, for a man of honour, a gentleman of worth ...

Familiar Descant on the Foregoing Character

> What fops and monsters do we see
> Sit lolling in their coaches
> And haughty apes, of high degree,
> Grow proud of their debauchees?

Reasons for the Growth of Sodomy

This text provides a detailed account of how boys used to be brought up to be men, contrasted with modern procedures in which boys are inducted into effeminate habits in infancy. The lack of discipline is harmful to their proper development as family men capable of serving king and country. Text from *Reasons for the Growth of Sodomy, in England* (1749).

Our fore-fathers were trained up to arts and arms; the scholar embellished the hero; and the fine gentleman of former days, was equally fit for the council as the camp; the boy (though perhaps a Baronet's son) was taken early from the nursery and sent to the grammar-school, with his breakfast in his hand, and his satchel at his back; subject to order and correction, he went regularly through his studies; and, if tardy, spurred up: the school hours over, and his exercise made, he had his moments of play allotted him for relaxation; then sought he the resort of other boys, either in the fields, or public squares of the city; where he hardened himself against the inclemency of the weather, and inured himself to athletic exercises; wholesome as well as pleasant: this has sent him home with his blood in a fine circulation, and his stomach as sharp as a ploughman's; supper over, and jogged down with t'other frolic, he went to bed and slept sweetly; after which he rose early the next morning, fresh, and fit for study, hurried on his clothes, and away to school again: no matter if his hands and face were now and then a little dirty, so his understanding was clean: if his clothes were sometimes torn with some skirmish, his heart was whole, and the frequent battles between school and school (which were then in vogue) inured him to courage, gave him a thirst after honour, and a proneness to warlike exercises.

I would not from this have my little hero esteemed a bully; no, his learning tempered his passions; with all this spirit, the boy was bashful to the last degree; dutiful and humble to his parents, mannerly to his elders and superiors; he knew no vice, being trained up in a series of virtue; the authors he read inspired him with notions of honour; the heroes and sages, whose lives he found transmitted with such applause, through so many ages, filled him with an emulation to knowledge, and a thirst after glory; familiarized to temperance and exercise, he was no valetudinarian[25] in his constitution, but a stranger to debauch; and as he grew to riper years, where the virtuous object of his first wishes crowned his virtuous love, there, in the flower of his health, and vigour of his youth, stamped he his maker's image: behold our schoolboy now become a father, blest with an endearing wife, and a dutiful, beautiful offspring; his love and care for them, now makes him ready to pursue whatever state of life Heaven has allotted him, his abilities of mind and body, render him capable of serving his King, his Country, and his Family. His application to business keeps him from debauch, and his success so spurs him on, that he soon sees a fine provision made for himself and family; and his (perhaps small) patrimony amply augmented: this shows the advantages of a proper education; I am sorry to say an old fashioned one.

Now let us take a sketch of the modern modish way of bringing up young gentlemen.

Little master is kept in the nursery 'till he is five or six years old, at least, after which he is sent to a girl's school, to learn dancing and reading, and, generally speaking, gets his minuet before his letters; for whereas boys of old went to school at six in the morning, and came home at eleven; master goes at eleven and stays 'till twelve; for the poor child must not get up till all its things are aired, and 'tis barbarous to let him breakfast without his mamma; so that if he is dressed by tea-time, 'tis well enough: to let him have milk-porridge, water-gruel, or such like spoon meats, is vulgar and unpolite; well, by eleven, or a little after breakfast, is over, and master taken to school, though very often breakfast is drilled on till it is too late, unless they dance in a morning, and then the whole family is up sooner than ordinary. When he comes to school, he stands by his mistress, who is generally working and looking another way all the while, he repeats the alphabet after her not without some interruption, though without the least attention; for the child is looking at its school-fellows, and the mistress directing the young ladies in their samplers, or other fiddle faddles.

Here he continues till the age at which boys formerly went to the Universities, at last (with great reluctance) he is sent to a master, probably to a writing school, for fear he should break his head with *Latin*; besides, *Grammar-masters* are harsh; and the child is of a tender constitution: well may it be so, when the tone of his stomach has been spoiled with tea, when his blood is curdled with now and then a dram, to keep the mother in countenance; when the boy's constitution is half torn to pieces with apothecary's *slip slops*, occasioned by early intemperance, sitting up late on nights, eating meat *suppers*, and drinking wine, and other strong liquors of most pernicious consequence to infant constitutions.

Besides, his whole animal fabric is enervated for want of due exercise; and he is grown so chilly by over nursing, that he gets cold with the least breath of wind; for, till he went to the *girls' school*, he seldom or never was out of the nursery, unless to pay a visit, in a coach, with his mamma: for, at the mistress's *school*, he was brought up in all respects like a *girl* (needleworks excepted), for his mamma had charged him not to play with rude boys, for fear of spoiling his *Clothes*; so that hitherto our young gentleman has amused himself with dolls, assisted at mock christenings, visits, and other girlish employments, inviting and being invited to drink tea with this or that school-fellow; insomuch, that his whole life hitherto has been one series of ignorance, indolence, and intemperance.

But here the master being doubly bribed, by the father to bring him forward, and by the mother not to *correct* him; with much a-do, makes a shift to teach him to read and write a little *English*, by which time he is almost too big to go to school; however, for form's sake, 'tis fit he should learn his accidence before he goes to the University, or to travel.

The boy, thus spoiled, becomes *company* for none but women, and even of those, only the fantastical and impertinent; for, to the glory of the sex be it spoken, the generality of 'em seeing the depravity of *men*, have set themselves to thinking, and got the upper-hand of our *Petits Maitres*, not only in common understanding, but even in liberal acquirements and polite conversation; and are, in all respects, fitter for the management of public and private affairs, than the *Milksops* beforementioned.

Far be it from me to arraign all mankind for the faults of a few! No, our public schools, such as *Westminster, Eton*, &c. still retain the same manly spirit: a milksop there, is like an owl among the birds: 'tis just the same at our Universities; there are real students, as well as fops; the former being the glory, as the latter are the shame of their age, or country.

When our young gentleman arrives to marriage; I wish I could say fit for it; what can be expected from such an enervated effeminate animal? What satisfaction can a woman have in the embraces of this figure of a man? Should she at last bring him a child, what can we hope from so crazy a *constitution*? But a feeble, unhealthy infant, scarce worth the rearing; whilst the father, instead of being the head of the family, makes it seem as if it were governed by two women: for he has sucked in the spirit of *Cotqueanism*[26] from his infancy: as for supporting them, his indolence won't let him undertake anything laborious; his ignorance denies him all hopes of any thing of *consequence*; and his pride won't accept of what is mean: (at least what he thinks so.) Thus, unfit to serve his king, his Country, or his Family, this man of *Clouts*[27] dwindles into nothing, and leaves a race as effeminate as himself; who, unable to please the women, choose rather to run into unnatural vices one with another, than to attempt what they are but too sensible they cannot perform.

The Effeminacy of our Men's Dress and Manners, particularly their Kissing each other

I am confident no age can produce any thing so preposterous as the present dress of those gentlemen who call themselves pretty fellows: their head-dress especially, which wants nothing but a suit of pinners to make them down-right women. But this may be easily accounted for, as they would appear as soft as possible to each other, any thing of *Manliness* being diametrically opposite to such unnatural practices, so they cannot too much invade the dress of the sex they would represent. And yet with all this, the present garb of our young gentlemen is most mean and unbecoming. 'Tis a difficulty to know a gentleman from a footman, by their present habits: The low-heeled pump is an emblem of their low spirits; the great harness buckle is the height of affectation; the silk waistcoat all belaced, with a scurvy blue coat like a livery frock, has something so poorly preposterous, it quite enrages me; I blush to see 'em aping the running footman, and poising a great oaken plant, fitter for a bailiff's follower than a gentleman. But what renders all more intolerable, is the hair stroked over before and cocked up behind, with a *comb* sticking in it, as if it were just ready to receive a head-dress: nay, I am told, some of our tip-top beaus dress their heads on quilted *hair caps*, to make 'em look more *womanish*; so that Master *Molly* has nothing to do but slip on his *head clothes* and he is an errant woman, his rueful face excepted; but even that can be amended with paint, which is as much in vogue among our gentlemen, as with the ladies in France.

But there is no *joke* like their new-fashion'd *joke hats*, equally priggish as foppish; plainly demonstrating, that notwithstanding the *bustle* they make about *jokes*, they have them only about their *heads*. But to see them dressed for a *ball*, or assembly, in a *party coloured silk coat*, is the height of my aversion: they had better have a *Mantua* and *petticoat* at once, than to mince the matter thus, or do things by halves.

But of all the customs *Effeminacy* has produced, none more hateful, predominant, and pernicious, than that of the men's *kissing* each other. This *fashion* was brought over from *Italy* (the *Mother* and *Nurse* of *Sodomy*); where the *master* is oftener *intriguing* with his *page*, than a *fair lady*. And not only in that *country*, but in *France*, which copies from them, the *contagion* is diversified, and the ladies (in the *nunneries*) are criminally *amorous* of each other, in a *method* too gross for expression. I must be so partial to my own *country-women*, to affirm, or, at least, hope they claim no share of this *charge*; but must confess, when I see two ladies *kissing* and *slopping* each other, in a *lascivious manner*, and *frequently* repeating it, I am shocked to the last degree; but not so much, as when I see two *fulsome* fellows *slavering* every time they meet, *squeezing* each other's hand, and other like *indecent symptoms*. And though many gentlemen of worth, are oftentimes, out of pure good *manners*, obliged to give into it; yet the land will never be purged of its *abominations*, till this *unmanly, unnnatural* usage be totally abolished: for it is the first *inlet* to the detestable sin of *Sodomy*.

Under this pretext vile *Catamites* make their preposterous *addresses*, even in the very *streets*; nor can anything be more shocking than to see a couple of *creatures*, who wear the shapes of *men, kiss* and *slaver* each other, to that degree, as is daily practised even in our most public places; and (generally speaking) without reproof; because they plead in excuse, *that it is the fashion*. Damned *fashion!* Imported from *Italy* amidst a train of other *unnatural vices*. Have we not *sins* enough of *foreign nations*, to fill up the cup of our *abominations*, and make us yet more ripe for *divine* vengeance.

'Till of late years, *sodomy* was a *sin*, in a manner unheard of in these nations; and indeed, one would think where there are such *angelic women*, so foul a sin should never enter into imagination: on the contrary, our *sessions-papers* are frequently stained with the *crimes* of these *beastly Wretches*; and though many have been made examples of, yet we have but too much reason to fear, that there are numbers yet undiscovered, and that this *abominable practice* gets ground every day.

Instead of the *pillory*, I would have the *stake* be the punishment of those, who in contradiction to the laws of *God* and *man*, to the order and course of *Nature*, and to the most simple principles of *Reason*, preposterously *burn* for each other, and *leave* the *field*, the *charming sex*, neglected.

But as loss of appetite is inseparable from a feeble and depraved *stomach*: so is this *vice* most predominant in those, to whom *Nature* has been so sparing of her blessings, that they found not a call equivalent to other *men*. And therefore, rather than expose themselves, they take the *contrary road*; and, like eunuchs, out of mere madness and disappointment, loathe the dear sex they have no power to please.

This must be the case, if we consider that the majority of persons suspected of this vice, are antiquated lechers; who have out-lived the power of enjoyment; are so conscious of their own insufficiency, they dare not look a woman in the face.

But so numerous are they grown, it is high time to put a stop to them, lest the growing generation be corrupted; and *England* rival *Italy*, in this most unnatural and wicked practice.

No step will be more effectual than at once to abolish the fulsome custom of *men kissing* each other, and to admit of no plea or exception in favour of so detestable practice.

Is not the old custom of shaking hands more manly, more friendly and more decent? What need have we of *Judas* like a practice? For my part, I hold it so ridiculous foolish custom for a man to *Kiss* even his own brother, it savours too much of *effeminacy*, to say the best of it. I know some worthy gentlemen so scrupulous, they will not on my account *kiss* any friend or relation of the same *Sex*, and I saw myself, two brothers take a very solemn leave of each other without one *kiss*, though not without tears; and I dare say with more friendship than ten thousand *kisses* could express. I am of a society of gentlemen, and with pride I declare it; who have made a solemn vow, never to give or take from any man a *kiss*, on any account whatever; and so punctual have we been in observation of this injunction, that many times at the expense of a quarrel, this rule has been most inviolably kept among us.

If such a resolution was more universal, the sons of *Sodom* would lose many *Proselytes*, in being baffled out of one of their principal advances; for under pretence of extraordinary friendship, they entice unwary youth from this first step, to more detestable practices, taking many times the advantage of their necessities, to decoy them to their ruin.

I know a thousand objections will be brought against what I say; I shall be laughed at by the votaries[28] of *Sodom* and effeminacy; but I hope the manly and generous *Britons*, who yet survive, will take what I say into consideration, and show themselves *friends to the* FAIR SEX; by opposing all inlets to the sin of *Sodomy*, of which *man-kissing* is the very first.

With this, all other *Effeminacies* should be abolished; and each sex should maintain its peculiar character: I hope the ladies will not stand in need of any advice from me; yet I could wish that some among them would seem less amorous of one another; for though woman *kissing* woman, is more suitable to their natural softness, and indeed more excusable than the like practice in the contrary sex; yet it ought to be done (*if at all*) with modesty and moderation, lest suggestions, which I hope are false, and which to me seem improbable, should bring such ladies under censure; who give themselves too great liberties with each other: for as the age increases in wickedness, new vices may arise; and since they themselves see how fulsome it is in gentlemen, I hope they will abstain *from all appearance of evil*, and contribute to the intended reformation; not only by scorning and deriding such *wretches* of *men*, who shall openly affront them, by *kissing* each other in their presence: but that they will set the gentlemen a pattern, and shame them out of it by using a *kiss*, if it must be used, in so decent a manner, and with so great restraint, that the most envious shall find no cause of censure.

The Italian OPERAs, and Corruption of the English Stage, and other Public Diversions

How famous, or rather how infamous Italy has been in all ages, and still continues in the odious practice of *Sodomy*, needs no explanation; it is there esteemed so trivial, and withal so modish a sin, that not a cardinal or churchman of note but has his *Ganymede*;[29] no sooner does a stranger of condition set his foot in *Rome*, but he is surrounded by a crowd of *Pandars*,[30] who ask him if he chooses a *woman* or a *boy*, and procure for him accordingly; this practice is there so general, they have little else in their heads or mouths, that *Casto* and *Culo* which they intermix with almost every sentence (a beastly and withal most stupid interjection!) for, let them be talking on never so serious a subject, these two syllables must come in, though never so foreign to the purpose; these they use just as the *French* do the Word *foutre*,[31] which must come in by head and shoulders in every company and sentence. Nay, there are those who will intermingle it word for word, to the no small improvement of conversation; we are not yet arrived to this pitch of perfection; but much may be hoped in time: for since the introduction of ITALIAN OPERAS here, our men are grown insensibly more and more *effeminate*; and whereas they used to go from a good *comedy* warm'd with the fire of love; and from a good *tragedy*, fir'd with a spirit of glory; they sit indolently and supine at an OPERA, and suffer their souls to be sung away by the voices of the *Italian Syrens*; 'twas just the same in *Greece*, when they left their noble warlike moods, and ran into soft compounds of *chromatic music*; of this the philosopher complains, and to this attributes the loss of so many battles, and dwindling of the *Grecian glory*. *Rome* likewise sank in honour and success, as it rose in *luxury* and *effeminacy*; they had women singers and eunuchs from *Asia*, at a vast price: which so softened their youth, they quite lost the spirit of manhood, and with it their empire. For they grew so *womanish* in mind, gesture, and attire; and withal so fearful of hurting their sweet faces, which were nurs'd up with all the *cosmetics* art or nature could invent or produce, that their enemies killed 'em with their very looks, and for fear of having their *faces* gashed, or their *fine Clothes* spoiled, they turned their backs upon those *ugly dirty fellows*, and gave up their liberty to preserve their *effeminacy*. Heaven grant the application may never extend to England; but I leave any reasonable person to judge, if the *similitude* is not too close.

As the ITALIAN OPERAS have flourished, the *English* stage has diminished. Where is that life, fire and spirit which adorned our *Plays* of old? Look over the productions of this last age (Mr ADDISONS's *Cato* excepted) and you will see nothing worthy to be call'd a *play*, or proper to be exhibited to a *British* audience: they are rather *drolls* or *farces*, than *tragedies* and *comedies*; so that it may well be said *comedy* and *tragedy* died with *Addison* and *Congreve*, and *action* with *Booth* and *Oldfield*. Our *players* are now turn'd *ballad-singers*; our *theatres* are transform'd to *puppet-shows*, improperly called *pantomimes*; for the *pantomimes* of the ancients were clever fellows, that would exactly mimic, or imitate, the voice and gesture of any man they had an intent to *ridicule*. But in these *pantomime entertainments*, there is neither head or tail, meaning or connection: *Gods*, *harlequins*, *priests*, and *sailors*, are all jumbled together, even in *temples*, in the most incoherent manner, ten times more extravagant than the most extravagant dream that ever was yet dreamt: however, these *drolls* have *crowded houses*, while the best *plays* of *Shakespeare* are exhibited to *empty boxes*.

This shows the taste of the Town, and the genius of the people who, grown quite *lethargic* with *luxury*, and in a state of *perdition*, dare not *think*, and only seek to be *diverted*.

The *masquerades*, *ridottos*, and *assemblies* of late so much the mode, at once explain and condemn themselves. 'Tis the greatest *Reproach* imaginable to the *British* nation, that they have suffered themselves to be bubbled at this rate by a vagabond *Swiss*, who has lived *profusely* for many years past, at the expense of the *English* fools; a public *cock-bawd*, who while others of his profession have been punished by Justices, &c. has gone on with impunity, caressed by the chief (I was about to say best) of our *quality*; but for what reasons may be easily imagined.

Next to the abuse of *public diversions*, is that of *private conversation*, which is now reduced to these two important heads, *tittle tattle* and *Quadrille*.[32]

This *whistling* away of time renders us such useless *animals*, that we live to no purpose; for, as our *Senses* grow depraved, so will our *appetites* and *inclinations*: for it is evident to men who have the free use of their *faculties*, that as there is no pleasure on earth equal to the possession of an *agreeable woman*; so it must be confessed, that whoever runs into any *extreme* of a contrary nature, it is because he is neither *worthy* or *capable* of enjoying so great a *blessing*.

The Petit Maitre, an odd sort of poem, in the Trolly-Lolly Stile, by a gentleman commoner.

I

Tell me, gentle Hob'dehoy!
Art thou girl, or art thou boy?
Art thou man, or art thou ape;
For thy gesture and thy shape,
And thy features and thy dress,
Such contraries do express:
I stand amaz'd, and at a loss to know,
To what new species thou thy form
    dost owe?

II

By thy hair, comb'd up behind,
Thou should'st be of *Womankind*:
But that damn'd forbidding face,
Does the charming sex disgrace;
Man, or woman, thou art neither;
But a blot, a shame to either:
Nor dare to *Brutehood*, even to make
    pretence;
For brutes themselves, show greater
    signs of sense.

III

By thy *jaws* all lank and thin;
By that forc'd unmeaning grin:
Thou appear'st to humane eyes,

Like some ape of monstrous size;
Yet an ape thou can'st not be,
Apes are more adroit than thee;
Thy oddities so much my mind
    perplex;
I neither can define thy kind or sex.

IV

Art thou substance, art thou shade?
That thus mounst'rouly array'd,
Walking forth in open day,
Dost our senses quite dismay?
Unghastly yet, thou only can'st
    provoke,
Our rage, our detestation, and our joke.

V

If thou art a man, forbear
Thus, this *motly garb* to wear;
Do not reason thus displace,
Do not man-hood thus disgrace;
But thy sex by dress impart,
And appear like what thou art:
Like what thou art, said I, pray pardon
    me;
I mean appear, like what thou ought'st
    to be.

A Learned Dissertation upon Old Women, Male and Female

The dissertation was designed as satire on the Whigs, but manages to produce a tour of sexual waywardness and political weakness throughout history. Text from *A Learned Dissertation upon Old Women, Male and Female, Spiritual and Temporal, in all Ages; whether In Church, State, or Exchange-Alley. Very seasonable to be read at all Times, but especially at particular Times. To which is added, An Essay upon the present Union of the Whig Chiefs* (1720)

There is a waggish acquaintance of mine, who carries the analogy between Old Women and grave barristers further than, in my judgement, need requires he should. 'Don't you observe, says he, that they have the same enmity to silence, and possess the same eternal wetness of beard? Pray, distinguish, if you can, between pleading and scolding; and, whatever you do, mark that hobling amble in their gate; that involuntary nod of the head; that contracted plodding forehead; that wise unmeaning face, and these desolate gums! and then, confess the invisible likeness' ...

Queen Semiramis was the greatest king that ever swayed the sceptre of Assyria, and exceeded by far all that succeeded her. She was indeed a most valiant man, but very lewd, which is no fault in princes; what is very common being very pardonable. To her succeeded her son, King Sardanapalus the Queen, who from his infancy was an Old Woman, and very naturally spent all his time, and his spinning, amongst young ones. But for all the harmlessness of this He-queen, he met an untimely Fate, and violent hands were laid upon the Lord's Anointed, to the great grief of all the true churchmen ... Those who came after him were for the most part like him; and from Semiramis to the end of the Babylonian monarchy, which lasted for several ages, all the kings proved to be of the female gender, except herself ... But as every old woman that totters under a crown, rules, or scolds, or blasphemes, or murders, or burns, by divine appointment; so the old women, alias emperors of Persia, continued to plague mankind, and misgovern, as heaven's lieutenants, till Alexander the Great, who in the beginning of his reign, was indeed a king of the masculine gender, came with all the violence of war, as heaven's lieutenants also, to dethrone and put an end to them: for he that was strongest always happened to have the divine authority on his side, contrary, and yet agreeable, to the orthodox system ... Alexander himself soon degenerated, and before he arrived to the flower of his age, grew an old woman, like the rest; became wonderfully addicted to scolding, and doating upon nothing but fine gowns, and citron water. His immediate successors resembled him; they were at first men, and at last drivelers; and, so those kings who succeeded them, they were old wives from their cradles ...

There never was, in all the East, a braver race of men than the Amazons, whose queens were also the bravest of kings. Tamerlane too happened to be a prince of a male genius; but excepting as before excepted, there has scarce ever been known such a character as a king in all the great continent of Asia, though abounding in monarchs. Their frequent exercising of craft and cruelty does in no degree determine them men; the same being also exercised, though in a smaller measure, by crocodiles, wolves, kites, adders, and the like emblems and patterns of such imperial old women as play the devil by divine right.

But these royal vermin, who sucked the blood of their subjects, and were the relentless foes of mankind, became all in their turn, the booty and vassals of the Romans, who knocked them on the head or imprisoned them, or suffered them to enjoy a precarious and slavish sovereignty, just as they had behaved themselves. The Romans were a nation of men, and friends to their species, lovers of liberty and despisers of life, when these two blessings were incompatible. They propagated politeness and laws; and hunted down tyrants and barbarity, wherever they came. They taught mankind to distinguish between manly obedience, proceeding from rational consent, which is the allegiance of subjects; and involuntary submission, extorted by fears and force, which is the lot and condition of slaves ... Every principle and every action which promoted their present liberty and prosperity was lawful, virtuous, and religious, in the eyes of that noble people; who had no idea of the encroachment of liberty upon religion, or of the church's clashing with the state, or of the creature's contending for superiority with its creator. These were monsters yet unborn, and absurdities as yet uninvented, which lived not till liberty was dead, and till old women succeeded heroes ... The Romans preserved their liberty so long as they preserved their virtue. At last ambition and bribery seized the senate house, and were followed by every civil art and every wicked purpose: the corruption began at the great, who spread it among the people, and debauched them in order to enslave them. Shows, farces, and masquerades, made them idle, and depending upon those who gratified them with these fine sights and diversions.[33] At long run, their highest ambition was to live and see shows. In the end, being fully purged of all sense of virtue and freedom, the whole Roman people, who had conquered the world, and polished it; they who had deposed tyrants, and set mankind free, became themselves an easy prey to a traitor of their own raising.

Men have been, and are, generally taught (from their early youth) to admire and reverence the first Caesar: at which I am astonished; for he was one of the most wicked and bloody men that ever the earth bore. He stuck at no villainy, no vileness, no destruction, to gain ends, and ruin his country ... In short, Julius Caesar, like most other conquerors, is intitled, in an humbler degree, to that sort of glory, which is due to Belzebub, for daring the Almighty, and defacing the creation. Those who succeeded him in the usurpation of Rome, were for the most part such an execrable race of vermin, that there is scarce any other character to be given of them, than that emperor and Old Women were terms synonymous, ever afterwards.

The empress Claudius deserves particular notice. She left the empire to the administration of whatever person happened to be most in her good graces, for the time being: and so sometimes her wife was queen, and sometimes her footman; while the good woman Claudius herself turned author, and scribbled, and gormandized, and got drunk, every day of her life ... Just like the learned and valiant monarch of another country, I mean Queen James the first of Magnagascar ... Queen James was also a royal benefactor to Grub-Street, and president of the learned society there. She writ books, and made speeches, and was greatly subject to the looseness; which last I take to be the true reason why the learned Queen James's performances smell but little of the conjurer ... To Queen James succeeded another queen; I mean he who was nick-named the confessor. Like king, like counsellors! this sucking monarch got him a wife, and yet went still in leading-strings:[34] mother William Laud,[35] and Madam the Duke of Buckingham, who had been his father's mistress, were his governors, unlimited and uncontrollable.

The kingdom grew ashamed and weary of being governed and oppressed by such a grizzel,[36] and so pulled her out of the elbow-chair, and never suffered her to set her breech in it afterwards; though she tried all means whatsoever, sometimes scolding, sometimes beseeching, sometimes tricking, and sometimes hiring bullies to fight for her.

After a long civil contention for liberty and dominion, which I pass over in silence, because it was between men and men, who do not belong to this my subject; come we, in the next place, to the riotous reign of Queen Sardanapalus the IInd, who neglected God and men to drink French wine, and play with French harlots and lap-dogs. There began then to be a great decay of sobriety, virtue and manhood; and nothing triumphed but the excise, fornication and the church.

After a long reign of luxury and feminine weaknesses, Queen Sardanapalus departed this life, by the pious assistance of the priests and her brother the Princess James; who mounted the throne, and showed herself as errant an Old Wife as ever shook the sceptre ... Queen James ... let loose his inclinations, and devilized with all his might ... driving furiously over the life and limb of every subject that stood in his way, without any resistance ...

I have thus, with great labour of body and brain, searched into the records of the time, and given my attentive reader an edifying abstract of universal history, of which I have shown Old Women to have been the principal heroes. If we look now into the disputes and transactions between nation and nation, we shall assuredly find that they ever prevailed, or miscarried, according as they employed men or Old Women in the management of their affairs civil and military.

To come now, towards the end, to speak of my own country, of which I have not hitherto said one word; I am sorry to say, that the increase of Old Women grows marvellously great amongst us. It is moreover grievous to consider, by what heavy and contemptible instruments this shameful change is wrought. Lo! our evil cometh from the dull heart of the city, and we are enchanted by a stupid kennel of Stock-Jobbers, who cheat us out of our money and our sex, and then stand godfathers to us, and, by way of tender derision, christen us bubbles!

A Genuine Narrative

The poem celebrates love for a young man. Text from *A Genuine Narrative of All the Street Robberies Committed since October last, by James Dalton, And his Accomplices* (1728).

Let the fops of the town upbraid
Us, for an unnatural trade,
We value not man nor maid;
    But among our own selves we'll be
free,
        But among, &c.

We'll kiss and we'll Sw[iv]e,[37]
Behind we will drive,
And we will contrive
    New ways of lechery,
        New ways, &c.

How sweet is the pleasant sin?
With a boy about sixteen,
That has got no hair on his chin,
    And a countenance like a rose
        And a countenance, &c.

Here we will enjoy
The simpering boy,
And with him we'll toy;
    The Devil may take the froes,

The devil &c.

Confusion on the stews,[38]
And those that whores do chuse,
We'll praise the Turks and Jews,
    Since they with us do agree,
        Since they &c.

They're not confin'd,
To water or wind,
Before or behind,
    But take all liberty,
        But take &c.

Achilles that hero great,
Had Patroculus for a mate;[39]
Nay, Jove he would have a Lad,
    The beautiful Ganymede,
        The beautiful &c.

Why should we then
Be daunted, when
Both gods and men
    Approve the pleasant deed,
        Approve the &c.

Hell upon Earth

A general satire on social life in London, with a special focus on sodomy. Effeminate conversations are recorded; together with the excessive, luxurious lifestyle of the fop. Text from *Hell upon Earth: Or, the Town in an Uproar. Occasioned by the late horrible Scenes of Forgery, Perjury, Street-Robbery, Murder, Sodomy, and other shocking Impieties* (1729).

The late proceedings in our Courts of Law have furnished us with ample proofs, that this Town abounds too plentifully with a sect of brutish creatures called SODOMITES; a sect that ought to be excluded from all civil society and human conversation. They exceed the worst beasts of the field in the filthiness of their abominations. The birds of the air couple male and female to propagate generation, and every animal moves by a natural instinct; but man, exclusive of all others, forms ideas destructive to himself, and grows fond of new inventions which are repugnant to divine institution and the fundamental laws of nature; he is grown hardened in iniquity, having abandoned himself to all manner of vice, and is not ashamed to act crimes which expose him to the severity of the laws and the contempt of the world. I have heard that one *Tolson*, who lately kept a brandy-shop at *Charing-Cross*, and was transported for felony, whose constitution was so depraved and ruined that he could contain nothing within him, and who was not ashamed to confess, that he received that debility by human conversation and the vile practice of buggery; and that once having caught a foot-soldier in bed with his wife, he insisted upon no other satisfaction than to commit the detestable sin of sodomy with him, which the other complied with, and so the affair was made easy. It is a melancholy sight to see men in full strength and vigour go to public executions unpitied and unlamented, loaded with the highest guilt, that can neither hope or expect any mercy in this, and may justly dread the punishments in the world to come: the greatest criminal has some people that may drop some pitying expressions for his unhappy and untimely fate and condole his dismal circumstances; while those persons who fall by the laws for *Sodomy*, can expect neither pity or compassion. It would be a pretty scene to behold them in their clubs and cabals, how they assume the air and affect the name of *Madam* or *Miss*, *Betty*, or *Molly*, with a chuck under the chin, and *O you bold Pullet*[40] *I'll break your eggs*, and then frisk and walk away to make room for another, who thus accosts the affected lady, with *Where have you been you saucy Queen? If I catch you strouling and caterwauling, I'll beat the milk out of your breast I will so*; with a great many other expressions of buffoonery and ridiculous affectation. If they can procure a young smug-faced fellow they never grudge any expense, and it is remarkable these effeminate villains are much fonder of a new *convert* than bully would be of a new *mistress*.

They have also their *walks* and *appointments*, to meet and pick up one another, and their particular houses of resort to go to, because they dare not trust themselves in an open tavern. About twenty of these sort of houses have been discovered, besides the nocturnal assemblies of great numbers of the like vile persons, what they call *markets*, which are the *Royal-Exchange*, *Lincoln's-Inn bog-houses*, the South-side of St *James's-Park*, the Piazzas of *Covent-Garden*, St *Clement's Church-Yard*, &c.

* * *

As a glittering appearance gains a popular esteem amongst the vulgar, it is no wonder to see our vain-glorious coxcombs so fond of a gaudy equipage; but to anatomize these animals, and show them in their proper colours, may possibly afford some diversion; for when a fool sets up for a fop he is no more the subject of a wise man's esteem, than a caterpillar after it is transformed to a butterfly.

The Character of a FOP

HE is the superficies of a man, and the magazine of superfluities, and consults his tailor with as much care as the ancient *Greeks* did the Oracle at *Delphos*: he has a particular regard to the Sabbath, especially after he has purchased a new Peruke,[41] and is never so devout as when he prays for fair weather yet he is very wavering in his religion for he visits half a dozen churches in sermon-time, and never tarieth long in a place, but where he can show his dress to some advantage: he looks upon rain and the wind as the greatest judgements of heaven, and had rather run against the D-l in a dark night than a chimney-sweeper; for which reason he passes *Cheapside-Conduit* with the same precaution as a poor citizen does *Woodstreet Compter*: His politics are upon the same foot with his religion, for before noon he runs his head into twenty coffee-houses, and has no small ambition to be thought a news-monger: he is no great friend to the tobacconist, for fear of his lungs, yet he holds a pipe in his mouth to make his diamond ring the more conspicuous, and to that end he has an excellent faculty in playing upon the table with his fingers: he is very careful in adjusting his phiz,[42] and takes a pinch of snuff with the utmost curiosity; and, at the same time, reckons him an unmannerly clown that will not praise his snuff box: his habiliments are mostly foreign, and nothing is admirable but what done by an outlandish artificer; the blade of his sword was tempered at Toledo, and the handle was wrought by the best workman in Andalusia; nay, the very head of his cane was dug out of a mine in the Pharsalian fields, and afterwards polished by an Aethiopian in Prester John's country. If his patrimony will allow him a footman, the poor fellow is hurried off his legs with carrying *Billet Doux* to the ladies, and often gets his head broke for his master's impertinence; however, he gets a snatch of his master's airs, and is initiated in the pride of powder, essence, snuff and washballs: if the fop keeps a mistress, according to fashion, his pride is too great to be over-courteous; so she must never expect him to dispense his favour in the day-time, for a true fop will starve a thousand other sins to support his vanity; and by consequence he had rather be gelt than discommode a Flanders lace chitterling.[43] His wit is like his habit, of the newest fashion; and was it treason to adulterate our language, as it is to counterfeit the coin, he would stand a notable chance to be guarded up Holbourn-Hill by the sheriff's officers; for he affects unintelligible terms of speech, and, like an apothecary, will reduce a whole sentence into a monosyllable; yet, if a man of honour will afford him a smile, he is not so concise in his compliments of French, Italian and broken Latin, to adorn his peacock's feathers with a little pedantry. If he hears a second-hand saying at the coffee-house, he immediately takes the minutes down in short-hand; for having but little brains in his head he has a natural tendency to forgetfulness, and nothing less than a new invented oath will make a lasting impression upon his mind, without the use of his common-place book. He goes to the play like a true critic, and pretends to distinguish what is genuine and what is sophisticated; and to prove himself one of a penetrating judgement he'll curse the actors, and damn the whole performance; nay the celebrated *Wilks* and *Booth* cannot escape his censure, though all the time his eyes are upon the ladies, and his thoughts lifted up that some of them *per* chance, may be smitten with his fine appearance. Thus the simple animal is composed of pride, ignorance, conceit, vain-glory and imagination, and Men of Sense withdraw from him as from a pestilential infection; and indeed nothing can give a prodigal fop more mortification than to take no notice of him, for he knows no other end of his being than to swagger in the streets, and resort to public places to be gazed at; for which reason he is the only person that rejoiceth at Adam's Fall, otherwise he must have gone naked; and his soul is too narrow to take a view of things beyond brutality: his greatest enemy is poverty; and death itself is not so formidable as a coat that is worn thread-bare: thus his misfortunes once attack him, the burden is insupportable, and the last extremity is to steal a rope to hang himself. Thus a supercilious life brings an ignominious death, and for want of reason to guide his passions, Sir Foppington falls into despair, and dies in suicide.

Lord Hervey

Hervey was for a time influential at court, and a friend of Lady Wortley Montagu who once said that there were men, women and Herveys. He also fought a duel with William Pulteney who accused him of being a delicate hermaphrodite, and of practising an unnatural vice. Text from Alexander Pope's *Epistle to Dr Arbuthnot* (1735). See Norton (1992: 146–58).

Let *Sporus* tremble – "What? that thing   *Sporus*, that mere white curd of ass's
    of silk,   milk?

Satire or sense alas! can *Sporus* feel?
Who breaks a butterfly upon a wheel?"
Yet let me flap this bug with gilded
    wings,
This painted child of dirt that stinks
    and stings;
Whose buzz the witty and the fair
    annoys,
Yet wit ne'er tastes, and beauty ne'er
    enjoys,
So well-bred spaniels civilly delight
In mumbling of the game they dare
    not bite.
Eternal smiles his emptiness betray,
As shallow streams run dimpling all
    the way.
Whether in florid impotence he
    speaks,
And, as the prompter breathes, the
    puppet squeaks;
Or at the ear of Eve,[44] familiar toad,
Half froth, half venom, spits himself
    abroad,

In puns, in politics, or tales, or lies,
Or spite, or smut, or rhymes, or
    blasphemies.
His wit all see-saw between *that* and
    this,
Now high, now low, now master up,
    now miss,
And he himself one vile antithesis.
Amphibious thing! that acting either
    part,
The trifling head, or the corrupted
    heart!
Fop at the toilet, flatt'rer at the board,
Now trips a lady, now struts a lord.
Eve's tempter thus the Rabbins have
    exprest,
A cherub's face, a reptile all the rest;
Beauty that shocks you, parts that none
    will trust,
Wit that can creep, and pride that licks
    the dust.

A View of the Town

The poem laments the transformation of London into the new Sodom; why do men choose each other rather than the charms of the fair sex? Text from *A View of the Town: In an Epistle to a Friend in the Country. A Satire* (1735).

O Pope, thou scourge to a licentious
    age,
Inspire these lines with thy severest
    rage;
Arm me with satire keen as *Oldham*[45]
    wrote
Against the curst *Divan*, with poignant
    thought;

To lash a crime which filthy lechers
    use,
Sworn foes to mother *Haywood*'s and
    the stews;
Inverting nature to a foul design,
They stop the propagation of their
    kind.
Forlorn *Saphira* with reclining head

Sighs for her absent lord in bridal bed;
He to *St James's-Park* with rapture flies,
And roams in search of some vile
    ingle[46] prize;
Courts the foul pathick in the fair one's
    place,
And with unnat'ral lust defiles his race.

    From whence cou'd such polluted
      wretches spring,
How learn to propagate so foul a sin!
The sons of *Sodom* were destroy'd by
    fire,
Gomorrah felt the Lord's destructive
    ire,
The great metropolis of *England*'s isle
Had like to've been the nation's funeral
    pile.
Bold race of men! whom nothing can
    affright,
Not e'en their consciences in dead of
    night.
Let *Jesuits* some subtler pains invent,
For hanging is too mild a punishment:
Let them ly groaning on the racking-
    wheel,
Or feel the tortures of the burning
    steel;
Whips, poisons, daggers, inquisitions,
    flames,

This crime the most exalted vengeance
    claims;
Or else be banish'd to some desart
    place,
And perish in each other's foul
    embrace.

    'Tis strange this sin should flourish
    in our isle,
Where *Cyprian Venus* and the *Graces*
    smile,
Where tender virgins in the bloom of
    youth
Are fam'd for virtue, innocence, and
    truth,
With all the charms that nature can
    provide
For the gay mistress, or the lovely
    bride:
Can yet this savage race obdurate
    prove,
And beauty have no pow'r their hearts
    to move
To warm transports of a female love!

    By such foul slaves our species is
    disgraced,
And may they all be damn'd for want
    of taste.

FINIS.

The State of Rome under Nero and Domitian: A Satire

The poem continues the themes developed in the previous extracts. Text from *The State of Rome under Nero and Domitian: A Satire* (1739).

Here *Sporus* live – and once more feel
  my Rage
Once and again I drag thee on the
  stage;
Male-Female thing, without one virtue
  made,
Fit only for the *Pathick's*[47] loathsome
  trade:
Feeble and weak in all that's good and
  right,

And only strong in impudence and
  spite.
What tho' thy blood thou strut'st a
  gaudy peer?
What tho' thou nestlest in the master's
  ear?
No ill man's happy – least of all are
  they
Whose study's to corrupt, revile,
  betray.

The Pretty Gentleman

Garrick had played the part of Mr Fribble in *Miss in her Teen; or, The Medley of Lovers* (1747). The 'pretty gentleman', like the 'fribble', named a range of characteristics of manner, behaviour and outlook, behind and in which sodomy lurked. See Senelick (1990: 58) and Staves (1982). Text from *The Pretty Gentleman: or, Softness of Manners Vindicated from the false Ridicule exhibited under the Character of William Fribble, Esq.* (1747).

I AM led into these reflections, by a late performance exhibited on our stage, wherein the author attempts to laugh out of countenance that *mollifying elegance* which manifests itself with such a bewitching grace, in the *refined* youths of this *cultivated age*. It is in defence of these injured gentlemen that I have taken up my pen; and how well qualified I am to execute such an undertaking, the reader will be convinced, if he has but patience to peruse carefully the following sheets.

Amidst all my researches into the history of this country, I do not find one PRETTY GENTLEMAN, till the glorious reign of King James I. The prince had an odd mixture of contrary qualities. In some respects he retained the rusticity of *Gothic* manners; in others, he was very refined.

Lord *Clarendon* assures us, 'That His *Most Sacred* MAJESTY was so highly delighted with a beauutiful person and fine clothes, that these were the chief recommendations to the great offices of state.' A convincing proof (begging the noble historian's pardon) of that monarch's superior talents for government.

In the Reign of *Charles* I this refinement sunk in reputation: for how indeed was it possible, that a genuine taste could be cultivated, when *Falkland* was beheld with general admiration, and *Waller*[48] read with general delight?

HARDER still was her Fate, under the rebukes of an austere republic, and a sour protector.[49] The very *Loyalists* themselves were treated with less rigour, and not a man of any elegance durst even now show his head.

BUT when monarchy was restored, *taste* emerged from her obscurity, and shone with some degree of lustre. For tho' the prince was somewhat inelegant in himself, yet that *downy ease*, which was cherished under his auspicious influence, was highly favourable to the cultivation of *soft manners*; notwithstanding the malicious efforts of *Milton, Denham, Dorset, Buckingham* and *Dryden*.

FROM this period, to the beginning of the present century, her progress was now and then checked by the blasts of envy; yet, upon the whole, she made some tolerable shots; when at last, a set of malevolent spirits arose, who (under the forms of *Tatlers, Spectators*, and *Guardians*[50]) with a cruel and bloody-minded zeal, entered into a combination to destroy this lovely plant, both root and branch. The better to effect their barbarous revolution, they set up an *idol* of their own fancy, ascribed to it all the attributes of the *graces*, and with the artifice of deceiving blandishments, allured the majority of the nation to fall down and worship the image they had set up.

HENCE it was that *elegance* became a neglected character, and the *pretty gentleman* an object of general contempt, and barbarous raillery.

BUT no sooner were these enemies removed, than the sons of delicacy made an attempt to rise again: and how successful; they have been, every place of polite report does fully witness; and notwithstanding all opposition, they are determined to push on their designs, and polish the British manners. Now the better to carry on this glorious scheme of reformation, these gentlemen have erected themselves into an amicable society, and from the principles, on which it is founded, have pertinently styled it,

The Fraternity of PRETTY GENTLEMEN

AS no associated body can possibly subsist, unless they are cemented by a union of hearts, the grand principle of this fellowship is mutual love, which, it must be confessed, they carry to the highest pitch ... Such an harmony of temper is preserved amongst them, such a sameness is there in all their words and actions, that the spirit of *one* seems to have passed in to the *other*; or rather, they *all* breathe the *same* soul.

THEY do not indeed consume their hours in such points of vain speculation, wherein the *pride* of *reason* and *learning* has room to operate. And indeed there is something in the drudgery of *masculine* knowledge, by no means adapted to youths of so *nice* a frame, that it cannot be said, they are ever invigorated with perfect health. The enfeebled tone of their organs and spirits does therefore naturally dispose them to the softer and more refined studies; furniture, equipage, dress, the tiring room, and the toy-shop. What a fund is here for study!

It is an established maxim in this school of manners, never to oppose the sentiments of the company. Every gentleman assents to everything that is said. Sometimes indeed, you may hear what appears, at first, like a difference of judgement: But have a little patience, and you will find, it is only the genteel interchange of sentiments ...

A PRETTY GENTLEMAN therefore scarce ever dissents. He will indeed sometimes say, 'Oh! pard'n me, mi Dear! I ke'n't possibly be of that apinion!' But then this is only a polite artifice, that he may flatter your judgement with a finer address, when he afterwards suffers himself to be convinc'd by your superior reasoning. To give him his due, he has not attachment to any one opinion in the world, but *that* of preserving the rules of good-breeding. In all other cases, he has an assent entirely at your service; and you cannot change sides oftener, than this most obsequious humble servant will follow you. A transgression of decorum is indeed so shocking to his Nature, that he cannot let it pass without correction; but then it is always inflicted with a gentle hand.

The gravity of dull knowledge is at last happily exploded: masculine sense and wit are rejected as obsolete and unfashionable talents; and better supplied by the more engaging charms of the contrary qualities. Nothing is now heard, but sweet chit-chat, and tender prittle-prattle, shreds of sentiments, and cuttings of sentences – all soft and charming, elegant and polite.

BY this short abstract of the prevailing turn in polite conversation, the reader sees, that the *Pretty Gentleman* must necessarily be the best company; because he will neither offend by the abominable coarsness of *manly* reason, nor the ungrateful poignancy of keen repartee: but tho' he is not such a fool, or so ill-bred as to be downright witty, he will now and then indulge himself in what he calls, *The little escapes of fancy*, which I will not injure so much as to rank them under the denomination of *Wit*. If the company happens to grow languid, *Fannius* has an admirable talent at reviving their spirits by some pretty familiar remark or other; which, obvious as it is, would never have entered into the head of an unrefined mortal. On such an occasion this little wag will pat a lady over the shoulder, and tell her with the most facetious leer.

'I vew, Me'me, yur'e immoderately entertaining.'

AND tho' this is all he says, yet there is something in the manner, and in the accent, and in the – *I don't know what*; that the company instantly revive, and begin again to exchange their words. Nor let any man imagine that this is a trifling talent, which can raise something out of – nothing, and restore a society to cheerfulness and pleasantry; for good manners require that conversation should be kept up at any rate.

BY what I have already advanced, the reader may probably perceive, that their language and diction has the most essential requisite of style, and that *the sound always echos to the sense*. But since this part the character has been a subject of our mimic's raillery, I shall produce such instances, as will incontestibly demonstrate the truth of my assertion.

AND what now have the sons of Momus to object against the style of a *Pretty Gentleman*? Here is every requisite in fine writing: here is brevity, softness, propriety, and ease. Happily freed from the shackles of *connecting* and *restraining* rules, the diction roves and wanders, now here, now there, and with a wond'rous facility glides so imperceptibly from one flower to another, that the most subtle penetrator would be at a loss to find, where *This* ends, and where *That* begins. Some negligences there are indeed; but they are such as must be allowed the truest ornaments of speech. Let any man examine the letters I have here faithfully transcribed, and tell me whether he does not admire the little carelessnesses which are beautifully interspersed in these pretty compositions. If there are faults, it must be owned that they are truly charming: one cannot but delight in the lovely errors ...

ANOTHER object of this mimic's raillery, is that sweet placability of temper, which obliges a refined gentleman to put up even repeated injuries and affronts, rather than avenge them by the usual method of demanding satisfaction.

I AM not apprehensive that this part of his character is less definable than the rest. I could produce some tolerable arguments against duelling, drawn from certain principles, which were once looked upon to be the rules of human conduct. I could easily prove, that the single combat is derived from *Gothic* manners, and is absolutely inconsistent with the character of a gentleman. But such reasonings as these are neither so well adapted to the times, nor so pertinent to the cause I have undertaken. Waving then this kind of defence, upon this single argument I lay my whole stress – 'The *Pretty Gentleman* will not fight – because – He is not *able*.'

AND can any man produce a better reason for not doing a thing, than to make it manifest – that he *cannot*?'

BEHOLD that tender frame! those trembling knees! Those feeble joints! Observe that fine complexion! Examine that smooth, that velvety Skin! View that *Pallor* which spreads itself over his countenance! Hark, with what a feminine softness his accents steal their way thro' his half-opened Lips! Feel that soft palm! those slender fingers, accustomed only to handle silks and ribbons, the easy-piercing needle, or soft-gliding shuttle; but unpractised in the rough exercises of warlike Weapons! Mark all these, and a thousand other gentle imbecillities, and then tell me, impartial reader, whether such a being is formed for battle? – You cannot think it: you will not say it. I will therefore venture to affirm, that he is so far from deserving contempt and ridicule, when he declines the combat, that he merits our esteem and applause. He therefore who is so base as to affront, or send a challenge to *such* a person, is an arrant coward. For would a man of honour draw his upon a *Lady?* And to say the truth, *The Pretty Gentleman* is certainly formed in a different mould from that of common men, and tempered with a purer flame. The whole system is of a finer turn, and superior accuracy of fabric, insomuch that it looks as if Nature had been in doubt, to which sex he should assign *Him*.

I HAVE already detained the reader so long, that I shall not trespass upon his patience by giving a detail of the numerous artifices, which are exhibited in the important hours that are employed in decorating their persons. Were you to behold *Narcissus*[51] at his toilet, how would you be charmed with the order and disposition! Did you view this lovely youth whilst he takes his exterior form into a most exact adjustment, you must stand amazed at all the pretty wonders of his art. What pains! What care! What study! What address! To arch that eyebrow! To soften that hand, and to curl those lovely locks! Whilst all the Graces attend as invisible handmaids, to finish the work of elegance ...

THUS have I presented to the reader's view an enumeration of the several qualities which constitute

A PRETTY GENTLEMAN

FROM whence it is easy to collect the true Notion of genuine elegance; which, without any apprehension of being disproved, I do not hesitate to define thus –

ELEGANCE is the absence or debilitation of *Masculine* strength and vigor; or rather, the happy metamorphosis; Or, the Gentleman turn'd lady; that is, female softness adopted into the breasts of a *Male*, discovering itself by outward signs and tokens in feminine expressions, accent, air, gesture and looks. Or, as the French more clearly define it, *A je ne sais quoi*.

AND now I appeal to the Judgement of the impartial, whether this be a character which deserves that contempt and ridicule some rude and undisciplined spirits have endeavoured to throw upon it? It is impossible that any *serious* person can entertain such a thought,

I CALL therefore upon the wisdom of the nation: I call upon the L–ds, K——ts, and B——s, now assembled in P———t, to interpose in this important cause, this truly *national* concern.

THE Question is, whether we shall become more than *Men*, that is, *Pretty Gentlemen*; or worse than brutes, *i.e.* masculine, robust creatures with unsoftened manners. The latter will infallibly be the case, if an effectual stop be not put to that licentious raillery, which would laugh out of countenance the generous endeavours of a race of virtuous youths, to polish our asperity, mollify us into gentle obsequiousness, and give us a true relish of all the dulcet elegancies of life? I will speak without reserve: should not the theatres be *absolutely demolished?* We have already in vain tried the lenient measures of restriction. Why then should we not now have recourse to the last Remedy, and cut down the trees, which after all our pruning and culture, still continues to produce *poisonous fruit?*

THE indulgent reader, I dare say, will approve the method I prescribe. But perhaps so many difficulties arise to his imagination, that he will conclude it impracticable.

Two Young Gentlemen

Fanny, a prostitute, is the privileged and disgusted voyeur of two men who practise sodomy. Text from *Memoirs of a Woman of Pleasure* (1748). See Kopelson (1992). Foxon (1963b) provides an account of the book's publication and censorship.

Whilst I was amusing myself with looking out of the window, a single horse-chaise stopped at the door, out of which lightly leaped two young gentlemen, for so they seemed, who came in as it were only to bait and refresh a little, for they gave their horse to be held in a readiness against they came out: and presently I heard the door of the next room to me open, where they were let in and called about them briskly, and as soon as they were served, I could just hear that they shut and fastened the door on the inside.

A spirit of curiosity far from sudden, since I did not know when I was without it, prompted me, without any particular suspicion, or other drift, or view, to see who they were, and examine their persons and behaviour. The partition of our rooms was one of those moveable ones that when taken down, served occasionally to lay them into one, for the convenience of a large company; and now my nicest search could not show me the shadow of a peep-hole, a circumstance which probably had no escaped the review of the parties on the other side, whom much it stood upon not to be deceived in it; but at length I observed a paper-patch of the same colour as the wainscot, which I took to conceal some flaw, but then it was so high, that I was obliged to stand on a chair to reach it, which I did as softly as possible, and with the point of a bodkin soon pierced it, and opened myself espial-room sufficient: and now applying my eye close, I commanded the room perfectly, and could see my two young sparks romping, and pulling one another about, entirely to my imagination, in frolic, and innocent play.

The eldest might be, on my nearest guess, towards nineteen, a tall comely young man, in a white fustian frock, with a green velvet cape, and a cut bob-wig.

The youngest could not be above seventeen, fair, ruddy, compleatly well made, and to say the truth, a sweet pretty stripling: he was, I fancy too, a country lad, by his dress, which was a green plush frock, and breeches of the same, white waistcoat and stockings, a jockey cap, with his yellowish hair long, and loose, in natural curls.

But after a look of circumspection which I saw the eldest cast every way round the room, probably in too much hurry and heat not to overlook the very small opening I was posted at, especially at the height it was, whilst my eye too close to it, kept the light from shining through, and betraying it; he said something to his companion that presently changed the face of things.

For now the eldest began to embrace, to press, to kiss the younger, to put his hands in his bosom, and give such manifest signs of an amorous intention, as made me conclude the other to be a girl in disguise, a mistake that nature kept me in countenance in, for she had certainly made one, when she gave him the male stamp.

In the rashness then of their age, and bent as they were to accomplish their project of preposterous pleasure, at the risk of the very worst consequences, where a discovery was nothing less than improbable, they now proceeded to such lengths as soon satisfied me, what they were.

For presently the eldest unbuttoned the other's breeches, and removing the linen barrier, brought out to view a white shaft, middle-sized, and scarce fledged, when after handling, and playing with it a little, with other dalliance, all received by the boy without other opposition, than certain wayward coynesses, ten times more alluring than repulsive, he got him to turn around with his face from him, to a chair that stood hard by, when knowing, I suppose, his office, the Ganymede now obsequiously leaned his head against the back of it, and projecting his body, made a fair mark, still covered with his shirt, as he thus stood in a side-view to meet me but fronting his companion, who presently unmasking his battery, produced an engine, that certainly deserved to be put to better use, and very fit to confirm me in my disbelief of the possibility of things being pushed to odious extremities, which I had built on the disproportion of parts; but this disbelief I was now cured of, as by my consent all young men should likewise be, that their innocence may not be betrayed into such snares, for want of knowing the extent of their danger, for nothing is more certain than, that ignorance of a vice, is by no means a guard against it.

Slipping then aside the young lad's shirt, and tucking it up under his cloaths behind, he showed to the open air, those globular, fleshy eminences that compose the mount pleasants of *Rome*, and which now, with all the narrow vale that intersects them, stood displayed, and exposed to his attack: nor could I, without a shudder, behold the dispositions he made for it. First then, moistening well with spittle his instrument, obviously to render it glib, he pointed, he introduced it, as I could plainly discern, not only from its direction, and my losing sight of it; but by the writhing, twisting, and soft murmured complaints of the young sufferer;

159

but, at length, the first streights of entrance being pretty well got through everything seemed to move, and go pretty currently on, as in a carpet-road, without much rub, or resistance: and now passing one hand round his minion's hips, he got hold of his red-topt ivory toy, that stood perfectly stiff, and showed, that if he was like his mother behind, he was like his father before; this he diverted himself with, whilst with the other, he wantoned with his hair, and leaning forward over his back, drew his face, from which the boy shook the loose curls that fell over it, in the posture he stood him in, and brought him towards his, so as to receive a long-breathed kiss, after which, renewing his driving, and thus continuing to harass his rear, the height of the fit came on with its usual symptoms, and dismissed the action.

When I came home again, and told Mrs *Cole* this adventure, she very sensibly observed to me, that there was no doubt of due vengeance one time or other, overtaking these miscreants, however they might escape for the present; and that, had I been the temporal instrument of it, I should have been, at least, put to a great deal more trouble and confusion than I imagine: that as to the thing itself, the less said of it was the better; but that though she might be suspected of partiality, from its being the common cause of woman-kind, out of whose *mouths* this practice tended to take something more precious than bread, yet she protested against any mixture of passion, with a declaration extorted from her by pure regard to truth, which was, '*that* whatever effect this infamous passion had in other ages, and other countries, it seemed a peculiar blessing on our air and climate, that there was a plague-spot visibly imprinted on all that are tainted with it, in this nation at least; for that among numbers of that stamp who she had known, or at least were universally under the scandalous suspicion of it, she could not name an exception hardly of one of them, whose character was not in all other respects the most worthless and despicable that could be, stript of all the unmanly virtues of their own sex, and filled up with only the very worst vices and follies of ours: that, in fine, they were scarce less execrable than ridiculous in their monstrous inconsistency, of loathing and contemning women, and all at the same time, apeing their manners, airs, lisp, skuttle, and, in general, all their little modes of affectation, which become them at least better, than they do these unsexed male-misses.'

The Destruction of Sodom Improved

Luxury and entertainment are shown to corrupt the natural spirit of the nation. Text from *The Destruction of SODOM improved, as a warning to GREAT BRITAIN. A Sermon Preached on the Fast-Day, Friday, February 6, 1756, at Hanover Street, Long Acre. By the Rev. Dr Allen, morning preacher there. Published at the request of the congregation* (1756).

God has happily thrown his own wall of waters round about everywhere for our defence; and, what is not the produce of our soil and climate, commerce, the child of liberty, and which makes the whole world our own, readily imports and brings in. And O now that I could stop here, and be able to trace the parallel no further! but who, that reads the account of Sodom's sins, the PRIDE, FULLNESS OF BREAD and ABUNDANCE OF IDLENESS which was in Sodom and her daughters, HER HAUGHTINESS, and COMMITTING ABOMINATIONS – has not his thoughts directly carried into the vices of our modern times? Who can help thinking – of MIDNIGHT MASQUERADES; secret assignations for GAMING; ROUTS, RIOTS, and other diversions of strange names, names contrived as one would think, to insult all decency; names too of follies in which the DAUGHTERS OF BRITAIN are observed even to take the lead? Who can help thinking – of our luxury in dress and high expensive living – of our lewdness, which is so open, so avowed by many, and even boasted of as a *comparative virtue*; lastly, of the *unnatural* vices, which are more practised than sober people can well conceive of; vices, till lately, strangers to our colder climate, and which are the abomination of god and man: are decorum and order necessary to the well being of society? Do vices of the kind I have mentioned, waste the strength, impair the spirit, and root out the vitals of any nation? They certainly do: if therefore, these are the iniquities of England and of London, it is the breaking its own constitution, and, without fire from heaven or earthquakes from under the ground, it must die of itself: above all if there's a righteous God in Heaven, the cry of such sins must come up before him, and for *these things He will visit*; and we must be beyond conception stupid, if with what has fallen out so lately abroad, and in the uncertain tottering state of every thing among us, we do not consider ourselves under a divine visitation for our sins.

Love in the Suds

Isaac Bickerstaffe had fled to France following a sexual encounter with a soldier which was publicized in the *The Daily Advertiser* and *St James Chronicle* in 1772. Later, William Kenrick accused Bickerstaffe (author of the comic opera *Love in a Village*) and David Garrick of being lovers. Nyky was a nick-name for Isaac, and also designated a fool. Senelick notes that Garrick 'so fully shared the common notion that sodomites and effeminates were identical that his astonishment was considerable when he learned that one of his closest collaborators was the former' (1990: 58). See also Norton (1992: 171–4). Text from *Love in the Suds. A Town Eclogue. Being the Lamentation of Roscius for the Loss of his Nyky* (1772). See also Charles Chuchill's *Rosciad* (1763) and Garrick's *The Fribbleriad* (1761).

The compliments passed between these celebrated geniuses indeed were mutual; Mr A. commending Roscius[52] for his fine acting, and Roscius in return Mr A. for his fine writing. The panegyric on both sides was equally modest and just; and yet some snarling epigrammatist could not forbear throwing out the following ill-natured jeu d'esprit on the occasion.

On the Compliments Lately Passed between Mess. G. and A.

When mincing masters, met with
　misses,
Pay mutual compliments for kisses;
Miss Polly sings no doubt divinely,
And master Jacky spouts as finely.

But how I hate such odious greeting,
When two old stagers have a meeting
Foh! out upon the filthy pother!
What! men beslobber one another!

A Letter to David Garrick, Esq.

We have indeed no knight errants but in politics ... It is no wonder, therefore, if the monsters and pests of society have so greatly of late gained ground upon us: nor will it be more to be wondered at, if, their enormities being winked at as they have been, they should still gain greater ground, to the utter destruction of our national character, and the diffusion of an universal degeneracy of manners. Nothing can more contribute to this, than our mistaken lenity, in treating suspicious character with personal respect

Till their broad shame come staring in the face

and they expose themselves to the objects of public detestation. What would become of the chastity, and what would we think of the modesty, of the fair sex, if coquetry were to be countenanced, and female levity encouraged, till they ripened into prostitution? What would become even of the morals of men, if vices of every kind were not nipped in the bud, and immorality discountenanced in the first and earliest stages of guilt? Are we to wink at theft till it grow bold enough for robbery? to put up with violence till it proceed to murder? It is thus indeed that the mercenaries of justice eventually co-operate to promote the perpetuation of capital crimes; a petty criminal is not worth their pursuit . . .

It is observed, as a remarkable instance of the modesty of our English laws, that the crime against nature is denominated *nameless*, or not fit to be named among Christians: an argument this in favour of the virtue of our ancestors; in times when so unnatural a fact was hardly ever heard of, it was natural to forbear giving so abhorred an idea a name. The language of the divine law, however, is less modishly delicate; nor can I think the squeamishness of our municipal style, in times so grossly depraved as the present, of any utility, either political or moral. It is indeed attended with a palpable absurdity, while our courts of justice treat so gross a depravity with evident lenity, on the completion of the horrid act, it is true, the laws give the judges no discretionary power; but surely there is the same criminality, as far as concerns the intention of the assailant, which in this case chiefly constitutes the crime, in a palpable attempt as in the actual perpetration! And yet such attempts, though *in actu proximo*, are usually punished by a short imprisonment and momentary penance; as if the law had thought it sufficient to expose, as a scandal to society, the wretch, who must have already digested the shame of being a disgrace to human nature.

Again, with respect to the public; shocking as the reflection on such subjects must be to true sensibility, the affectation of burying the shame and guilt in forgetfulness together, is certainly a piece of false delicacy; it is in fact rescuing the culprit from the infamy, and is an alleviation of a punishment, which will almost bear every possible aggravation. It is besides inconsistent with our notions of justiciary punishment in every case. That of common felony ends with death; to that of one attended with cruelty or murder, is added the gibbetting of the criminal, in order that the remembrance of his punishment may prevent the repetition of his crime. In the case in question, confessedly the most odious of all crimes, both that and its punishment are carefully hid under the veil of secrecy; as if justice itself were ashamed of avenging the outrages which the monsters of society commit against nature.

Now, Sir, it will hardly be denied, that the fair countenance and familiarity, which long subsisted between Roscius and Nyky (setting the odious idea of criminality out of the question) was become at length a public nuisance. The parasitical servility, to say no worse of it, with which the latter clung round the heels, and was ever at the beck, of the former, is well known to those, who, disgusted at such ungentlemanlike, such unmanly behaviour, absented themselves on this account from the theatrical and domestic levees of the manager. At the same time, the affected bursts of adulation and intemperate applause, with which the admiring Nyky used to alarm and disturb the audience, when his patron performed, are sufficiently notorious.

WHITHER away, now, GEORGE, into the city
And to the village, must thou bear my ditty.
Seek NYKY out, while I in verse complain,
And court the Muse to call him back again.
  Boeotian nymphs, my favourite verse inspire;
As erst ye Nyky taught to strike the lyre.
For he like Phoebus' self can touch the string,
And opera-songs compose – like any thing!
What shall I do, now Nyky's fled away?
For who like him can either sing or say?
For me, alas! who well compos'd the song
When lovely Peggy liv'd, and I was young;
By age impair'd, my piping days are done,
My memory fails, and ev'n my voice is gone.
My feeble notes I yet must strive to raise;
Boeotian Muses! aid my feeble lays:
A little louder, and yet louder still,
Aid me to raise my failing voice at will;

Aid me as loud as Hercules did bawl,
For Hylas[53] lost, lost Nyky back did call;
While London town, and all its suburbs round
In echoes, Nyky, Nyky, back resound.
Whom fliest thou, frantic youth, and whence thy fear?
Blest had there never been a grenadier![54]
Unhappy Nyky, by what frenzy seiz'd,
Couldst thou with such a monstrous thing be pleas'd?
What, tho' thyself a loving horse-marine,
A common foot-soldier's a thing obscene.
Not fabled nymphs, be spleen turn'd into cows,
Bellow'd to nasty bulls their amorous vows;
Tho' turn'd their loving horns upon each other,
Butting in play, as brother might with brother.
Unhappy Nyky, whither dost thou stray,
Lost to thy friends, o'er hills and far away? . . .
Mean-time do thou beware, while I bemoan,
How far thou trustest seas or lands unknown.

To Tyber's stream, or to the banks of Po,
Safe in thy love, safe in thy virtue, go;
Yet even there with caution be thou
    kind,
And look out sharp and frequently
    behind.
But ah, beware, nor trust, tho' native
    Mud,
The banks of Liffy, or of Shannon's
    flood;
Or there, if driv'n by fate, be hush'd thy
    strain?
Nor of thy wayward lot, nor mine
    complain.
Lest female Bacchanals, when flush'd
    with wine,
Serve thee, like Orpheus, for thy song
    divine;
Nay back return, lest my too plaintive
    verse
Entail on me the same Orphean curse;
Lest Venus' train of Drury and the
    Strand
Attack my house by water and by land;
Hot with their midnight orgies, madly
    tear
My little limbs, and throw them here
    and there;
Casting, enrag'd at my provoking
    theme,
Th'inditing brain into the
    neighbouring stream:
When, as my skull shall float the tide
    along,
Thy much-lov'd name, the burthen of
    my song,
Shall still be flutter'd, later than my
    breath;
Nyky— Nyk— Ny— till stopt my
    tongue in death:

Through London-bridge shall Wapping
    Nyky roar,
And Nyk be even heard to Hampton's
    shore.
On Hebrus' banks so tuneful Orpheus
    died;
His limbs the fields receiv'd, his head
    the tide . . .
Oh, horror, horror! Nyky back return;
Nor more for grenadiers imprudent
    burn.
    And yet, ah why should Nyky thus
    be blam'd?
Of manly love ah! why are men
    asham'd?
A new red coat, fierce cock and killing
    air
Will captivate the most obdurate fair;
What wonder then if Nyky's tender
    heart
At such a fight should feel a lover's
    smart:
No wonder love, that in itself is blind,
Should no distinction in the difference
    find;
No wonder love should Nyky thus
    enthrall;
Almighty love, at times, subdues us all;
While, vulgar prejudices soar'd above;
Nyk gave up all the world – well lost for
    love.
Yet slight the cause of Nyky's late
    mishap;
Nyk but mistook the colour of the cap:
A common error, frequent in the park,
Where love is apt to stumble in the
    dark.
Why rais'd the haughty female head so
    high,
With the tall caps of grenadiers to vie?

Why does it like tremendous figure
     make,
To subject purblind lovers to mistake?
Or rather why, in these enlighten'd
     times,
Should rigid Nature call such errors
     crimes?
"Thou Nature art my goddess," saith
     the play;
But even Shakespeare's text hath had
     its day.
More gentle custom no such rigour
     knows;
And custom into second nature grows.
Let vulgar passions move the vulgar
     mind,
Superior souls feel motives more
     refin'd:
Among the low-bred English slow
     advance
Th'Italian *gusto* and *bon ton* of France.
Strange to the classic lore of Greece
     and Rome,
And rudely nurs'd in ignorance at
     home,
The tasteless herd e'en construe into
     sin,
That poets should in metaphor lie in,
While I, their best man-midwife, must
     be sham'd
Whene'er the fashionable lover's
     nam'd.
But candour's veil love's foibles still
     should cover
And Nyk be stil'd a fashionable lover.
To polish'd travellers is only known
That taste which makes the ancient
     arts our own;
Which shares with Rome in every gem
     antique;

Which blends the modern with the
     ancient Greek;
Improves on both, and greatly soars
     above,
In pure philanthropy, Platonic love;
That love which burns with
     undistinguish'd rage,
And spares in fondness neither sex nor
     age?
Ah! therefore why in these
     enlighten'd times
Should rigid Nature call such errors
     crimes?
Must not the taste of Attic wits be nice?
Can ancient virtue be a modern vice?
The Mantuan bard, or else his scholiast
     lies,
Virgil the chaste, nay Socrates the wise,
The gay Petronius, sophists, wits and
     bards,
Of old, bestow'd on youth their soft
     regards;
In modish dalliance pass'd their
     harmless time
Ev'n modish now in soft Italia's clime.
Could lightenings ever issue from
     above
To blast poor men for such a crime as
     love;
When the lewd daughters of
     incestuous Lot
Were both with child by their own
     father got?
Poor goody Lot indeed might be in
     fault,
And justly turn'd to monumental salt:
The matrimonial emblem of a wife:
Needs must be salt a dish to keep for
     life!
A fable Sodom's fate: in Heav'n above

All is made up of harmony and love;
That such its vengeance I believe not, I;
Historians err and Hebrew Jews will lie.
    Sing then, my Muse, a more
    engaging strain
To lure my Nyky back to Drury-lane.
Tell him the fancied danger all is o'er;
Home he may come and love as
    heretofore.
In vain the vulgar shall for vengeance
    call,
Or move the justices at Hickes's-hall;
In vain grand juries shall be urg'd by
    law
In his indictment not to leave a flaw.
Ev'n at the bar should Nyky stand
    arraign'd,
No verdict 'gainst him should be there
    obtain'd;
Nay, by the laws and customs of the
    land,
Tho' trembling Nyky should convicted
    stand,
The candid jury shall be mov'd t'acquit
A gentleman, an author, and a wit:
For liberal minds with candour ever
    see
The milder failings of humanity! ...
    Nor need my Nyky fear a London
    jury
Will e'er be influenc'd with a female
    fury.
Can they who let a prov'd assassin
    'scape
Hang upon poor Nyky for a friendly
    rape?
If in the dark to stab, be thought no
    crime,
What may'nt be hop'd from jurymen
    in time?

Soon Southern modes, no doubt,
    they'll reconcile
With the plain manners of our
    Northern isle;
And e'en new-married citizens be
    brought
To reckon S——y a venial fault ...
    Sing then, O Muse, a more pathetic
    strain,
To lure my gentle Nyky back again.
For, sure as Thames resembles Tyber's
    tide,
Shall macaronis[55] soon possess
    Cheapside;
As petty-jury-men in judgement sit,
And ev'ry Corydon, with Nyk, acquit ...

Curse on that Kenrick, with his caustic
    pen,
Who scorns the hate, and hates the
    love of men;
Who with such ease envenom'd satire
    writes,
Deeper his ink than acqua fortis bites.
Stand his perpetual-motion ever still;
Or, if it move, oh, let it move up hill.
The curse of Sisiphus, oh, let him feel;
The curse of Fortune's still recurring
    wheel;
That upward roll'd with anxious toil
    and pain,
The summit almost gain'd, rolls back
    again.
Ne'er shall his Falstaff come again to
    life;
Ne'er shall be play'd again his Widow'd
    Wife;
Ne'er will I court again his stubborn
    Muse,
But for a pageant would his play refuse.

While puff and pantomime will gull
the town,
'Tis good to keep o'erweening merit
down ...
    Bring Nyky back, O Muse! by verse
divine,
The Trojan-Greeks were once
transformed to swine.
By verse divine B—-tti scap'd the rope:
Now love is known, what may not
lovers hope!
Ev'n as with *Griffins* stallions late have
join'd
With blood-hounds goats may litter, as
in kind;
Nay wanton kids devouring wolves
may greet,
And wolves with loving lionesses meet.
By different means is different love
made known.
And each fond lover will prefer his own.

Strange lot of love! two friends, my
soul's delight,
Men call that M——-r, this a Catamite!
Yet bring him back; for who chaste
roundelay
Shall sing, now B—-st–ff is driv'n away?
Who now correct, for modest Drury-
lane,
Loose Wycherly's or Congreve's looser
vein?[56]
With nice decorum shunning naughty
jokes,
Exhibit none but decent, dainty folks?
Ah me! how wanton wit will shame the
stage,
And shock this delicate, this virtuous
age!
How will *Plain-dealers* triumph, to my
sorrow!
And Paphos rise o'er Sodom and
Gomorrah!

The Latin Epitaph on Bob Jones

On 11 August 1772, Robert Jones was pardoned, having been found guilty of sodomy with 13-year-old Francis Hay. Text from *The Latin Epitaph on Bob Jones versified into English* (1773).

Underneath this stone there lies
A face turn'd downwards to the skies;
A captain who employ'd his parts
Upon male b—-s, not female hearts:
Who tunrn'd his arms not against his
foes,
But against friends, whence Sodom
rose,
And vile Gomorrah horrid fell,

To court th'unnatural flames of hell.
Because he err'd from nature's ways,
Nature despis'd him all his days,
Till being to Jack Ketch[57] consigned,
For crime of crimes, and dirty mind,
He was repriev'd from gallows death,
At Tyburn had resign'd his breath;
But George, in vengeance, let him live,
Like Cain, till conscience should
forgive.

The Times

Charles Churchill used parts of his long satirical poem *The Times* to express his sense that 'Go where we will, at ev'ry time and place, SODOM confronts, and stares us in the face' (1763). Sodomy has been imported from overseas with the result that men now prefer a Ganymede to a woman.

With our island vices not content,
We rob our neighbours on the
    Continent;
Dance Europe round, and visit every
    court,
To ape their follies and their crimes
    import.
To diff'rent lands for diff'rent sins we
    roam,
And, richly freighted, bring our cargo
    home,
Nobly industrious to make vice appear
In her full state, and perfect only
    here ...

Nor stop we here – the soft luxurious
    EAST,
Where man, his soul degraded, from
    the beast
In nothing diff'rent but in shape we
    view,
They walk on four legs, and he walks
    on two,
Attracts our eye; and flowing from that
    source,
Sins of the blackest character, sins
    worse
Than all her plagues, which truly to
    unfold,
Would make the best blood in my
    veins run cold,
And strike all manhood dead, which
    but to name,

Would call up in my cheeks the marks
    of shame,
Sins, if such sins can be, which shut
    out grace;
Which for the guilty leave no hope, no
    place
E'en in God's mercy; sins 'gainst
    Nature's plan
Possess the land at large; and man for
    man
Burns in those fires, which Hell alone
    could raise
To make him more than damn'd;
    which, in the days
Of punishment, when guilt becomes
    her prey,
With all her tortures she can scarce
    repay ...

So public in their crimes, so daring
    grown,
They almost take a pride to have them
    known,
And each unnat'ral villain scarce
    endures
To make a secret of his vile amours.
Go where we will, at ev'ry time and
    place,
SODOM confronts, and stares us in
    the face;
They ply in public at our very doors
And take the bread from much more
    honest whores.

Those who are mean high paramours
  secure,
And the rich guilty screen the guilty
  poor;
The sin too proud to feel from reason
  awe,
And those, who practise it, too great for
  Law.

Woman, the pride and happiness of
  Man,
Without whose soft endearments
  Nature's plan
Had been a blank, and life not worth a
  thought;
Woman, by all the loves and Graces
  taught,
With softest arts, and sure, tho' hidden
  skill
To humanize, and mould us to her
  will;
Woman, with more than common
  grace form'd here,
With the persuasive language of a tear
To melt the rugged temper of our Isle,
Or win us to her purpose with a smile;
Woman, by fate the quickest spur
  decreed,
The fairest, best reward of ev'ry deed
Which bears the stamp of honour, at
  whose name
Our ancient Heroes caught a quicker
  flame,
And dar'd beyond belief, whilst o'er the
  plain,
Spurning the carcases of Princes slain,
Confusion proudly strode, whilst
  Horror blew
The fatal trump, and Death stalked full
  in view;

Woman is out of date, a thing thrown by
As having lost its use; no more the eye
With female beauty caught, in wild
  amaze,
Gazes entranc'd, and could forever
  gaze;
No more the heart, that seat where
  Love resides,
Each breath drawn quick and short, in
  fuller tides
Life posting through the veins, each
  pulse on fire,
And the whole body tingling with
  desire,
Pants from those charms, which Virtue
  might engage
To break his vow, and thaw the frost of
  age,
Bidding each trembling nerve, each
  muscle strain,
And giving pleasure which is almost
  pain.
Women are kept for nothing but to
  breed;
For pleasure we must have a
  GANYMEDE,
A fine, fresh HYLAS, a delicious boy,
To serve our purposes of beastly joy.

Is a son born into a world of woe?
In never-ceasing streams let sorrow
  flow,
Be from that hour the house with
  sables hung,
Let lamentations dwell upon thy
  tongue,
E'en from that moment that he first
  began
To wail and whine, let him not see a
  man.

Lock, lock him up, far from the public
  eye;
Give him no opportunity to buy,
Or to be bought; B—, though rich, was
  sold,
And gave his body up to shame for
  gold.
  Let it be bruited all about the Town,
That he is coarse, indelicate, and
  brown,
An antidote to lust; his face deep
  scar'ed
With the small pox, his body maim'd
  and marr'd;
Eat up with the king's-evil,[58] and his
  blood,
Tainted throughout, a thick and putrid
  flood,
Where dwells corruption, making him
  all o'er,
From head to foot, a rank and runing
  sore.
Should'st thou report him, as by
  Nature made,
He is undone, and by that praise
  betrayed:
Give him out fair, lechers, in number
  more,
More brutal, and more fierce, than
  thronged the door
Of Lot in SODOM, shall to thine
  repair,
And force a passage, tho' a God is
  there.
  Let him not have one servant that is
  male;
Where Lords are baffled, servants oft
  prevail.
  Give him no tutor – throw him to a
  punk,

Rather than trust his morals to a monk;
Monks we all know – we, who have
  liv'd at home,
From fair report, and travellers, who
  roam,
More feelingly – nor trust him to the
  gown,
'Tis oft a covering in this vile town
For base designs: ourselves have liv'd
  to see
More than one parson in the pillory.
Should he have brothers (image to thy
  view
A scene, which, though not public
  made, is true)
Let not one brother be to t'other
  known,
Nor let his father sit with him alone ...

But if, too eager in my bold career,
Haply I wound the nice, and chaster
  ear;
If, all unguarded, all too rude, I speak,
And call up blushes in the maiden's
  cheek,
Forgive, ye fair – my real motives view,
And to forgiveness add your praises
  too.
For you I write – nor wish a better
  plan,
The cause of woman is most worthy
  man;
For you I still will write, nor hold my
  hand
Whilst there's one slave of SODOM in
  the land.
  Let them fly far, and skulk from
  place to place,
Not daring to meet manhood face to
  face,

171

Their steps I'll track, nor yield them
 one retreat
Where they may hide their heads, or
 rest their feet,
Till God, in wrath, shall let his
 vengeance fall,
And make a great example of them all,
Bidding in one grand pile this town
 expire,

Her tow'rs in dust, her Thames a lake
 of fire;
Or they (most worth our wish)
 convinc'd tho' late,
Of their past crimes and dangerous
 estate,
Pardon of women with repentance
 buy,
And learn to honour them as much as I.

The Fruit Shop

A bizarre publication touching on a number of topics, mainly sexual. The author quoted extensively and approvingly from Churchill's *The Times*. He also deals with eunuchs and the evils of celibacy. Text from *The Fruit-Shop, A Tale; or, a Companion to St James's Street* (1766).

The unnaturalists, or the deserters of the fruit shop

When things were even arrived at the pitch where we left them, at the close of the last chapter, the iniquity of the human race was not as yet completed; for, while a fair intercourse is kept up between the *Fruit-shop* and its natural customers, this world is an object of the Deity's mercy: but of his wrath when, through a misconceived notion of self-sufficiency, either attempts to be actuated to blissful rapture without the friendly concurrence of the other. To all such selfish and uncommunicative transgressors, we cannot more energetically convey our disapprobation, than in the words of a learned, ingenious, and modest *Scot*, which the most exasperated among the *South-Britons* must allow to be a phenomenon both rare and valuable!

– Banish from thy shades
Th'ungenerous, selfish, solitary joy:
Hold, parricide, thy hand – For thee
alone
Did nature form thee? For thy narrow
self

Grant thee the means of pleasure? –
Impious forbear –
To shed thy blossoms thro' the desart
air,
And sow thy perish'd off-spring in the
winds.

A still greater degree of criminality (than even what misguided and erroneous groping after a chymerical but destructive *self-sufficiency* implieth) is chargeable to *unnaturalism*; which horrid form of sin stigmatiseth with public infamy, and calls aloud for heavenly vengeance on its followers ... Now let us see how, against such execrable subjects, our Herculean satyrist, as his friends are pleased to call him, wields his formidable mass, or club in vulgar phrase.[59]

The violent resentment of some against *The Times*, and palliative arguments made use of by others, as well as our own private judgement upon the whole, we reserve for another place; wishing to all culprits of that diabolical fraternity here fulminated against, the title of our ensuing chapter.

Nature's revenge on disobedient children

In the preceding chapter we have seen instances of the apostate vagaries pursued by those who go wilfully astray from the sacred impulse of nature. Here it follows in order, to show a striking example of her punishing such from time to time. None was ever made a more signal example of by her than St *Anthony*; as appeareth by all those pictures we see of him, persecuted by the devil, in such a variety of forms. But the Devil had nothing at all to do in the affair. His nocturnal sufferings arose from the suppressed sensations of manhood during the day; they then usurped with the assistance of nature, and by her direction, an absolute empire over his body while asleep.

Certain animal spirits being let loose, and twitching the nerves this way and that, in various directions, made him to undergo such a successive crowd of imaginary tortures. A female bed fellow properly applied to, would soon have put an end to his persecution in the flesh.

Hysteric fits, &c. are the frequent punishment of those females who delay too long to obey nature's dictates. In popish convents, as well as nunneries abroad, how many are the diseases attendant on celibacy; all which there is but one way of curing: and that nature points out to every member of society, however savage; to which the more civilized give a sanction by laws.

Eunuchism

That parents can be so far divested of all feeling, and remonstrances of nature, as to consent; or that surgeons can be found barbarous enough to perform the execrable operation of unmanning an innocent object that had never given any offence, is shocking to thought. Wherever this horrid deed, inspired by the prince of darkness, is executing, young girls of the neighbourhood should assemble and urge somewhat, alike in sense to these words of our elegant and classic *Pope*, which he makes *Eloisa* write on the occasion of *Abelard*'s maltreatment by her relations.

> Barbarians hold, restrain your butch'ring rage –
> Cut from its fount my ravish'd joy I see,
> And love's warm tide for ever stopped in thee.

Why the antivenereal critic W-rb-n[60] hath omitted these lines in his masked edition of that poet appears not to us; but it is perhaps from kindred motives of insufficiency, and no doubt for reasons best known to himself.

Should any advocate for *Eunuchism*, oppose to us that their state is not so deplorable as we imagine, for that they are capable of love, and become beloved objects of the fair. They are it seems often admitted into their intimacy, beds, and embraces of ladies who rank in the highest life. Nay some have been even separated from their husbands, in consequence of such insulting familiarities; and others committed outrageous extravagancies on their account . . .

Eunuchs can but affect a passion, because deprived of that procreant *stimulus* by which we are goaded on to love. Who would not envy *Manzoli* the ravishing powers of his voice, but for the irreperable damage necessary to so enrapturing an acquisition.

4 SAPPHIC TEXTS

Introduction

Two pamphlets from the early seventeenth century begin this section. Both are concerned with the issue of cross-dressing in men and women. In a comprehensive study of the cultural context of the pamphlets, Sandra Clark noted, 'For the last few years of King James's reign ... satire against women's clothing temporarily developed a new aspect: women were fiercely accused of dressing and behaving like men' (1985: 157). She argues that 'the destruction of sexual barriers readily suggested itself as further evidence of imminent social disintegration' (159). The satires were not simply rooted in the traditions of misogynistic writing; rather, they suggest a new twist in relations between the sexes. In one sense, the last echo of the controversy was in William Austin's *Haec Homo* ... (1637) which operated 'not to dispraise the exchange of sexual characteristics, but to assert the essential similarity of men and women' (183). The debate began to contest the notion that we should simply follow custom, to examine the hegemony of the natural (which turns out to be always already culturally constructed) disputing or resisting its foundations.

Sapphic issues are often displaced, becoming feminist challenges to patriarchal models. In the case of *Roxana* (1724), J.Z. Zhang concludes that Roxana becomes 'a paradoxical figure who rejects the distinctive either/or thinking in gender studies and is both subjected to the laws of matrimony and at the same time capable of destroying male power that is mandated by those same laws' (1993: 273). Yet he does not discern latently disruptive lesbian readings of the text. Similarly, romantic friendships often operated in a seemingly autonomous way, but the lesbian component in them has not always been susceptible to analysis from the surviving documents. Donoghue, in reclaiming a number of these has noted that 'many of the romantic friends ... might have shared sex, "genital" and otherwise. It is crucial to distinguish between the dominant ideology's explanation of romantic friendship – that it was sexless, morally elevating, and no threat to female power – and the reality of such bonds between women' (1993: 109). She has also argued that 'there was a strand of misogamist (marriage-hating) women's writing throughout this period that linked the love of friends to a revulsion for marriage' (121). The short extract from *A Serious Proposal to the Ladies* (1696) begins to explore the issue. For Donoghue, Astell was the first to theorize 'the prototype of the spinster as a respectable figure' (122).

The lesbian direction of female husbands has also been underplayed in influential studies by Wheelwright (1989) and Dugaw (1989). Emma Donoghue helps to reclaim this component: in her view, 'researchers can be made uneasy by female husbands' profound deceptions (sometimes, it seems, even of their wives), by their misogyny and exploitation of male privilege, and by those worrying phallic dildos' (59). Yet many of these issues were openly discussed. *Monsieur Thing's Origin*, for instance, explored the dildo's passage from France to England and its many adventures. The main direction of the text was misogynistic, but it nonetheless tests out (at length!) the competition between the natural and the artificial; perhaps women don't need men, after all! In the case of Catherine Vizzani the phallus is hidden away, but its discovery provides a curious twist to the tale:

> The leathern machine, which was hid under the pillow, fell into the hands of the surgeon's mates in the hospital, who immediately were for ripping it up, concluding that it contained money, or something else of value, but they found it stuffed only with old rags ...

The passage does more than mock Catherine; rather, it exposes the material foundations on which the phallus is grounded. Perhaps patriarchy itself is threatened if its content is nothing more than the rags discovered within it. Vizzani elopes with not one but two women and despite boasting of venereal infections, is discovered (in some detail) to be a virgin at her death. It is difficult to know finally how to place her. Garber (1992: 44–5) noted that 'psychologists and psychiatrists still deny the existence of female-to-male transvestites, alleging that any woman who consistently cross-dresses as a man is actually a transsexual – that is, a woman who wishes that she were a man ... Women who cross-dress must thus fall into two ... categories: the occasional, recreational cross-dresser who does not wish or try to pass, and the transsexual.' The tale concludes with a warning about unnatural behaviour and provides a guide to proper conduct in the upbringing of one's offspring.

Sex between women is discussed in the dialogue between Cleonarium and Leaena from *Lucian's Works*, translated by Ferrand Spence (1684), and in the conversation between Angelica and Agnes from Jean Barrin's *Venus in the Cloister; or, the Nun in her Smock* (1725 originally published 1683). Characteristically these narratives operate in such a way as to illustrate an autonomy that merely precedes proper knowledge of men; women can arouse each other, but this is a pale shadow of the real thing. Moreover, it is not clear how far such scenes were designed merely to titillate male heterosexuals. Yet we should not rule out the possibility that female readers experimented themselves in the light of such episodes, or that they found a measure of legitimation in these textual/sexual encounters. In *The Progress of Nature* a boarding school provides the setting for a young woman learning to explore her body, and her sexuality. As I have noted, the direction of many of these texts is towards heterosexuality, but the effect of prior phases is never fully erased.

Moreover, it is indisputable that women did live together, sometimes for long periods of time in contented companionship, sometimes undergoing sacrifice and hardship. In the case of *The Unaccountable Wife* (1723) the heterosexual relationship is disrupted by a female servant who changes places with the wife while the latter does all the domestic chores. The ambiguous sexual relationship that develops radically constructs a social 'world turned upside down'. In the report of *A discovery of a very extraordinary nature* (1766) it is recorded that two women lived together for thirty-six years. Was this a romantic friendship? They certainly seemed to have coped admirably in their 'performance' of a heterosexual relationship. The suggestion that 'both had been crossed in love' need not rule out that they found their own sexual pleasures together. As Hitchcock noted in the concluding remark of his survey of sex in the eighteenth century, 'The rise of romantic friendships from mid-century can likewise be seen as part of the process of redefining all forms of sex. As heterosexuality became more and more dominated by the phallus, new and different definitions and categories were needed to accommodate lesbian love' (1996: 85).

The Man-Woman

The text begins by exploring the grammatical form of its own ambiguous mis-naming. Text from *Hic Mulier: or, The Man-Woman: Being a medicine to cure the coltish disease of the Staggers in the Masculine-Feminines of our times. Exprest in a brief declamation. Non omnes possumus omnes. Mistris, will you be trim'd or truss'd?* (1620). See Clark (1985: 158–83); Dekker and de Pol (1989); Garber (1992); Lucas (1988); Shapiro (1987); Traub (1992).

Since the days of Adam women were never so masculine; masculine in their genders and whole generations, from the Mother, to the youngest daughter; masculine in number, from one to multitudes; masculine in Case, even from the head to the foot; masculine in mood, from bold speech, to impudent action; and masculine in tense: for (without redress) they were, are, and will be still most masculine, most mankind, and most monstrous. Are all women then turned masculine? No, God forbid, there are a world full of holy thoughts, modest carriage, and severe chastity; to these let me fall on my knees, and say; You, O you women; you good women; you that are in the fulness of perfection, you that are the crowns of nature's work, the complements of men's excellencies, and the seminaries of propagation; you that maintain the world, support mankind, and give life to society; you, that armed with the infinite power of virtue, are castles impregnable, rivers unsailable, seas immovable, infinite treasures, and invincible armies; that are helpers most trusty, sentinels most careful, signes deceitless, plain ways fail-less, true guides dangerless; balms that instantly cure, and honours that never perish: O do not look to find your names in this declamation, but with all honour and reverence do I speak to you: you are Seneca's Graces, women, good women, modest women, true women: ever young, because ever virtuous, ever chaste, ever glorious: when I write of you, I will write with a golden pen; now I write with a rough quill, and black ink on iron sheets, the iron deeds of an iron generation.

Come then, you masculine-women, for you are my subject, you that have made admiration an asse, and fooled him with a deformity never before dreamed of, that have made your selves stranger things than ever Noah's Ark unladed; or Nile ingendred;[1] whom to name, he that named all things, might study an age to find you a right attribute; whose like are not found in any antiquaries study, in any sea-man's travel, nor in any painter's cunning; you that are stranger than strangeness itself; whom wisemen wonder at; boys shout at, and goblins themselves start at; you that are the gilt dirt, which embroiders play-houses; the painted statues which adorn caroches,[2] and the perfumed carrion that bad men feed on in brothels: 'tis of you, I intreat, and of your monstrous deformity; you that have made your bodies like antic boscadge, or crotesco worke,[3] not half man, half woman; half fish, half flesh; half beast, half monster: but all odious, all devil, that have cast off the ornaments of your sexes, to put on the garments of shame; that have laid by the bashfulness of your natures, to gather the impudence of harlots; that have buried silence, to revive slander; that are all things but that which you should be, and nothing less than friends to virtue and goodness, that have made the foundation of your highest detested work, from the lowest despised creatures that record can give testimony of . . .

But such as are able to buy all their own charges, they swim in the excess of these vanities, and will be man-like not only from the head to the waist, but to the very foot, & in every condition: man in body by attire, man in behaviour by rude complement, man in nature by aptness to anger, man in action by pursuing revenge, man in wearing weapons, man in using weapons: and in brief, so much man in all things, that they are neither men, nor women, but just good for nothing . . .

But when they thrust virtue out of doors, and give a shameless liberty to every loose passion, that either their weak thoughts engenders, or the discourse of wicked tongues can charm into their yielding bosoms (much too apt to be opened with any pick-lock of flattering and deceitful insinuation) then they turn maskers,[4] mummers,[5] nay monsters in their disguises, and so they may catch the bridle in their teeth, and run away with their rulers, they care not into what dangers they plunge either their fortune or reputations, the disgrace of the whole sex, or the blot and obloquy of their private families, according to the saying of the poet:

Such is the cruelty of women-kind,
When they have shaken off the shamefac't
*   band*
With which wise nature did them strongly
*   bind,*
T'obey the hests[6] of man's well-ruling
*   hand;*

That then all rule and reason they
*   withstand*
To purchase a licentious liberty;
But virtuous women wisely understand,
That they were born to mild humility,
Unless the heavens them lift to lawful
*   sovereignty.*

To you therefore that are fathers, husbands, or sustainers of these new *Hermaphrodites*, belongs the cure of this impostume;[7] it is you that give fuel to the flames of their wild indiscretion. You add the oil which makes their stinking lamps defile the whole house with filthy smoke, and your purses purchase these deformities at rates, both dear and unreasonable. Do you but hold close your liberal hands, or take a strict account of the employment of the treasure you give to their necessary maintenance, and these excesses will either cease, or else die smothered in prison in the tailors' trunks for want of redemption . . .

The Womanish Man

Text from *Haec-Vir: or the Womanish-Man: Being an answer to a late booke intituled Hic-Mulier.* See Clark (1985: 158–83); Dekker and de Pol (1989); Garber (1992); Lucas (1988); Shapiro (1987); Traub (1992).

Hic Mulier . . . you condemn me of *unnaturalness*, in forsaking my creation, and contemning[8] custom. How do I forsake my creation, that do all the rights and offices due to my creation? I was created free, born free, and live free: what lets me then so to spin out my time, that I may die free?

To alter creation, were to walk on my hands my heels upward, to feed myself with my feet, or to forsake the sweet sound of sweet words, for the hissing noise of the serpent: but I walk with a face erected, with a body clothed, with a mind busied, & with a heart full of reasonable and devout cogitations; only offensive in attire, in as much as it is a stranger to the curiosity of the present times, and an enemy to custom. Are we then bound to be the flatterers of time, or the dependants on custom? O miserable servitude chained only to baseness and folly! for than custom, nothing is more absurd, nothing more foolish . . .

Now since according to your own inference, even by the laws of nature, by the rules of religion, and the customs of all civil nations, it is necessary there be a distinct and special difference between man and woman, both in their habit and behaviours: what could we poor weak women do less (being far too weak by force to fetch back those spoils you have unjustly taken from us) then to gather up those garments you have proudly cast away, and therewith to clothe both our bodies and our minds; since no other means was left us to continue our names, and to support a difference? for to have held the way in which our fore-fathers first set us, or to have embraced the civil modesty, or gentle sweetness of our soft inclinations; why, you had so far encroached upon us, and so over-bribed the world, to be deaf to any grant of restitution, that as at our creation, our whole sex was contained in man our first parent, so we should have had no other being, but in you, and your most effeminate quality. Hence we have preserved (though to our own shames) those manly things which you have forsaken, which would you again accept, and restore to us the blushes we laid by, when first we put on your masculine garments; doubt not but chaste thoughts and bashfulnesse will again dwell in us, and our palaces being newly gilt, trimmed, and re-edified, draw to us all the Graces, all the Muses; which that you may more willingly do, and (as we of yours) grow into detestation of that deformity you have purloined; to the utter loss of your honours and reputations; mark how the brave Italian poet, even in the infancy of your abuses, most lively describes you;

About his neck a carknet⁹ rich he ware
Of precious stones, all set in gold well tried;
His arms that earst¹⁰ all warlike weapons
   bare,
In golden bracelets wantonly were tied:
Into his ears two rings convayed are
Of golden wire, at which on either side,
Two Indian pearls, in making like two
   pears,
Of passing price were pendant at his eares.

His locks bedewed with waters of sweet
   savour

Stood curled round in order on his head;
He had such wanton womanish
   behaviour,
As though in valour he had ne'er been
   bred:
So chang'd in speech, in manners and in
   favour,
So from himself beyond all reason led,
By these enchantments of this amorous
   dame;
He was himself in nothing, but in name.

Thus you see your injury to us is of an old and inveterate continuance, having taken such strong root in your bosoms, that it can hardly be pulled up, without some offence to the soil: ours young and tender, scarce freed from the swaddling clouts,[11] and therefore may with as much ease be lost, as it was with little difficulty found. Cast then from you our ornaments, and put on your own armours: be men in shape, men in show, men in words, men in actions, men in counsel, men in example: then will we love and serve you; then will we hear and obey you; then will we like rich jewels hang at your ears to take our instructions, like true friends follow you through all dangers, and like careful leeches pour oil into your wounds: then shall you finde delight in our words; pleasure in our faces; faith in our hearts; chastity in our thoughts, and sweetness both in our inward and outward inclinations. Comeliness shall be then our study; fear our armour, and modesty our practice: then shall we be all your most excellentest thoughts can desire, and have nothing in us less than impudence and deformity . . .

A Dialogue between Cleonarium and Leaena

Classical texts provided a rich range of examples of same-sex relationships; translation opened them to a wider readership, often without losing the sexual charge of the original. Text from 'A Dialogue between *Cleonarium* and *Leaena*' in *Lucian's Works* translated by Ferrand Spence (1684).

Cleonarium: Strange rumours run of thee Leaena; how Megilla that rich lady of Lesbos, carresses thee as a man would do; how is't for Gods sake? But tell me, is't true?

Leaena: Ay, some such business.

Cleonarium: But I can't apprehend, to what all these carresses tend? if you loved me, you'd tell me all, and make me your confident.

Leaena: I love ye as much as any body living, but I'm ashamed to tell it – well, 'tis a strange female.

Cleonarium: I can't imagine what you mean, unless she's a *Tribadian,*[12] as there are said to be many in that island, who will not have to do with men, and only commit with women.

Leaena: Why truly y'are near the mark.

Cleonarium: Prithee tell me then, how she declared her passion, the returns you made, and the rest of that adventure.

Leaena: She was junketing[13] with Demonassa of Corinth, Melissa's twin in

181

humour, and they sent for me as a minstrel, to sing and play upon instruments during their repast. After they grew a little bowsey,[14] they kept me all night, and told me I should be their bedfellow, and that they would put me in the midst; which I durst not refuse, as thinking they honoured me very much. When we were in bed, they began to toy, kissing me as men are wont, not barely applying the lips, but opening the mouth, biting and pressing my bosom, with all other testimonies of a violent passion, whereat I was strangely amazed, as not being able to guess the matter. At last Megilla all raving mad, pulling off her head-gear, appeared stark naked, and her pate shaved like any champion; which surprized me still more. Then cried she, Leaena, did you ever see a brisker, handsomer fellow. Don't offend me continued she, by taking me for a woman, I am not called Megilla but Megillus, and there's my wife, showing Demonassa. I fell a laughing at this discourse, and told her, what, you have deceived us all the while, being a man, and passing for a woman, like Achilles among the maids. But have you the *Ballum Raneum*, the virility you wot, and can you not like a man perform with Demonassa. No, said she, there's no need of that; and if you try, you'll find I want nothing for the accomplishing thy and my desires. You are no hermaphrodite sure, said I to her, as there are said to be several? or like that Theban soothsayer, who I've heard my companion Ismedora talk of, who became a man after having been a woman. No, said she, but I've all the passions and inclinations of men, and something that will serve instead of manhood. Then she made me a present of a necklace, and some dainty fine linen, and embracing me with all imaginable transport, kissed and satisfied her passion.

Cleonarium: But what did she and how? for there's the main mystery.

Leaena: Paw, paw! enquire no farther; for it's neither handsome for me to say, nor you to hear it.

A Serious Proposal to the Ladies

Text from *A Serious Proposal to the Ladies* (1696) by Mary Astell (1666–1731), who wrote a number of influential and popular treatises on women and marriage. The extract is a defence of spinsterhood, which was usually mocked by male and female writers alike.

For the poor lady having past the prime of her years in gaiety and company, in running the circle of all the vanities of the town, having spread all her nets and used all her arts for conquest, and finding that the bait fails where she would have it take; and having all this while been so over-careful of her body, that she had no time to improve her mind, which therefore affords her no safe retreat, now she meets with disappointments abroad, and growing every day more and more sensible, that the respect which used to be paid her decays as fast as her beauty; quite terrified with the dreadful name of *Old Maid*, which yet none but fools will reproach her with, nor any wise woman be afraid of; to avoid ... the scoffs that are thrown on superannuated virgins, she flies to some dishonourable match as her last, though much mistaken refuge, to the disgrace of her family and her own irreparable ruin.

Sappho

Text from the entry in Pierre Bayle's *An Historical and Critical Dictionary* (1710, first published in 1695). Sappho's poetry was widely admired in the eighteenth century; her sexual persona and history were nonetheless open to dispute. See Page (1955); Cavin (1985); Lipking (1988); Bremner (1989); DeJean (1989); Harvey (1989); Donoghue (1993: 243–68); Semple (1994).

There remains nothing of so many poems she made but some small fragments which the ancient scholiasts have cited, a Hymn to Venus, and an ode to one of her mistresses; for you must know that her amorous passion extended even to the persons of her own sex, and this is that for which she was most cried down. Suidas has preserved the names of 3 of her mistresses, who spoiled her reputation and defamed themselves by a strange singularity which was imputed to their commerce. He also preserved the names of 3 of her female, scholars whom she did, without doubt, initiate in her mysteries. Since Lucian does not observe that the women of the isle of Lesbos, who he says were very subject to this passion, learned it of Sappho, 'tis better to imagine that she found it already established in her country than to make her the inventer of it. Be it as it will, Sappho always passed for a famous Tribas, and some think that it was for this reason, that some sirnamed her Mascula[15] Sappho. If her design was to pass by and neglect the other half of mankind, she was frustrated of her expectation; for she fell desperately in love with Phaon, and did all in vain she could to make him love her: but he despised her and forced her by his coldness to throw herself from a high rock to extinguish her devouring flame.

Blest as the Immortal Gods Is He

Sappho's poem may have been written originally to one of her mistresses. Emma Donoghue notes that it reads 'like an expression of passion between women' (1993: 247). Text from the translation by Ambrose Phillips published in *The Spectator* (22 November 1711), with commentary by Joseph Addison.[16] See also *The Works of Anacreon and Sappho* (1713); Page (1955); Cavin (1985); Lipking (1988); Bremner (1989); DeJean (1989); Harvey (1989); Donoghue (1993: 243–67); Semple (1994).

I

Blest as th'immortal Gods is he,
The youth who fondly sits by thee,
And hears and sees thee all the while
Softly speak and sweetly smile.

II

'Twas this depriv'd my soul of rest,
And rais'd such tumults in my breast;
For while I gaz'd, in transport tost,
My breath was gone, my voice was lost:

III

My bosom glow'd; the subtle flame
Ran quick through all my vital frame;
O'er my dim eyes a darkness hung;
My ears with hollow murmurs rung.

IV

In dewy damps my limbs were chill'd;
My blood with gentle horrors thrill'd;
My feeble pulse forgot to play;
I fainted, sunk, and dy'd away.

The Fable of Iphis and Ianthe

From her birth (with which this extract commences), the girl Iphis is brought up secretly as a boy to placate her father's need for a male heir. He plans to marry 'him' to Ianthe, but in the nick of time Iphis is metamorphosed into a man! The poem manipulates and dramatizes the erotic (the spectre of lesbianism), and the ambiguous, 'secret', body. Text: John Dryden's translation from Book 9 of *Ovid's Metamorphoses in Fifteen Books. Translated by the most eminent hands* (1717).

'Twas of the beauteous kind, and
   brought to light
With secrecy, to shun the father's
   sight.
Th'indulgent mother did her care
   employ,
And pass'd it on her husband for a boy.
The nurse was conscious of the fact
   alone;

The father paid his vows as for a son;
And call'd him Iphis, by a common
   name,
Which either sex with equal right may
   claim.
Iphis his grandsire was; the wife was
   pleas'd,
Of half the fraud by fortune's favour
   eas'd:

The doubtful name was used without
  deceit,
And truth was cover'd with a pious
  cheat.
The habit show'd a boy, the beauteous
  face
With manly fierceness mingl'd female
  grace.
  Now thirteen years of age were
  swiftly run,
When fond father thought the time
  drew on
Of settling in the world his only son.
Ianthe was his choice; so wondrous
  fair,
Her form alone with Iphis cou'd
  compare;
A neighbour's daughter of his own
  degree,
And not more bless'd with fortune's
  goods than he.
  They soon espous'd; for they with
  ease were join'd,
Who were before contracted in the
  mind.
Their age the same, their inclinations
  too;
And bred together, in one school they
  grew.
Thus, fatally dispos'd to mutual fires,
They felt, before they knew, the same
  desires.
Equal their flame, unequal was their
  care;
One lov'd with hope, one languish'd in
  despair.
The maid accus'd the ling'ring days
  alone:
For whom she thought a man, she
  thought her own.

But Iphis bends beneath a greater
  grief;
As fiercely burns, but hopes for no
  relief.
Ev'n her despair adds fuel to her fire;
A maid with madness does a maid
  desire.
  And, scarce refraining tears, alas,
  said she,
What issue of my love remains for me!
How wild a passion works within my
  breast,
With what prodigious flames am I
  possest!
Cou'd I the care of providence deserve,
Heav'n must destroy me, if it wou'd
  preserve.
And that's my fate; or sure it would
  have sent
Some usual evil for my punishment:
Not this unkindly curse; to rage and
  burn,
Where nature shows no prospect of
  return.
Nor cows for cows consume with
  fruitless fire,
nor mares, when hot, their fellow-
  mares desire:
The father of the fold supplies his
  ewes;
The stag through secret woods his hind
  pursues;
And birds for mates the males of their
  own species choose.
Her females nature guards from
  female flame,
And joins two sexes to preserve the
  game:
Wou'd I were nothing, or not what I
  am!

Crete, fam'd for monsters, wanted of
her store,
Till my new love produc'd one monster
more.
The daughter of the sun a bull desir'd,
And yet ev'n then a male a female fir'd:
Her passion was extravagantly new,
But mine is much the madder of the
two.
To things impossible she was not bent,
But found the means to compass the
intent.
To cheat his eyes she took a different
shape;
Yet still she gain'd a lover and a leap.
Shou'd all the wit of all the world
conspire,
Shou'd Daedalus assist my wild desire,
What art can make Ianthe to a boy?
Extinguish then thy passion, hopeless
maid,
And recollect thy reason for thy aid.
Know what thou art, and love as
maidens ought,
And drive these golden wishes from
thy thought.
Thou canst not hope thy fond desires
to gain;
Where hope is wanting, wishes are in
vain.
And yet no guards against our joys
conspire;
No jealous husband hinders our
desire:
My parents are propitious to my wish,
And she herself consenting to the bliss.
All things concur to prosper our
design;
All things to prosper any love but
mine.

And yet I never can enjoy the fair;
'Tis past the pow'r of heav'n to grant
my pray'r.
Heav'n has been kind, as far as heaven
can be;
Our parents with our own desires
agree;
But nature, stronger than the gods
above,
Refuses her assistance to my love;
She sets the bar that causes all my
pain;
One gift refus'd, makes all their bounty
vain.
And now the happy day is just at hand,
To bind our hearts in Hymen's holy
band:
Our hearts, but not our bodies: thus
accurs'd,
In midst of water I complain of thirst.
Why com'st thou, Juno, to these barren
rites,
To bless a bed defrauded of delights?
But why shou'd Hymen lift his torch
on high,
To see two brides in cold embraces lie?
Thus love-sick Iphis her vain
passion mourns;
With equal ardour fair Ianthe burns,
Invoking Hymen's name and Juno's
pow'r,
To speed the work, and haste the happy
hour.
She hopes, while Telethusa[17] fears
the day,
And strives to interpose some new delay:
Now feigns a sickness, now is in a
fright
For this bad omen, or that boding
sight.

186

But having done whate'er she cou'd
   devise,
And empty'd all her magazine of lies,
The time approach'd; the next ensuing
   day
The fatal secret must to light betray.
Then Telethusa had recourse to pray'r,
She, and her daugher with dishevell'd
   hair;
Trembling with fear, great Isis they
   ador'd,
Embrac'd her altar, and her aid
   implor'd ...
   Her tears pursu'd her words; and
   while she spoke
The Goddess nodded, and her altar
   shook:
The temple doors, as with a blast of
   wind,
Were heard to clap; the lunar horns
   that bind
The brows of Isis, cast a blaze around;
The trembling timbrel made
   murm'ring sound.
   Some hopes these happy omens did
   impart;
Forth went the mother with a beating
   heart:
Not much in fear, nor fully satisfy'd;
But Iphis follow'd with a larger stride:

The whiteness of her skin forsook her
   face;
Her looks embolden'd, with an awful
   grace;
Her features and her strength together
   grew,
And her long hair to curling locks
   withdrew.
Her sparkling eyes with manly vigour
   shone,
Big was her voice, audacious was her
   tone.
The latent parts, at length reveal'd,
   began
To shoot, and spread, and burnish into
   man.
The maid becomes a youth ...
   Now when the star of day had
   shown his face,
Venus and Juno with their presence
   grace
The nuptial rites, and Hymen from
   above
Descending to complete their happy
   love:
The Gods of marriage lend their
   mutual aid;
And the warm youth enjoys the lovely
   maid.

Venus in the Cloister; or, the Nun in her Smock

This extract takes the form of a dialogue between an older and a younger nun, concerning sexual pleasures, which are described so as to titillate the reader's imagination. Later dialogues in the collection provide a transition to heterosexual practices: dialogue 5, in particular, rehearses the idea that bachelors should be forced to marriage and propagation. Text from Dialogue 1, *Venus in the Cloister; or, the Nun in her Smock*, translated by Robert Samber (second edition, 1725); see Jean Barrin, *Venus dans la Cloitre* (1683). The English editions were prosecuted in 1725 and 1745 for obscene libel. See Thomas (1969) and Foxon (1963a); Donoghue (1993: 198–200; 221–32).

Agnes: Ah Lard! Sister Angelica, for heaven's sake do not come into our cell; I am not visible at present. Ought you to surprise our people in the condition I am in? I thought I had shut the door.

Angel: Be quiet, my dear, what is it gives thee this alarm? The mighty crime of seeing thee shift thy self, or doing somewhat more refreshing? Good friends ought to conceal nothing from one another: sit down upon the mattress, I'll go and shut the door.

Agnes: I'll assure you, Sister, I should have died with confusion, had any one but your self thus surprised me; but I know you love me, and therefore I have no cause to fear any thing from you, whatever you might have taken notice of.

Angel: Thou hast reason, my child, to talk after this manner; and though I had not all the affection for thee, a tender heart is sensible of, yet shouldst thou apprehend nothing on that account. Seven years are now past since I was professed a nun: I came into the convent at thirteen, and I can say, I have made no creature in the house my enemy by my ill conduct, having ever an utter aversion of speaking ill of people, and taking the most inward pleasure and satisfaction in the world to serve any one of the community. This manner of acting has gained me the affection of the greatest number, and above all, entirely engaged me that of our superior, the abbess, which stands me in no small stead upon occasion.

Agnes: I know it; and have often wondered how you could even manage those of a different party; undoubtedly you must have a great deal of wit and address to win such people. For my part, I could never torture myself in my affections, or labour to make friends of those who were indifferent to me. This is my *foible*, who am enemy to restraint, and would always act with liberty.

Angel: It is certainly very agreeable, to let oneself be guided by that pure and innocent Nature, by following the inclinations which she gives us; but honour and ambition, which have long since troubled the repose of cloisters, oblige those who come into them to divide themselves, and do often that with prudence, which they cannot do by inclination.

Agnes: Which is as much as to say; that a great many who believe themselves mistresses of your heart, possess only the picture of it; and that all your protestations assure them very often of a good which in reality they do not enjoy. I should be afraid, I assure you, to be of that number, and fall a victim to your politics.

Angel: Ah! my dear, thou dost me wrong; dissimulation has nothing to do with friendships so strong as ours. I am entirely thine; and had nature made me of the same blood and spirits with thee, she could not have given me more tender sentiments than those I now perceive with such excess of pleasure. Let me embrace thee, that our hearts may talk to each other in the tumult of our kisses.

Agnes: Ah Lud! how you squeeze me in your arms: don't you see I am naked to my smock? Ah! you have set me all on fire.

Angel: Ah! how does that vermilion, which at this instant animates thee, augment the brilliancy of thy beauty? That fire which sparkles in thy eyes, how amiable does it make thee? How lovely! must a young creature so accomplished be thus reserved? No, no, my child, I'll make thee acquainted with my most secret actions, and give thee the conduct of sage and prudent religious; I do not mean that austere and scrupulous sageness which is the child of fasting, and discovers itself in hair and sackcloth: there is another less wild and savage, which all people of better informed judgement make profession to follow, and which does no less suit thy amorous inclination.

Agnes: My amorous inclination! certainly my physiognomy must be very deceitful, or you do not perfectly understand the rules of that art. There is nothing touches me less than that passion; and since the three years that I have been in religion [having taken vows] it has given me the least inquietude.

Angel: That I doubt very much, and if thou wouldst speak with greater sincerity thou wouldst own that I have spoke nothing but the truth. What, can a young girl of sixteen, of so lively a wit, and a body so well formed as thine, be cold and insensible? No, I cannot persuade myself to think so: everything thou dost, however so negligent it is, convinces me of the contrary, and that *Je ne sais quoi* that I saw through the Crevice[18] of the door, before I came in, convinces me that thou art a dissembler.

Agnes: Ah dear! I am undone!

Angel: Indeed thou hast no reason to say so. Tell me a little whether thou couldst apprehend anything from me, or hadst any cause to be afraid of a friend? I spoke this to thee with design to make thee my confident in a great many other things relating to myself. Really these are pretty *Bagatelles*;[19] the most scrupulous make use of them, and they are called in conventual terms, *The Amusement of the Young, and the Pastimes of the Old.*

Agnes: But pray what did you perceive through the crevice?

Angel: Thou perfectly tirest me with this conduct. Know for certain, that love banishes all fear; and that if we would both of us live with that harmony and perfect understanding, as I desire we should, thou must keep nothing from me, nor I hide anything from thee. Kiss me, my little heart; in the condition thou art at present, a discipline[20] would be of good use to chastise thee for the small return thou makest me for the friendship I show thee. Ah Lard! in what good plight thou art! what delicate proportion of shape! Let me –

Agnes: For Heaven's sake let me alone, I am not able to recover from my surprise. But in good earnest what did you see through.

Angel: Dost thou not know, my little fool, what it was I could see? Why I saw thee in an action, in which I will serve thee myself, if thou wilt, and in which my hand shall now perform that office which thine did just now so charitably to another part of thy body. This is that grand crime which I discovered, and which my Lady Abbess * of **** practises, as she says, in her most innocent diversions, which the Prioress does not reject, and which the mistress of the *Novices* called *The Ecstatic Intromission*. Thou wouldst not believe that such holy souls were capable of employing themselves in such profane exercises. Their carriage and outside have deceived thee; and this exterior of sanctity, with which they do so well know how to deck themselves on occasion, has made thee believe that they live in their bodies, as if they were only made up of nothing but the spirit. Ah! my child, how shall I instruct thee in a great many things of which thou art ignorant, if thou wilt but place a little confidence in me, and discover to me the present disposition of thy mind and conscience? After this I will be thy penitent, and I protest thou shalt see my heart as open, as if thou thy self wert sensible of its genuine movements.

Agnes: After all this, I think I ought not to doubt your sincerity; for which reason I shall not only inform you what you desire to know of me, but I would also do myself that sensible pleasure to communicate to you even my most secret thoughts and actions. This will be a general confession of which I know you have no design to make any advantage, but of which the confidence I shall repose in you, will only serve to unite us both in the strictest and most indissoluble chains of friendship.

Angel: Without doubt, my dearest soul; and thou wilt observe as we proceed, that there is nothing more sweet and agreeable in the world, than a true friend, who might be the depositary of our secret thoughts, and even our very actions. Ah how comfortable are the openings of hearts in the like occasions! Speak then, my minion, I am coming to sit down by thee on the mattress: there is no necessity to dress thee, the weather gives thee leave to continue as thou art; I think thou art the more lovely for being so, and the more thou approach to the state in which nature produced thee, thou hast more charms and beauty. Embrace me, my dear Agnes, before we begin, and confirm by thy kisses the mutual protestations we have given to love each other for ever. Ah! how pure and innocent are thy kisses! how full of tenderness and sweetness! what excess of pleasure do they afford me! Truce a moment, my little heart, I am all on fire, thou makest me mad with thy caresses. Ah Lard how powerful is love! and what will become of me if simple kisses thus lively animate and transport me!

Agnes: Ah! how difficult it is to contain ourselves within the bounds of our duty, when we give ever so little the reins to this passion! Would you believe Angelica, how wonderfully these toyings, which in the main are nothing, have wrought upon me: Ah, ah, ah, let me breathe a little; methinks my heart is too much locked up at present! Ah how do these sighs comfort me! I begin to feel within me a new affection for you, more strong and tender than before! I know not whence it proceeds, for can simple kisses cause such disorder in the soul? It is true you are very artful in your caresses, and all you do is extraordinarily engaging; for you have gained me so much, that I am now yours more than my own. I am even afraid that in the excess of that satisfaction which I have tasted, there may be somewhat intermixed, that may give me cause to reflect upon my conscience; this would give me a great deal of trouble: for when I am obliged to speak to my confessor of these matters, I die with shame, and know not how to support myself. Lord how weak we are, and how vain are our efforts to surmount the smallest sallies and lightest attacks of corrupted nature?

Angel: Thou art now arrived where I expected thee, I know thou wert always a little scrupulous on many things, and that a certain tenderness of conscience hath not given a little pain. Thus it is to fall into the hands of an ill-instructed and ignorant director. For my part, I tell thee, that I was instructed by a very learned man, with what air I ought to comport myself to live happily all my life, without doing anything, notwithstanding that might shock the observation of a regular community, or which might be directly oposite to the commandments.

Agnes: Do me the favour, sister Angelica, to give me a perfect idea of this good conduct; believe me entirely disposed to hear you, and suffer myself to be persuaded by your reasonings, when I cannot refute them by stronger. The promise that I made you to open myself fully to you, shall be no less observed; since you will insensibly in my answers to you, remark on what foot I stand, and you will judge by that sincere discovery in all things I shall make you, of the good or bad ways I am to follow.

Angel: My child, thou wilt be perhaps surprised at the lessons I am going to give thee, and thou wilt be astonished to hear a girl between nineteen and twenty, so intelligent, and to have penetrated into the deepest secrets of religious policy. Do not believe, my dear, that a spirit vain of glory inspires my words: no, I am satisfied I was less enlightened than thou wert at thy age, and that all I have learnt, hath succeeded an extreme ignorance; but I must also tell thee, that I should accuse myself of stupidity, if the care which several great men had taken to form me, had not produced some fruit; and if the understanding of several languages which they have taught me, had not caused to make some progress, by the reading of good books.

Agnes: My dear Angelica, begin your instructions, I desire you, I die with impatience to hear you; you never had a scholar more attentive than I shall be to your discourse.

Angel: As we are not born of a sex to make laws, we ought to obey those we find, and follow as known truths, a great many things, which pass a number of people only for opinions; we know we are indispensibly to do good, and avoid evil. But as all do not agree, what to call good or evil, and that there is an infinity of actions for which we have the utmost horror, that are notwithstanding received and approved of by our neighbours; I shall teach thee in a few words, what a reverend father Jesuit, who had a particular affection for me, told me at the time when he endeavoured to open my understandings, and make me capable of the present speculations ... 'In obeying the commands of God, we must consider whether his will be written with his own finger, or proceeds from the mouth of his son; or whether only from the voice of the people: so that sister Angelica may without scruple, lengthen her chains, embellish her solitude, and giving herself a gay air in all things, make herself familiar with the world. She may, as much as prudence will permit her, dispense herself with putting in execution that *Fratras*[21] of vows and promises which she indiscreetly made between the hands of men, and resume the same liberty she was in before her engagement, by following only her original obligations. This is what, continued he, regards interior peace: as for the exterior, you cannot without sinning against prudence, dispense with the laws, customs, and manners to which you submitted yourself at your entrance into the monastery. You ought also to appear zealous and fervent in exercises the most painful; if any interest of glory or honour depend on those employments; you may furnish your cell with hair and sackcloth, thorns and briars, and merit by that devout equipage, as much as they who indiscreetly wound and lacerate their bodies.'

Agnes: Ah! how I am ravished to hear you! the extreme pleasure which I take makes me interrupt you, and that liberty of conscience which you begin to give me by your discourse, hath rid me of almost an infinite number of troubles which tormented me. But continue, I beseech you, and teach me what was the design of policy, in establishing so many orders, the rules and constitution of which, are so rigorous.

Angel: One must consider in the foundation of all monasteries, two master workmen, that is to say, the founder and the policy. The intention of the former was very often pure, holy, and far distant from the designs of the other; and without having any other rules and manners of life, which he believed necessary, or at least useful for advancing in the spiritual warfare, and the good of our neighbour; it was for this end that deserts were peopled, and cloisters erected. The zeal of one alone inflamed a great many, and their principal employment being to sing continually the praises of the true God, they drew by these pious exercises, to them, whole companies, which united themselves to them, and became one body. I speak of what past in the fervour of the first ages; for as to others one must reason differently, and not think that this primitive innocence, and this fine character of devotion preserved itself very long, which gradually mixed itself with what we see at present. Policy, which cannot suffer anything defective in the state, seeing the increase of these recluses, their disorder and irregularity, was obliged to make use of its power; it banished a great many, and retrenched the constitutions of others, as to what it did not think necessary for the common interest: it had a mind to rid itself entirely of those *Leaches*, who through laziness and horrible sloth, would live on the labour of poor people; but this buckler of religion with which they cover themselves, and the judgement of the vulgar, of which they had already made themselves masters, gave things another turn; so that these communities were not entirely unuseful to the common-weal. Policy, then looked upon these houses as so many common-sewers, into which it might discharge itself of its superfluities; it makes use of them to ease families, whom a great number of children would make poor and indigent, if there were not places for them to retire to; and that their retreat may be secure, without any hopes of return, it invented vows, by which it pretends to bind us, and tie us indissolubly, to that state which we have embraced: it makes us even renounce the rights which nature has given us, and separates us from the world in such manner, that we make no part of it. You comprehend all this very well.

Agnes: Yes, but whence comes it that this cursed policy, which of free people hath made us slaves, approves more of those rules which are rude and austere, than those which are less rigorous?

Angel: The reason is this, policy, considers monastics of both sexes, as so many members cut off from its body, and as parts divided; the life of which it does not esteem in particular to be useful to anything, but rather prejudicial to the public. And as it would appear to be an action very inhuman, to rid itself of them openly, it had recourse to stratagems; and under pretence of devotion, it engaged these poor victims to be their own murderers; to macerate themselves with so many fastings, penances and mortifications, that at last the poor innocents sink under the burden, and make room by their death, for others, who must be as miserable as themselves, if they are not more enlightened. Thus, a father is often an executioner of his children, and without thinking of it, sacrifices them to policy, when he believes he offers them to God.

Agnes: Ah wretched effect of a detestable government! you give me life, my dear Angelica, in drawing me by your reasons out of the broad road I was in; very few people put in practice more than myself all kinds of mortifications, even the most rude and violent. I am torn to pieces with stripes of the discipline, in order to combat often the innocent movements of nature, which my director passed upon me for horrible disorders. Ah! why should I have been thus abused! without doubt it is from this cruel maxim, that moderate orders are despised, and those which have every thing in them frightful and horrid, praised and elevated to the skies. Oh God! dost thou suffer thy holy name to be thus abused in such unjust executions! dost thou permit men thus to personate and mock thee!

Angel: Ah! my child, these exclamations, plainly convince me that thou wantest yet some ray to enlighten thee universally in all things: but let us rest here; thy mind is not capable at present of a more delicate speculation. *Love God and thy Neighbour*, and be satisfied, that the whole law is included in these two commandments.

Agnes: What Angelica, would you leave me in my error?

Angel: No, my dear heart, thou shalt be fully instructed, and I will put into thy hands a book which shall completely make thee intelligent, and, by which thou shalt learn with ease, what I cannot explain to thee but very confusedly. Here it is, take it.

Agnes: Enough. Ha! what is it I see, I have dipped into that passage you were just now mentioning: *That cloisters are the common-sewers, whereinto policy discharges itself of its Ordures!* and I think no one could speak after a lower and more abject manner.

194

Angel: It is true, the expression smells a little strong; but it is no more shocking than that of another author, who says, that *Friars and Nuns were in the Church, what Cats and Mice were in Noah's Ark.*

Agnes: You are in the right, and I admire the easiness with which you discourse of these things, and would not for all that is dear to me, that the crevice in the door had not given birth to this entertainment: yes, dear Angelica, I have penetrated into the sense of every word you spoke.

Angel: Very well; will you make a good use of what hath been said? And shall this beautiful body which hath been guilty of no manner of crime, be again treated like the most infamous and most consummate villain in the world?

Agnes: No, I design to make it amends for the bad weather I caused it to suffer. I beg its pardon, and particularly for a very rude discipline which I made it very sensible of by the advice of my confessor.

Angel: Kiss me, poor child, I am more touched at what thou telleth me, than if I had experienced it myself; this correction must be the last thou shalt inflict upon thyself: but does it still pain thee?

Agnes: Alas! my zeal was indiscrete, I thought the more I laid on, the more I merited; my good plight of health, and my youth made me sensible of the least stroke; so that at the conclusion of this fine exercise, I found my back apartment all on fire: I don't know whether I have not some wound in those parts, for I was altogether transported when I committed this so sensible an outrage upon it.

Angel: You must let me make it a visit, my mignonne, that I may see how far an ill-managed zeal may carry one.

Agnes: Oh Lud! must I suffer this! you speak then in earnest. I cannot bear it without confusion. Oh! Oh!

Angel: To what purpose is all what I have been saying, if you are still enslaved by a foolish shame-facedness? What harm is there in granting what I ask of you?

Agnes: 'Tis true, I am in the wrong, and your curiosity is no wise blameable; take then that satisfaction you desire.

Angel: Oh! let us see then unveiled that beautiful countenance that has hitherto been always covered! kneel down upon the mattress, and hold down thy head a little, that I may observe the violence of thy stripes! Ah! Goodness of heaven, what patch-work is here? what variety of colours? Methinks I see a piece of China taffeta: sure one must have a great deal of devotion to *the Mystery of Flagellation,*[22] thus to illuminate one's thighs.

Agnes: Well, and hast thou sufficiently contemplated that innocent outrage? Oh God! how you handle it, let it alone, that it may recover from its former

195

complexion, and divest itself of this strange colour. What, dost thou kiss it?

Angel: Do not be against it, my child, I am a soul the most compassionate in the world; and as it is a work of mercy to comfort the afflicted, I think I could not carress them too much to acquit myself willingly of that devoir. Ah! how well formed is that part! and what *eclat* and beauty does that whiteness and good plight that there appears bestow upon it! I perceive also another place which is no less participant of the kindness of nature, it is Nature itself.

Agnes: Take away your hand, I beseech you, from that place, if you would not blow up a fire not easily to be extinguished. I must own my own weakness, I am a girl the most sensible you ever knew; and that which would not cause in any other the least emotion, very often puts me entirely into the utmost disorder.

Angel: So! then thou art not so cold as thou wouldst have persuaded me at the beginning of our discourse! and I believe thou wilt act thy part as well as anyone I know, when I shall have put thee into the hands of five or six good friars. I could wish on that account, that the time of the retreat, into which, according to custom, I am going to enter, might be deferred, that I might go along with thee into the parlour: but no matter, I shall comfort myself with the recital thou wilt make me of everything that shall have passed; that is, whether the Abbé shall have acquitted himself better than the monk or the Feuillant,[23] than the Jesuit; and in short, if the whole *Fratraille*[24] shall have given thee plenary satisfaction.

Agnes: Ah! I fancy I shall be much embarrassed in these kinds of entertainments, and that they will find me a mere novice in feats of love.

Angel: Do not put thyself in pain about that, they know what methods to make use of with every body, and one quarter of an hour with them will make thee more knowing, than all the precepts thou couldst have from me in a whole week. There, cover thy back-side for fear it should catch cold: but stay, it shall first have this kiss from me, and this, and this.

Agnes: How toying thou art? Dost believe I would suffer these fooleries, unless I knew there was nothing criminal in them.

Angel: If there was, I should commit a sin every moment, for the charge I have over the scholars and pensioners, obliges me to visit their back-houses very often. It was but yesterday, I whipped one, more for my own satisfaction, than for any fault she had committed. I took a singular pleasure in looking on her; she was very pretty, and only thirteen years old.

Agnes: I long for that employment of school-mistress, that I might take the like diversion; I was struck with that fancy, and I should be even ravished to behold in thee, what thou hast so attentively considered in my person.

Angel: Alas! my child, what thou askest does not at all surprise me; we are all formed of the same paste. Hold, I'll put myself into thy posture. So! Take up my petticoat and smock as high as thou canst.

Agnes: I've a strong temptation to take my discipline, and so order it, that these twin sisters may have nothing to reproach me withall.

Angel: Ouf! ouf! ouf! what havoc thou makest; this kind of diversion does by no means please me, but when it is not too violent. Truce, truce, if thy devotion should tempt thee to renew this exercise, I should be ruined. Lud what an inflexible arm thou hast! I have a design to make thee partner to my office, but that requires a little more moderation.

Agnes: You have a great deal of reason to complain indeed, this is not the tenth part of what I received: I'll defer the rest to another opportunity, something must be allowed to your want of courage. You must know this place looks now more beautiful; a certain fire, which enlivens it, gives it a vermilion, more pure and brilliant than Spanish wool. Come a little nearer to the window, that the light may discover all its beauties: So, that's well. I could never be weary of looking at it: I see all I could wish even to its neighbourhood. Why do you cover that place with your hand?

Angel: Alas! thou mayest look upon it as well as the rest: if there be any ill in this operation, it cannot prejudice any body, and does not in the least trouble the tranquillity of the public.

Agnes: How can it, since we make no more a part of it? Besides, hidden faults are half pardoned.

Angel: You have reason, my dear, for if one practised in the world as many crimes, to speak conformably to our rules, as are committed in cloisters, the government would be obliged to correct the house, and cut off the current of these disorders.

Agnes: And I believe that parents would never suffer their children to come into our houses, and be professed amongst us, if they knew our disorders.

Angel: You need not doubt it; but as the greatest part of these faults are secret, and dissimulation reigns more in cloisters than elsewhere. All who live in these retirements do not see them; but serve themselves to decoy others. Besides, very often the particular interest of families prevails above all other considerations.

Agnes: Confessors and directors of convents have a particular talent to make those poor innocents fall into their snares, who snap at their bait, vainly imagining they have found an invaluable treasure.

Roxana

Roxana, the heroine of the tale, defends single women. text from Daniel Defoe's *Roxana* (1724). See Zhang (1993); Castle (1979) and Donoghue (1993: 174–6).

I returned, that while a woman was single, she was masculine in her politic capacity; that she had then the full command of what she had, and the full direction of what she did; that she was a man in her separated capacity, to all intents and purposes that a man could be so to himself; that she was controlled by none, because accountable to none, and was in subjection to none ...

I added, that whoever the woman was that had an estate, and would give it up to be the slave of a great man, that woman was a fool, and must be fit for nothing but a beggar; and that it was my opinion a woman was fit to govern and enjoy her own estate, without a man, as a man was without a woman; and that if she had a mind to gratify herself as to sexes, she might entertain a man as a man does a mistress; that while she was thus single she was her own, and if she gave away that power, she merited to be as miserable as it was possible that any creature could be.

Monsieur Thing's Origin

The dildo is here personfied as a French visitor to London. *The Daily Journal* recorded on 9 June 1722 that this publication offended one female bookseller and that she sent constables to attempt to suppress its sale. The author is largely contemptuous of women who reject the natural penis for the artificial dildo. As in many cases the unnatural is mapped from a national *other* which threatens to destroy solid native values. Text: *Monsieur Thing's Origin: or, Seignior D—o's Adventures in Britain* (1722).

Astraea's[25] kind, who taught me how
   to choose
This comic thesis, for my present muse.
Whoe'er they be, that do desire to trace
His pedigree, it's of the Gallick race:
Some say it was the Duchess Mazarine
Was first contriver of this fine
   machine;
From Italy it was that first it came,
And from that country it had first its
   name:

But if my information is but true,
A place it came from nearer to our
   view.
To France he owes his birth or first
   extraction,
By doctors there he had his first
   creation,
And is originally of that nation.
Experienc'd Aesculapians[26] did design
Him for the use of infants feminine,
Until they were fit to be put to nurses

Of males, most proper for to steer their
    courses.
He first was made, to put a help to
    nature,
But art of nature now has got the better:
His first progeny, and design'd
    descent,
Was to relieve the poor and innocent;
But now converted to a WORSE
    INTENT.

Satyr be kind, and be not too severe,
But lightly speak of SEIGNIOR's
    character:
Then once take wing, and soar o'er
    Albion's Isle,
To see how Virtue there seems in exile,
And view how D––o females there
    beguile,
Behold kind virtue weeping from on
    high,
Tears dropping from her, as from
    gloomy sky,
With eyes dejected, on the isles of
    Britain
Bare-faced cou'd not behold, but with a
    mask on:
Leering she gazes from her airy
    mansions,
Blushes to see strange introduc'd
    inventions.

When SEIGNIOR first at London did
    arrive,
Was put to shifts to know how to
    contrive,
Or find a place where family should
    live.

At length all day after they had been
    trudging,

Tired with fatigue, in seeking of a
    lodging
Were show'd a TOY-SHOP, nigh to
    Covent-Garden.

Where for some time they liv'd in
    private room,
But soon became unto the public
    known,
Because his qualities were really such,
Could with small help do *Little* or *do*
    Much:
For his capacity, made Denizen,
'Twas thus Monsieur became an
    Englishman.
Before 'twas long, the number did
    increase,
So the last brood were to choose a new
    place,
That he should not be taken for a
    clown,
A station chose, in middle of the town,
In TOY-SHOP large, and nigh unto a
    church,
In Fleetstreet did this lovely creature
    perch.

Although he is not like to owl or bat,
He's downy, smooth, and soft as any
    rat:
And tho' he is no bird of paradise,
Can do the lady's business in a trice:
He's often by'em so caress'd and
    fondl'd,
No child by them was e'er so dearly
    dandl'd,
Or e'er poor THING made use of or
    better handl'd.

The engine does come up so near to
    nature,

Can spout so pleasing, betwixt wind
and water,
warm milk, or any other liquid softer,
Slow as they please, or, if they please,
much faster.

In little time Monsieur came to be
known,
Then soon was visited by ev'ry one:
It was the darling of their great desire
To see our foreigner, in his attire;
As it's polite, to visit out of hand
A stranger new come from a foreign
land.

No sooner Monsieur grew to be of
fame,
But as soon was receiv'd by City Dame:
The serpent sooner did not beguile
Eve,
Than the kind sex blind SEIGNIOR did
receive.

They brought him quick to truckle to
their bow,
To feel what hidden treasures they'd
below:
The afterwards they taught him to
ascend
Towards a port, where pleasures did
portend:
When they had brought him so near
happiness,
They forc'd him in the summit of their
bliss;
And after they had tasted, made a
drudge
Worse than a waterman, who wears a
badge,
Or ticket-porter in the street that plies,

Burthen'd with loads, is in no worse
disguise,
Than to their lust he is a sacrifice.

By this time his good qualities were
known,
And much became belov'd by most of
'em:
A merchant's wife prevail'd on him to
sit,
His picture coveted, to please her wit.
So monsieur chose to be picted on
glass:
How you would laugh, to see how like
a Ta—e,
And ladies smile, as they did by it pass.
This greatly did explain their kind good
humour,
From the respect they paid unto his
honour;
For not a soul of them, as they past by,
But at the picture they wou'd cast an
eye.

Soon after this, he lodg'd in
merchant's house,
And did make friends between him
and his spouse:
He undertook the merchant's wife to
please,
Then the old doated fool liv'd at his
ease;
All that she wanted, was to please her
creature,
It was brimming full of her good
nature.
Our SEIGNIOR's duty was no sooner
done,
Than the lascivious heart of her he'd
won.
She boldly work'd him up unto an oil,

So did she make the creature slave and
    toil;
She wrought him till he was just out of
    breath,
And harrast SEIGNIOR almost unto
    death;
Until he was forc'd to choose a new
    place,
To alter somewhat of his slavish case.

Then he remov'd, to lodge with an old
    maid;
No sooner came, her virtue was
    betray'd:
So soon as he had popt but up his
    head,
Her modesty was vanish'd, and quite
    fled.
As soon as Monsieur had kiss'd
    wrinkl'd Nancy,
He so did tickle, and please Trulla's
    fancy,
That pleas'd her thoughts at the first
    very touch,
Her inclinations he'd gain'd very
    much:
Tire'd with old hagg, he went away by
    stealth,
He took his flight, and left her by
    herself.

Clear as Monsieur was, and free to
    range,
His tour he took towards the Great
    Exchange;
Ingratiated himself into the favour
Of milliners, by's complaisant
    behaviour:
He pitch'd his tent between two
    partners,

Indeed he took them not for to be
    whores;
But like two cows a playing in a field,
While the one rid, the other seem'd to
    yield:
This was itself complete
    encouragement,
To show what they'd be at, and their
    intent
Fully explain'd what it was that they
    meant.

One of these girls ty'd Monsieur to her
    middle,
To try if she the secret could unriddle:
She acted man, being in a merry mood,
Striving to please her partner as she
    cou'd;
And thus they took it in their turns to
    please
Their lustful inclinations to appease,
Until Monsieur was almost suffocated
With that, of all things, that at last he
    hated.
So did he leave these vile and lustful
    elves,
To run the frisk together by
    themselves.

Monsieur by chance came in a
    christening room,
Where he had like to have receiv'd his
    doom:
The midwife bellowing, open mouth'd
    she cry'd,
If you're encourag'd, villain, we're
    destroy'd:
The bedstaff took, and in her serious
    whim,
With all her force desig'd to fling at
    him.

The parson present, in this angry rage,
He interpos'd, her passion to assuage,
As likewise he did that of furious
    Nurse's
Whose mouth was open'd, nothing but
    for curses.
But all agreed to turn immediately
Poor SEIGNIOR out, as common
    enemy.
From hence Monsieur took moving to
    the court,
To see what pastime there was, or what
    sport:
So came he to the hand of lady's maid,
With whom some little time our
    Monsieur stay'd,
She like cade[27] lamb was pleas'd, with
    Monsieur play'd,
No sooner had she tasted of his favour,
But she embrac'd the sweetness of his
    savour;
To him alone she show'd her good
    behaviour.

By this time Monsieur having thus
    infus'd
His friendship in the maid, she
    introduc'd
Him to her kind mistress's first
    acquaintance,
As a fine thing of noted worth and
    sense:
So that the lady was to make a trial

Of Monsieur's skill, which was without
    denial
The best, most pleasing thing as e'er
    she felt,
Ever since she near to the court had
    dwelt.
If e'er you see a proud ambitious citt,[28]
And she pretend to triumph as a wit;
You may be sure SEIGNIOR is her
    friend,
On him alone she only does depend.

Or e'er you meet a proud and sconful
    maid,
And she but feign that virtue is her
    trade;
Then be assur'd, the jilt[29] is such a
    one,
Who shares of Seignior's smile, and
    not his frown,
And does make use of him to please
    her own:
Yet it's in women's nature to be civil,
If they're no instigated by the devil,
Or in the way, Monsieur he is the rival.
No doubt but this uncouth contriv'd
    new fashion
Was to destroy the end of the creation;
Like that foul sin which is as bad in
    men,
For which God did the eastern world
    condemn.

The Unaccountable Wife

Jane Barker learned Latin and medicine from her elder brother, and became proficient in herbal remdies. She suffered from blindness and breast cancer, but devoted herself to her religious faith, to writing (poems and novels), and to friends. She defended her spinsterhood alongside her deep and intense friendships. Galesia, the spinster heroine of the text, provides the story of a *ménage à trois*. The wife is well-born, her husband a soldier. Their relationship is disrupted by a female servant who changes places with the wife. The ambiguous sexual relationship that develops is, on another level, a social 'world turned upside down'. Emma Donoghue has read the tale as 'a veiled love story between two women whom the Master could not keep apart' (1993: 178); Janet Todd (1980: 326) sees the servant exploiting a sexually barren wife. The unsympathetic narrator nonetheless provides a sufficiently ambiguous story to permit 'unaccountable' readings. Text from Jane Barker's *A Patch-Work Screen for the Ladies; or, Love and Virtue Recommended . . .* (1723).

The Lady ... bad Galesia return to her story, of the gentleman that had married her kinswoman ... In short, married she was to the foresaid young man, whose person was truly handsome; and with part of her fortune he placed himself in the army, bestowed another part in furnishing her a house, and so lived very decently; and notwithstanding her indifferent person, he had children by her, though they did not live long. Thus they made a pretty handsome shift in the world, till a vile wretch, her servant, overturned all; as follows. This servant, whether she was a creature of her master's before she came to her mistress, is not known; but she became very fruitful, and had every year a child; pretending that she was privately married to an apprentice. Whether the wife knew the whole of the matter, or was imposed on, is uncertain; but which soever it was, she was extremely kind to this woman, to a degree unheard of; became a perfect slave to her, and, as if she was the servant, instead of the mistress, did all the household-work, made the bed, cleaned the house, washed the dishes; nay, farther than so, got up in the morning, scoured the irons, made the fire, &c. leaving this vile strumpet in bed with her husband; for they lay all three together every night. All this her friends knew, or at least suspected; but thought it complaisance, not choice in her; and that she considered her own imperfections, and deformity; and therefore, was willing to take no notice of her husband's fancy in the embraces of this woman her servant. But the sequel opens quite another scene: and now I come to that part of the story where he came to his mother. His business was, to desire her to come to his wife, and endeavour to persuade her to part with this woman ... In short, there my mother went; and there she found the servant sitting in a handsome velvet chair, dressed up in a very good laced linen, having clean gloves on her hands, and the wife washing the dishes. This sight put my mother into such a violent passion, that she had much ado to refrain from laying her hands on her. However, she vehemently chid the mistress; telling her, that she offended God, disgraced her family, scandalised her neighbours, and was a shame to woman-kind. All which she returned with virulent words; amongst other things, she stood buff in favour of that woman; saying, that she had been not only a faithful servant, but the best of friends, and those that desired to remove such a friend from her, deserved not the name of friends, neither did she desire they should come into her house: all which she uttered with such an air of vehemency, that there was no room left to doubt of the sincerity of her words; but that all proceeded from an interior thoroughly degenerated ... I went next day, hoping that a night's repose would calm the storm my mother's anger might have raised. But when I came I found it all the same: though I took her apart, and with the utmost mildness, persuaded her, and used the best reasons I could think on to enforce those persuasions, yet all was in vain; and she said, we all joined with her husband to make her miserable, by removing from her, the only friend she had in the world; and passionately swore by Him that made her, that if we combined to send the woman away, she would go with her ...

Long it was not, e'er Death made a true and substantial separation, by carrying the husband into the other world. Now was the time to make manifest, whether promises, flatteries or threatenings had made her act the foresaid scene: but it appeared all voluntary; for when he was dead, her friends and relations invited and persuaded her to leave that creature and her children, and come to live with them, suitable to her birth and education. But all in vain; she absolutely adhered to this woman and her children, to the last degree of folly; insomuch, that being reduced to poverty, she begged in the streets to support them. At last, some friend of her family told the Queen of the distressed way she was in; and in some degree, how it came to pass, that neither her dead husband nor her relations might be blameable. The Queen, with much goodness, told her friend, that if she would leave that woman, and go live with some relation, she would take care she should not want; and withal sent her five guineas, as an earnest of a monthly pension; but notwithstanding, this infatuated creature refused the Queen's favour, rather than part with this family: and so, for their support, begged in the streets, the remainder of her days.

Sure, said the Lady, this poor creature was under some spell or enchantment, or she could not have persisted, in so strange a manner, to oppose her husband, and all her nearest friends, and even her Sovereign ...

Letter from a Young Lady

A young lady writes of her addiction to masturbation, with herself and an associate. As a result she misses her periods and suffers from an extended clitoris, like a penis. The quack doctor warns of immoderate unnatural practices which may result in an unwanted change of sex. Text from *A Supplement to the Onania, or the heinous*

sin of self-pollution, and all its frightful consequences, in the two sexes, considered
(1725).

Just as this supplement, was as 'twere printed off, the following letter from a
young Lady, was left for me at the booksellers, which, for the particularity of the
case, and ingenuity of the writer, I thought I could do no less than make room for.

To the commendable Author of the ONANIA, Oct. 16, 1725,

SIR,

This Letter comes from a young female creature, but an old transgressor of the
practice of that filthy pleasure which you have so justly exploded and condemned,
in your ingenious book *Onania*, which I happily met with about 10 days ago: but
in all the cases therein enumerated, there is not one that is parallel to mine, which
as my welfare requires it, I must be obliged to relate, and is what I question, Sir,
whether you have ever once met with: nor could I tell it, though at the same time
I bless the opportunity, but that I am sure you no more know the writer of it, nor
ever will, than I know the author of *Onania*, or desire it. I began, sir, the folly at
11 years of age, was taught it by my mother's chambermaid, who lay with me from
that time all along until now, which is full seven years, and so intimate were we
in the sin, that we took the opportunities of committing it, and invented all the
ways we were capable of to heighten the titillation, and gratify our sinful lusts the
more. We, in short, pleasured one another, as well as ourselves, but whether by
the hard usage of my parts by her, or myself, or both, or whether from any thing
in nature more in my make, than is customary to the sex, I don't know, but for
above half a year past I have had a swelling that thrusts out from my body, as big,
and almost as hard, and as long or longer than my thumb, which inclines me to
excessive lustful desires, and from it there issues a moisture or slipperiness to that
degree that I am almost continually wet, and sometimes have such a forcing, as
if something of a large substance was coming from me, which greatly frightens
both me and my maid. She went to a midwife about it, but did not, she says, tell
her of our practice; the midwife said it was a bearing down of the womb, by
weakness, and told her what I should do, which I did, but to no purpose. Ever since
I have been so, I have not had the course of nature, have great pain in my back,
and my belly is swelled, am not near so strong as I was, my countenance much
paler, and appetite less. It has almost distracted me, and unfits me for my
learning, and am afraid I am so hurt, as that it cannot be remedied. O! that I
should be so wicked, I, who have had a much nobler education (and should know
better) than is common to most of my sex; that am versed in the classics, and
designed by my friends, who are very rich, for something above the common

station of my sex; I say, that I should so filthily debase myself, wrong my body, and, which is worse, my soul, is surprising even to myself. Had I read more the Bible, and less in *Martial, Juvenal, Ovid*,[30] &c. it had been better form, but those books Rochester,[31] and Plays, at first debauched my silly fancy. But I hope, as now, both myself and maid have, on consulting your curious discourse of *Self-Pollution*, abandon'd the practice, and resolved, through God's Grace, to commit it no more, we shall find pardon, and my infirm body, from your hands, good sir, relief. She ails nothing, is a strong wench of twenty-seven, myself of a tender make, and naturally inclined to be weakly, and but just turned of eighteen. I have with this, sent you a guinea fee, and desire your cordial advice, what I had best to do, and your opinion of my case, sealed up safe, directed to Mrs *E.N.* and I will send for it tomorrow morning, at the bookseller's where this is left; and, sir, I must needs desire you to send me this letter back, that I may have the satisfaction of committing it to the flames myself. According to your answer, you shall hear further from,

SIR,

Your ever obliged, and

Most obedient humble Servant,

E.N.

NOT, sir, but you may copy my letter first, and if you think worthwhile, to print it also in your next edition, as a caution to others; but would not that my hand be seen by any besides your self, the circumstances of the relation, so as not to be know 'tis me, I have taken care of and guarded against.

THIS young lady's case, though the height of her lust, and force and frequency of abusing herself, and probably the unnatural proponderance of the part, is no more, according to the account she gives, than a relaxation of the *Clitoris*, a thing common to many of the sex, both in the single and married, who are vigorous and lustful, and have given up themselves to the practice of *Self-Pollution* for any time. In some women it extends itself, and is enlarged when inflated to the exact likeness and size of a human *Penis* erect, except that it has no perforation (though it really looks, by the natural impression at the end, as if there was a passage) nor is altogether so long, but yet it erects and falls as that does, in proportion to the venereal desire or inclination of the woman. I have had in my time one or two under this circumstance, by the same practice, for cure, who upon their living afterwards chaste, and using some astringent foments, and a few internals, to regulate the inordinate and enraged venereal desires, have been brought to rights, and the parts restored to their pristine, natural state and condition. It was the like case of this lady's, that gave rise to the report of two *Nuns* at *Rome*, having changed their sex, and which had made such a noise in that city, that the Pope, upon hearing of it, gave orders for their being inspected by some cardinals. Dr Carr, in his medicinal epistles, translated by Dr Quincy, has in his answer to a letter sent him by a divine, upon the subject of it, wrote his opinion at large, which as it may confirm mine, in relation to the aforesaid lady's case, and be of some use both to practitioners and patients, I shall not think much to transcribe it, and give it to the reader, verbatim. It is his 6th Epistle, entitled, *Concerning two nuns reported to have changed their sex.*

The Toast

An extended attack on women as Sapphic monsters, demonstrating just how much was known about the topic; the poem provides us with a useful range of contemporary nomenclatures. Text from *The Toast. An Heroick Poem in four books, written originally in Latin, by Frederick Scheffer: now done into English, and illustrated with notes and observations, by Peregrin O'Donald Esq ... (1736).*

Myra, or Mira,[32] who is the heroine of the poem, was descended from a good family among the Coritani.[33] She was a woman of extraordinary stature, and of a vigour and strength of body superior to most of her contemporaries. 'Tis said that at eighteen years of age, she was a match for Milo; and, like that famous wrestler, could carry a full grown bull. Though I am apt to believe this is not to be understood literally ... Nor was our noble matron debilitated by age, or her concupiscible appetite decayed, though arrived to her grand climacteric; and she had so artfully repaired the ruins which the malice of time had made in her outward form, that *Apollo* himself was deceived by her first appearance; as he had been by the shining character which one of his favourite bards had bestowed on her. This mistake or misinformation, and the incidents which follow upon it, furnish the chief matter of Mr *Scheffer*'s Poem. For the God being rallied for toasting the old Dame, and thereupon making a nearer inspection, he discovered all the defects of her person, and the various arts which she used to disguise them: and examining into her conduct and constitution, and the frame and temper of her mind, he plainly perceived, that she had been guilty of all kind of pollutions; that, unsated by her male gallants, she daily practised that unnatural act the Spaniards call *Donna con Donna*.[34] His Godship was so ashamed and incensed to be thus disappointed, that in revenge he published the famous edict, which our author recites in his third book; where among other prohibitions, our old matron was for the future interdicted all commerce with men.

Thus dismiss'd the male gallants,
in-crawl'd her own *Imp*

In a scaly small body, contors'd like a
shrimp.

In a rapture she stroak'd it, and gave it
the teat,

By the suction to raise sympathetical
heat.

Then by *Hecate* she swore, *she was sated
with men;*

Sung a wanton *Sapphic*, and strok'd it
agen;

And agen – and then thrice she erected
her rod:

(For the numbers in magic must
always be odd.)

See the force of her spells mighty's
surpass,

And the Beldams, which made
Apuleius and Ass!

See a reptile transform'd to a shape
near the human,

And the imp, that erst enter'd,
resemble a woman!

Not a woman – like those, which the
Mussulmen use,

Or the grandees of *Britain* for
mistresses chuse:

The indelible mark, on her forehead
impress'd,

God's revenge, and old *Shylock*'s curs'd
lineage confess'd;

With the locks of a negress half
mingled with grey,

And a carcase ill-moulded of dirty red
clay;

Clammy, livid, cold lips, with a crooked
long nose;

And a skin full of spots from her head
to her toes.

Nor a daughter of *Eve* has a body so
foul;

Nor has *Envy* herself so envenom'd a
soul.

But to *Myra* most dear! nor so fair in
her sight,

Was *Anacthon* or *Cydno*[35] thus form'd
for delight:

O ma Vie, ma Femme! What a shape,
and a face!

Then impatient she rush'd to a closer
embrace.

Lest the rest be untold! – And thus
even forbear,

Lest thy numbers, O Scheffer, offend
the chaste fair.

And do thou, O my *Clara*, this freedom
excuse;

Since a vengeance so just has created
the muse;

Or a passion more noble. I hang out
my lights,

To direct foreign sailors in dreary long
nights:

I expose to their ken (and dear-bought
was my wit)

Both the pools, which ingulph'd me,
and the rocks, where I split.

When a pair of foul Tribads I rudely
unveil,

'Tis *Charybdis* I show you, 'tis *Scylla*'s
dog-tail . . .

Sappho was a famous Tribade, as appears by the testimonies of all the old poets,
but particularly from that beautiful ode (addressed to one of the ladies, with whom
she was in love) which *Longinus* has preserved, and which has ever been so highly

esteemed by all the critics. But though she had acquired so much glory by her verses, as to be styled the tenth muse, yet she acknowledges, that her love of the *Lesbian* women had destroyed her reputation ... As amorous and vicious as the Greeks were, yet they accounted this a most infamous passion. And there seems to have been a peculiar act of justice in the punishment of Sappho, who killed herself at last for the love of a man.

Travels into Turkey

Text from *Travels into Turkey: containing the most accurate account of the Turks, and neighbouring nations, their manners, customs, religion, superstition, policy, riches, coins, &c. The whole being a series of remarkable observations and events, interspers'd with great variety of entertaining incidents, never before printed. Translated from the original Latin of the learned A.G. Busbequius ... (1744).*

IT happened one time, that at the public baths for women, an old woman fell in love, with a girl, the daughter of a poor man, a citizen of Constantinople; and, when neither by wooing nor flattering her, she could obtain that of her which her mad affection aimed at, she attempted to perform an exploit, almost incredible; she feigned herself to be a man, changed her habit, hired an house near the maid's father, and pretended he was one of the Chiauxes of the Grand Seignior; and thus, by reason of his neighbourhood, she insinuated herself into the man's acquaintance, and after some time, acquaints him with the desire of his daughter. In short, he being a man in such a prosperous condition, the matter was agreed on, a portion was settled, such as they were able to give, and a day appointed for the marriage; when the ceremonies were over, and this doughty bridegroom went into the bride-chamber to his spouse; and after some discourse, and plucking off her headgear, she was found to be a woman. Whereupon the maid runs out, and calls up her parents, who soon found that they had married her, not to a *Man*, but a *Woman*: whereupon, they carried the supposed man, the next day, to the General of the *Janizaries*, who, in the absence of the *Grand Seignior*, was Governor of the city. When she was brought before him, he chide her soundly for her beastly love; what, says he, are you not ashamed, an old Beldam[36] as you are, to attempt so notorious a bestiality, and so filthy a fact?

AWAY, sir, says she! You do not know the force of love, and god grant you never may. At this absurd reply, the governor could scarce forbear laughter, but commanded her, presently, to be packed away and drowned in the deep; such was the unfortunate issue of her wild amours. For you must know, that the *Turks* make no noise when *secret* offences are committed by them, that they may not open the mouths of scandal and reproach; but *open* and *manifest* ones they punish most severely.

The Progress of Nature

Constrained by a life at boarding school, the narrator argues that our desires are natural, no matter what their object, or direction. Dreaming of an ideal man, she satisfies herself in the masturbatory pleasures that her own body affords her. Text from *The Progress of nature: exemplified in the life and surprizing adventures of Roger Lovejoy, Esq; natural son of the right reverend prelate, sometime deceased ... (1744)[37]*

I will not determine, said she, whether they are happy, or unhappy, whose constitutions are so framed, as they can easily run counter to nature, and glory in opposing her most exquisite sensations; but born with desires as we are, I am persuaded no perfect being is able to resist them. In vain they dogmatize, 'tis to pleasure we offer the first fruits of our inclinations. Our fears, indeed, may restrain us, but we enjoy it over and over in our wishes, which is equivalent by the law. The old exclaim against it, because they are past the sensibility of it; and the young will join them in decrying it, from a coldness of constitution. Now what is this coldness of constitution, but an imperfection in nature? and yet this same imperfection, without one other good quality, shall be called by the venerable name of virtue. What can be more chimerical? Can God make it criminal in a poor woman of a warm complexion, that she seeks to relieve herself in certain emergencies, when she is prompted by propensities, that were ordained invincible, and which are the very first principles of man's existence? A person has an appetite, another has not; it is neither a crime in him that has, nor in him that has not: 'tis only where you abuse nature, that you sin against her. We did not make ourselves: is it our fault, therefore, if we have desires? Is it our fault if we are in love, and occasion has not yet thrown us husbands in our way? 'Tis natural to quench a flame that devours us; and those are rather criminals against nature, who refuse to obey her soft dictates, than those who cheerfully comply with them.

You may suppose, Poll, continued she, that with such dispositions as these, a boarding school life could not be very agreeable to me. I was then at Salisbury. The constraint I was under, soon produced an utter distaste in me, arising from a deprivation of something, which, upon examination, I found to be that of a more intimate intercourse with the world. How did I wish myself enlarged from what I now looked upon as a state of slavery! But, why all these wishes? demanded I. Upon a nicer enquiry still, I perceived that man was at the bottom of them. And what is this same creature, man, pursued I. Why is he the eternal object of my thoughts by day, and dreams by night? And what is the reason my heart is always so in a flutter at the sight of one? Is it because he has a handsomer face than another? No, cried I, that can't be the sole reason; his having more or less charms, I find, excites only more or less emotions. This agitation of the heart at his presence, must certainly be independent of the accidents of beauty and ugliness, youth or age, since there's our old French Master, argued I, as frightful a mortal as ever nature formed, yet even he, all hideous as he is, had the same effect on me. Hence I concluded, that it must needs be the single quality of man, that produced this sensation; but for what end it was produced, remained a point I could not clear up, with all the reasoning I was mistress of. I felt the reason every moment in my heart, without being able to explain it. How did I struggle to break the bonds of ignorance, that fettered my understanding! Month after month, how did I give myself up to my reflections! But alas! still were my efforts fruitless. At last, thought I, though I can't discover for what end this sensation is produced in me, possibly I may gather some light, by a proper examination of the sensation itself.

Accordingly, one Sunday morning, it was in the month of May, the sun was about two hours high, darting into my chamber his animating beams, the sparrow was chirping, the linnet warbling, the raven kawing, the bells of the cathedral were ringing sweet changes, when, as I lay in bed, absorbed in my enquiries, I suddenly threw off the bed-clothes, and with curious eye, and feverish pulse, I surveyed every part of my extended body. My imagination all inflamed, presently brought to my idea, that charming creature, man, who seemed rather an angel than a man, and whom, fighting, I embraced a thousand times. Now it was I endured the most pungent inquietudes, yet without knowing how to assuage them. My roving hand a moment rested on the part most aggrieved, raging with a violent inflammation all around; but recollecting all the sage admonitions I had heard against such positions, I hastily withdrew it away. Resuming courage, I just put the tip of my finger upon it, but withdrew it away as before. Then I cautiously covered it with the hollow of my hand; but by often pressing it, the sensation at last was too powerful to be restrained by precept: with an intrepidity, bordering on rashness, I forced myself a passage, and the hurt which I did myself was swallowed up in the pleasure I felt; which, indeed, was so exquisite, that I thought I was going to expire; and I came to myself only with fresh inclinations to repeat the dear experiment, which I did as often as my strength would permit me.

I was transported with the discovery I had made, nor did I fail to amuse myself in this manner every night and morning during my stay at the boarding school. I let some other young misses into the secret, as I have done you, Poll, and they owned their obligations, as you have done to me. But see, Poll, continued she, see how one ray of knowledge begets another! Having found out the true road of pleasure, I went on from conclusion to conclusion, setting it down as a mathematical demonstration, that since I had procured to myself so many delicious moments by myself, doubtless the men must have something about them, with which they were able to afford us a much greater pleasure. Upon this, I was agitateed with a most violent desire to see the original of a thing, of which the copy had afforded me so much delight. Day after day I eagerly sought every occasion to gratify it: going to church, or a walking, wherever I went, my eyes were directed to every wall, to every corner, but still in vain: that was a satisfaction Salisbury was not to indulge me in.

A Spy on Mother Midnight

In a letter to his friend Jack, Mr F— explains how he cross-dressed in order to seduce Miss Maria. Comically, and subversively, the tale plays on the competition between a penis and the counterfeiting dildo. The end of the story demonstrates the inevitable victory of heterosexuality, but this does not fully erase all the transgressive ambiguities in the text. From A Spy on Mother Midnight: or, the Templar Metamorphos'd (1748).

Dear Jack,
I met the lovely sorceress at a country church the last time I was upon this circuit: she appeared so charming, so young, tempting and languishing, during all the time of a tedious dull sermon, that I lost my heart before the parson had split his text into half his unmeaning distinctions. I was quite lost in admiration, before I was aware of the danger, and paid my devotions to this she saint in inward ejaculations, with greater zeal and fervency than ever I did to anything else in my life ...

I passed the remaining part of the service in a kind of adoring rapture, flattering myself, that I should find my charmer as susceptible of the amorous flame as myself; for tho' I had treated her in my own mind as a divinity, yet I was resolved to approach her as if made of flesh and blood, and should have been most damnably vexed to have found her immaterial. But how transitory is all human joy! and how fleeting every shadow of human happiness! I had no sooner made inquiry who my mistress was, than I found her, by her character, as inaccessible as a seraphim, and that I might expect to thaw the frozen ocean as soon as soften, or make any warm impression upon her obdurate heart. She had baffled all the *Beaux Esprits* of the county, and had more slaves at her nod than the grand *Seignor* has in his galleys. In a word, my friend, my mistress is nothing less than a mere

Prude: she pretends to hate everything that's male, and is ready to swoon at the least hint that borders on the subject of procreation. She is delighted with nothing that's human, but pretends her mind is entirely devoted to heaven and the intellectual joys of another world . . .

In this situation I left my affairs when I came last to town, in the hands of a trusty female agent, who undertook to bribe the garrison, or undermine the out-works by sap and cunning. My negotiator, after three or four months' vain endeavours in my behalf, sent me word, two days before I left town, that my prude was just gone to a village about a dozen miles from her father's house, to be present at the inlying of an aunt's daughter, who kept the Crown and Anchor inn at B—, where she supposed she might stay some weeks; and hinted, that such a place might afford a better opportunity of prosecuting my scheme, than any hitherto had occurred, if I would take the trouble of passing a night or two there, as if by accident.

Upon receiving this intelligence a crotchet[38] stuck into my head, to attack my fair enemy by stratagem and masked batteries: I knew, by her complexion, she was no constitutional enemy to the joys of love; a moist palm, a prominent nose, and a leering eye, for all its devout aspect, were all symptoms which promised me friends within the fort, if I could give them an opportunity to exert themselves, in spite of the out-works of pride, religion, and the discipline of education and custom. Therefore to lull these ever-watchful dragons asleep, like *Jove*, I resolved on a metamorphosis, but it was neither into bulls nor birds, but it was into something more deceiving than all these, that of a woman; for by woman, woman's best betrayed.

You know I have got a tolerable smug face of my own, with very little hair upon my chin, and as I'm but a little dapper fellow, I assure you, I made no disagreeable figure in petticoats. I chose for my dress a blue riding habit of my sister Nancy's, which fitted me exactly, hat, a feather, and periwig, supplied the place of linen, and if I had anything masculine remaining in my impudent countenance, you know the habit was made answerable for it, and not I.

Thus, in an instant, your friend Dick was changed into a damsel, with all the ease imaginable; but I had still something about me, which declared an enmity to petticoats, and could not bear to be under them, without standing up in support of the royal prerogative of breeches. In short, the very idea of a petticoat, especially the inside of one, put that companion of mine into a mighty fume, and it was some time before I could persuade him that, at present, it was there, and his business to lie down.

Being myself equipped, I, and an old acquaintance of the female sex, who passed as my maid, (though, God knows, poor girl, I believe she could not remember when she was one) took seats in the Stage for B—.

Our journey was very entertaining, and a journal of it would certainly divert you, as our company consisted of a celebrated Methodist Preacher, a Quaker girl, a strolling player, and the very *Mother Midnight* who was to officiate at the Inn I was bound for; but have not time at present for that part ... [He records the shocking conversation of several old women.]

Know then, that my fair mistress made a proposal to me to be her bedfellow for the remainder of the night, or rather morning, for it was now about six o'clock. My heart beat the alarm at the motion, which I immediately closed in with, trusting to fortune to direct me in my future proceedings.

We were conducted to a chamber, from which I dismissed the maid, and locked the door, resolving to have no interruption. Miss Maria begun to undress, and discovered charms which would have subdued an anchorite, and made him break his vow of celibacy: I was in so great a perturbation of spirits, that I had not a word to utter; Maria begun the conversation, with well, miss, these are strange old women; I thought their clacks would never have done. The devil take them and their discourse, they have raised such a combustion within me, that if Mr F— (meaning your humble Servant) was here, I'm afraid he would find this the critical minute: if he was, replied I, with some hesitation, I'm afraid you would change your mind, and get into your very virtuous attitudes again. No, says she, I'm afraid I should not; but hang him, let's raise no more devils, but rather think of some way to lay those already conjured up: at these words, while she was rummaging in a dressing-box for some night cloaths, I cast my eyes on the image of manhood, an ivory substitute of virility, which astonished me prodigiously. I had often heard of such things, but little expected to find one in the hands of so young a creature, so complete a prude, and a country girl too. The sight of it raised a thousand odd emotions in my breast at once; but this she perceived not, and I quickly recovering my surprise, it immediately struck into my head, that this little incident might not a little facilitate my design. I snatched up the alluring implement, and laughing, said; Come, Courage Maria, here is at least some kind of comfort; now, if you get to bed quickly, I shall use this so artfully, that you shall not know the difference 'twixt me and Mr— (naming myself) nay, I'll be hanged, if *Mother Midnight* herself may not be deceived by good management, for all her knowledge in manhood. Miss Maria seemed at first a little changed at my discovering her instrument; however, seeing that I was not disconcerted, she laughed it off; but we soon came to so good an understanding as to its use, that she expressed great satisfaction at the promise I made her, and told me, she would call me Mr— to help the better to carry the deceit. Come then, my dear, says I, make haste to bed, lest you change your mind; for as I am to personate your lover, I'm afraid you intend to jilt me. No, no, my dear, replied she, I'll be true to myself this once, and, by my dispatch, show you the respect I have even for the representative of Mr F—;

with that she hastily got into bed. I put out the candle and soon followed, clasped her fast in my arms, and scarce permitted her to draw breath, before she might know the difference between Mr F— and a poor passive implement. 'Bless me!' says she, 'What!' She had not power to ask the question, but was immediately convinced what sort of a bedfellow she had got. Great was her confusion, but not so great as to spoil our sport; she had gone too far to recede. However we soon found leisure to come to an explanation of the mystery. She would have upbraided me for deceiving her, but I effectually silenced her, by observing that she had no reason to complain, since I had furnished her with the means of gratifying those inclinations she could not now conceal, in a manner, I thought, less sinful, and indisputably more natural, than I presumed she heretofore had recourse to. In short, it was, as you may suppose, all circumstances considered, no difficult matter to gain her pardon. For what with her consciousness that she had betrayed her whole soul to me, and what with the superior pleasure I gave her, in comparison with what she had been used to reap from her ivory substitute, she at length frankly owned, that I was a much more agreeable bedfellow, as Mr F—, than as Miss Polly.

I had more to add, but as my letter is extended to so enormous a length, and as I have carried you through this last scene, which is better imagined than described, I shall refer the further particulars of this amour till another opportunity offers; only I must acquaint you, that I am still in petticoats, and have had more than one affair with the females of this part of the world; nay, and have done some execution among those of my own sex.

The History of the Human Heart

The tale records at this point the early history of the hero, Camillo, whose attraction to the vulva is linked back to his mother's obsession with her own anatomy. Randolph Trumbach (Epstein and Straub 1991: 118) argues that the author follows the belief that pregnant women were subject to unnatural longings and that they might therefore seek out other women. Pregnant women were certainly attributed an irregular imagination but Emma Donoghue (1993: 202) points out that this is the only example of a *pregnant* woman seeeking a same-sex relationship. Text from *The History of the Human Heart: or, the Adventures of a Young Gentleman* (1749).

Camillo chanced to be called some days from home and Florinda made a young lady, a kinswoman of hers, her bedfellow for that time. This lady was young and frolicksome, and one night, when undressed for going to bed, playing some wanton tricks to make Florinda laugh, she discovered a certain promontory about her, more naturally coveted by a man than a woman but as the latter have sometimes very strange longings in their pregnancy, Florinda, casting her eyes on that seldom seen spot, was seized with an irresistable desire to taste it. She endeavoured to check the thought as soon as conceived, but in vain, the more she strove to banish the unnatural idea, the more it haunted her imagination. She grew very restless, and communicated her anxiety to the unborn infant, who wished and longed, it knew not for what, but still was sensible something was wanting to remove its uneasiness, little knowing at the time that what was so much its own and its mother's wishes, was destined for purposes much different from what its present notion of things could suggest. Florinda bore a great deal of pain, and grew so much out of order, that her life began to be in danger; the husband came home, and tried all means in his power to pick the secret out of his wife, what it was she longed for: for by the symptoms the physicians guessed that to be the disease. But she, ashamed of her unnatural appetite, and knowing it impossible to be gratified, even if she revealed it, kept an obstinate silence: for, though she had heard of men who had parted with a slice of their buttocks to satisfy a loved wife's longing, yet she could not imagine her young friend would part with a bit from from a part so sensible, to gratify her capricious taste; so she languished for some time, and at last, by the help of some old woman's receipt, became pretty well again.

Memoirs of a Woman of Pleasure

John Cleland's novel first appeared in 1748–9 in two volumes. It was also known as *Fanny Hill*. See David Foxon (1963a: 52–63). The view that prostitutes did not enjoy their sexual encounters is largely reversed in Cleland's work. Fanny explores her body with the assistance of a female; in the second extract she watches a man and woman making love, and reflects upon it, concluding with a preference for 'solid' heterosexuality, rather than the 'shadow' of sex between women. For other depictions of prostitutes see texts such as *The Whore's Rhetorick* and Eliza Heywood's *Fantomina; or, Love in a Maze* (1724). Text from *Memoirs of a Woman of Pleasure* (1749). See Mengay (1992).

To slip over minutes of no importance to the main of my story, I pass the interval to bedtime, in which I was more and more pleased with the views that opened to me of an easy service under these good people: and after supper, being showed up to bed, Miss Phoebe, who observed a kind of modest reluctance in me to strip, and go to bed in my shift before her, now the maid was withdrawn, came up to me, and beginning with unpinning my handkerchief, and gown, soon encouraged me to go on with undressing myself, and, still blushing at now seeing myself naked to my shift, I hurried to get under the bed-clothes, out of sight. Phoebe laughed, and was not long before she placed herself by my side. She was about five and twenty, by her own most suspicious account, in which, according to all appearances, she must have sunk at least ten good years, allowance too being made for the havoc which a long course of hacney-ship, and hot-waters, must have made of her constitution and which had already brought on, upon the spur, that stale stage, in which those of her profession are reduced to think of *showing* company, instead of *seeking* it.

No sooner then was this precious substitute of my mistress's lain down, but she, who was never out of her way when any occasion of lewdness presented itself, turned to me, embraced, and kissed me with great eagerness. This was not new, this was odd; but imputing it to nothing but pure kindness, which, for ought I knew, it might be the London way to express in that manner, I was determined not to be behind-hand with her, and returned her the kiss and embrace, with all the fervour that perfect innocence knew.

Encouraged by this, her hands became extremely free, and wandered over my whole body, with touches, squeezes, pressures, that rather warmed and surprised me with their novelty, than they either shocked or alarmed me.

The flattering praises she intermingled with these invasions, contributed also not a little to bribe my passiveness, and knowing no ill, I feared none; especially from one who had prevented all doubt of her womanhood, by conducting my hands to a pair of breasts that hung loosely down, in a size and volume that full sufficiently distinguished her sex, to me at least, who had never made any other comparison.

I lay then all tame and passive as she could wish, whilst her freedom, raised no other emotion but those of a strange, and till then unfelt pleasure: every part of me was open, and exposed to the licentious courses of her hands, which like a lambent fire ran over my whole body, and thawed all coldness as they went.

My breasts, if it is not too bold a figure to call so, two hard, firm, rising hillocs, that just began to show themselves, or signify any thing to the touch, employed and amused her hands a while, till slipping down lower, over a smooth track, she could just feel the soft silky down that had but a few months before put forth, and garnished the mount-pleasant of those parts, and promised to spread a grateful shelter over the sweet seat of the most exquisite sensation, and which had been, till that instant, the seat of the most insensible innocence. Her fingers played and strove to twine in the young tendrils of that moss which nature has contrived at once for use and ornament.

But not contented with these outer-posts, she now attempts the main-spot, and began to twitch, to insinuate, and at length to force an introduction of a finger into the quick itself, in such a manner, that had she not proceeded by insensible gradations, that enflamed me beyond the power of modesty to oppose its resistance to their progress, I should have jumped out of bed, and cried out for help against such strange assaults.

Instead of which, her lascivious touches had lighted up a new fire that wantoned through all my veins, but fixed with violence in that center appointed them by nature, where the first strange hands were now busied in feeling, squeezing, compressing the lips, then opening them again, with a finger between, till an Oh! expressed her hurting me, where the narrowness of the unbroken passage refused it entrance to any depth.

In the mean time the extension of my limbs, languid stretchings, sighs, short heavings, all conspired to assure that experienced wanton, that I was more pleased than offended at her proceedings, which seasoned with repeated kisses and exclamations, such as 'Oh! what a charming creature thou art! – what a happy man will he be that first makes a woman of you! – Oh! that I were a man for your sake – !' with the like broken expressions, interrupted by kisses as fierce and salacious as ever I received from the other sex.

For my part, I was transported, confused, out of myself: feelings so new were too much for me; my heated and alarmed senses were in a tumult that robbed me of all liberty of thought; tears of pleasure gushed from my eyes, and somewhat assuaged the fire that raged all over me.

Phoebe herself, the hackneyed, thorough-bred Phoebe, to whom all modes and devices of pleasure were known and familiar, found, it seems, in this exercise of her art to break young girls, the gratification of one of those arbitrary tastes, for which there is no accounting: not that she hated men, or did not even prefer them to her own sex; but when she met with such occasions as this was, a satiety of enjoyments in the common road, perhaps too a secret byass, inclined her to make the most of pleasure, where-ever she could find it, without distinction of sexes. In this view, now well assured that she had, by her touches, sufficiently inflamed me for her purpose, she rolled down the bed-clothes gently, and I saw myself stretched naked, my shift being turned up to my neck, whilst I had no power or sense to oppose it; even my glowing blushes expressed more desire than modesty, whilst the candle left, to be sure not undesignedly, burning, threw a full light on my whole body.

'No! (says Phoebe) you must not, my sweet girl, think to hide all these treasures from me, my sight must be feasted as well as my touch – I must devour with my eyes this springing *bosom* – suffer me to kiss it – I have not seen it enough – let me kiss it once more – what firm, smooth, white flesh is here – how delicately shaped! – then this delicious down! Oh! let me view the small, dear, tender cleft! – this is too much, I cannot bear it, I must, I must'. Here she took my hand, and, in a transport, carried it where you will easily guess; but what a difference in the state of the same thing! – a spreading thicket of bushy curls marked the full-grown complete woman: then the cavity, to which she guided my hand, easily received it, and as soon as she felt it within her, she moved to and fro, with so rapid a friction, that I presently withdrew it, wet and clammy, when instantly Phoebe grew more composed, after two or three sighs, and heart-fetched Ohs! and giving me a kiss, that seemed to exhale her soul through her lips, she replaced the bed-clothes over us.

What pleasures she had found I will not say; but this I know, that the first sparks of kindling nature, the first ideas of pollution, were caught by me that night, and that the acquaintance and communication with the bad of our own sex, is often as fatal to innocence, as all the seductions of the other: but to go on: – when Phoebe was restored to that calm, which I was far from the enjoyment of myself, she artfully sounded me on all the points necessary to govern the designs of my virtuous mistress on me, and by my answers, drawn from pure undissembled nature, she had no reason to promise herself all imaginable success, so far as it depended on my ignorance, easiness, and warmth of constitution.

After a sufficient length of dialogue, my bed-fellow left me to my rest, and I fell asleep, through pure weariness, from the violent emotions I had been led into, when nature (which had been too warmly stirred, and fermented to subside without allaying by some means or other) relieved me by one of those luscious dreams, the transports of which are scarce inferior to those of waking, real action.

When he had finished his stroke, and got from off her, she lay still without the least motion, breathless, as it should seem, with pleasure. He replaced her again breadthwise on the couch, unable to sit up, with her thighs open, between which I could observe a kind of white liquid, like froth, hanging about the outward lips of that recent opened wound, which now glowed with a deeper red. Presently she gets up, and throwing her arms round him, seemed far from undelighted with the trial he had put her to, to judge at least by the fondness with which she eyed, and hung upon him.

For my part, I will not pretend to describe what I felt all over me, during this scene; but from that instant, adieu all fears of what man could do unto me; they were now changed into such ardent desires, such ungovernable longings, that I could have pulled the first of that sex that should present himself, by the sleeve, and offered him the bauble, which I now imagined the loss of would be a gain I could not too soon procure myself.

Phoebe, who had more experience, and to whom such sights were not so new, could not however be unmoved at so warm a scene; and drawing me away softly from the peep-hole, for fear of being over-heard, guided me as near the door as possible; all passive, and obedient to her least signals.

Here was no room either to sit, or lie, but making me stand with my back towards the door, she lifted up my petticoats, and with her busy fingers fell to visit, and explore that part of me, where now the heat, and irritations were so violent, that I was perfectly sick and ready to die with desire: that the bare touch of her finger in that critical place, had the effect of fire to a train, and her hand instantly made her sensible to what a pitch I was wound up, and melted by the sight she had thus procured me: satisfied then with her success, in allaying a heat that would have made me impatient of seeing the continuation of transactions between our amorous couple, she brought me again to the crevice, so favourable to our curiosity.

For me, I could bear to see no more: I was so overcome, so inflamed at this second part of the same play, that, mad with intolerable desire, I hugged, I clasped Phoebe, as if she had had wherewithal to relieve me: pleased however with, and pitying the taking she could feel me in, she drew me towards the door and opening it as softly as she could, we both got off undiscovered, and she reconducted me to my own room, where unable to keep my legs, in the agitation, I was in, I instantly threw myself down on the bed, where I lay transported, though ashamed at what I felt.

Phoebe lay down by me, and asked me archly, if now that I had seen the enemy, and fully considered him, I was still afraid of him? Or did I think I could venture to come on to a close engagement with him? To all which not a word on my side: I sighed, and could scarce breath: she takes hold of my hand, and having rolled up her own petticoats, forced it half-strivingly towards those parts, where now grown more knowing, I missed the main object of my wishes; and finding not even the shadow of what I wanted, where every thing was so flat! or so hollow! In the vexation I was in at it, I should have withdrawn my hand, but for fear of disobliging her. Abandoning it the entirely to her management, she made use of it as she thought proper, to procure herself rather the shadow than the substance of any pleasure. For my part, I now pined for more solid food, and promised tacitly to myself that I would not be put off much longer with this foolery from woman to woman ...

Tonzenie

The extract includes a section from the preface to *A New Atalantis* followed by the sexual awakening of Tonzenie with the assistance of her French servant.[39] Text from *A New Atalantis*, for the Year one thousand and seven hundred and fifty-eight (second

edition, 1758). See also *A Spy on Mother Midnight* (1748) and Donoghue (1993: 206–12).

To all cynical readers, who, at the same time, that they cannot help chuckling and wriggling themselves about, as if they were seated on cow-itch, shall say, *cui bono?* where is the use of this book? What advantage can it be productive of to society? Will it not rather be prejudicial to such of the youth of both sexes, into whose hands it may fall, by inflaming their tender minds with premature desires of pledging each other in the circean cup of pleasure?

We grant the charge; stand impleaded: and offer the following defence.

As men of morality, we have for a long time been highly displeased at the illicit pleasures *a posteriori*;[40] which are not only unnatural, but also inconsequential. While from those *a priori*, the only genuine source of pleasures, all laudable effects are derived for the support and ornament of society.

The curse of barrenness is pronounced against the former; but the latter is the very cornucopia of the human species. Can therefore, in so depraved an age as ours is, a too early admiration of that productive and elegant system, be infused into the minds of young people, that they may apply early to a proper cultivation of it? Because those, who, while young, are initiated in the right path; in their advancing years, will never wish to deviate or risk themselves in ways of difficult access ...

The tender fibres of Tonzenie, while yet unborn, were so strongly impregnated with a salacious fluid, that from the moment of her birth, it was with the greatest difficulty the nurse could hinder her from separating her legs, and indecently agitating her little body, which put some persons of quality (who were witnesses to the infant's immodest wriggling) in mind of the sarcastic French epitaph ... which may be thus rendered in English.

Lascivious Anna lies within her tomb,
Who whilst a foetus in her mother's
   womb,
Had so well fix'd her source of fond
   desire,
That there she fornicated with her fire.

On all occasions young Tonzenie betrayed strong indications of a most lustful constitution, while in the nursery she used to put her male and female babies one on top of the other, and shake them violently together.

When a little more advanced in years, she was from time to time admitted to sit a while in company with the grave matrons, as soon as old lick-stink, a pug dog,[41] who had sipped up many a lady's privacy, was got upon the table, and while there panting, puffing, and ogling his intimates with eyes of grave lechery, his long red indelicacy used so spontaneously to unsheath itself; the sober dames would immediately incline their heads another way, and seeing, not seem to see, the pleasing remembrancer.

Young Tonzenie, impelled by instinct, and to ease the itching of her fingers, immediately fell a tickling it: pug grinned. The ladies tittered and whispered to each other, 'a rare girl i'faith, mother's own daughter.'

As soon as she was permitted to pay visits, she procured, pimped for, and carried with her to and fro in her chair, all the male and female dogs belonging to her acquaintance, that procreation might thrive; nay, she would scrupulously preside over, and assist until the consummation of each act, that no unhallowed interruption might happen.

One day in the country, as she, for the first time, beheld a bull tup a heifer, the impetuosity of his irruption filled her with such a sudden transport of sympathising joy, that she swooned in the arms of her attendants; nor was the pleasing image effaced from her memory, till about a month after the view of a large gifted stallion, who triumphantly forced his way into the conclave of his beloved, so fired her, that unable to restrain herself, and agitated like the Pythian priestess, she cried aloud, 'Good Gods! why am not I a mare?'

Having soon after reached her teens, and by means of her chamber-maid got a translation of Ovid's Art of Love, Rochester's works, and the Memoirs of a Woman of Pleasure, all her doubts about her inward feelings vanished; she was convinced what use she was designed for, and made acquainted with the canal thro' which it was to be admitted; which, with her new-disciplined fingers, she used so frequently to explore: whose capacity and wants increasing daily, one of the middle-sized dildo-tribe was procured for her private amusement; through it her French maid, well skilled in such practices, would in the moment of rapture, dart a warm injection, sometimes artfully gird it to her loins, and act the man with her young mistress, who grown too sensible of the inefficacy of all such weak representations, was determined to enjoy the essence ere long.

Catherine Vizzani

A tale of cross-dressing and sexual exploits, together with the death of the heroine, the dissection of her body and the discovery that her virginity was intact. Text from Giovanni Bianchi's *The True History and Adventures of Catherine Vizzani, a young gentlewoman a native of Rome, who for many years past in the habit of a man; was killed for an amour with a young lady; and found on dissection, a true virgin*, translated by John Cleland (1755).

The subject before me is an instance, that the wantonness of fancy, and the depravity of nature, are at as great a height as ever; and that our times afford a girl, who, far from being inferior to *Sappho*, or any of the *Lesbian* nymphs, in an attachment for those of her own sex, has greatly surpassed them in fatigues, dangers, and distress, which terminated in a violent death. This the following narrative will manifest, which is a pregnant example of the shocking ebullition[42] of human passions, yet, at the same time, of a most firm constancy and daringness in a young creature, though with a said alloy of guilt and precipitancy.

Our unfortunate adventurer's name was *Catherine Vizzani*; she was born at Rome, and of ordinary parentage, her father being a carpenter. When she came to her fourteenth year, the age of love in our forward climate, she was reserved and shy towards young men, but would be continually romping with her own sex, and some she carressed with all the eagerness and transport of a male lover; but, above all, she was passionately enamoured with one Margaret, whose company she used to court, under pretence of learning embroidery; and, not satisified with these interviews by day, scarce a night passed, but she appeared in man's cloaths, under her charmer's window; though in all appearance, her pleasure must be limited to the viewing of Margaret's captivating charms, and saying soft things to her. This whimsical amour went on very quietly for above two years, but at last Catherine being surprised by Margaret's father, just when her heart was overflowing with fervid expressions of love to his daughter, he rattled her severely, and threatened that the governor of the city should hear of her pranks. Catherine was so frightened with menaces of such a nature, that she absconded, and went to Viterbo, in a man's disguise, where she took upon herself the name of Giovanni Bordoni. After continuing till she imagined the noise of her gallantry was blown over, and she was at the bottom of her purse, which at first had not been too full to tie; she ventured to return to Rome, not to her father's house, but taking sanctuary, as an unfortunate young man, in the church of Santa Maria, in Transtevero ...

Never was Gentleman better fitted with a servant than the Vicar with Giovanni; for, besides reading, making of chocolate, and cookery, she was very dexterous at pen, comb, and razor; in a word, she was a thorough proficient in all branches of her employment. [The Vicar], however, being an austere man, who made no allowance for the impulses of nature, or the fervour of youth, was used not to spare her, for incessantly following the wenches, and being so barefaced and insatiable in her amours. She had recourse to several delusive impudicities, not only to establish the certainty, but raise the reputation of her manhood. The doctor enters into a nauseous detail of her impostures, which is the more inexcusable, they not being essential to the main scope of the narrative. These, if agreeable to the *Italian gout*, would shock the delicacy of our nation, with whom I hope the following lines will ever be in force, as the standard of criticism:

223

Immodest words admit of no defence;
And want of decency is want of sense.

Though a veil be drawn over such ordures,[43] yet as Giovanni's artifices cannot be one and all concealed, without an infraction of the laws of history; and would, besides, occasion too great a chasm in a translation; I return to the original, with saying, that she was two several times with a surgeon in that district, to buy medicaments for the removal of disorders, which she pretended to have contracted from infectious women, being but a raw soldier in the wars of *Venus*; to obviate any suspicions which her laundress might at certain times harbour, she told her, that it some way or other, having taken air, that nature had been very liberal to him, the girls teased him out of his very life, but that some of them had very ill rewarded his compliance; that, however, he hoped, by the care of the good doctor, and his own discretion, quickly to get clear of their present, and that he would be more upon his guard for the future ...

Within a short time, it was whispered about that Giovanni was the best woman's man, and the most addicted to that alluring sex of all the men in that part of the country. However, this character, the acquirement of which had cost her so many artifices, and in which she hugged herself with such pride and delight, was near proving fatal to her; for, being passionately enamoured with a girl, whose singular beauty attracted numerous adorers, one of her rivals, apprehending she would bear away the prize, in a fit of rage at seeing her use some endearments with the beloved object, which were permitted without so much as any feint of repulse, drew upon her, and gave her a very deep wound in the neck ...

The canon, being a person of unblemished sanctity, but so ready to all acts of kindness, as sometimes to overlook the proper cautions, immediately dispatched a servant to the carpenter, Giovanni's father, to come to his house without delay. He began, with the most serious concern, to lay open to him the particulars of his son's scandalous dissoluteness, charging it upon the want of timely instruction and chastisement, if not the influence of vicious example. The carpenter, who could hardly keep his countenance during a remonstrance delivered with a dictatorial solemnity, calmly answered, that, to his and his dear wife's inexpressible grief, their son was a prodigy of nature, and that, in his very childhood, they had observed some astonishing motions of lust, which had unhappily gathered vehemence with the growth of his body; that, however, since such was the case, and the vigour of his constitution was not to be repressed by words or blows, nature must e'en take its course; and, as for the vicious example you are pleased to insinuate, I hope I am no worse than my neighbours. I must tell you, Master Carpenter, replied the ecclesiastic a little moved, that you are in the wrong, ay, and very much so, to offer to extenuate your son's enormities, chiefly, as they are an offence to the God of Holiness, and, as such, may plunge the youth into misery inexpressible, and without end; but also, which is not beneath consideration, they reflect a dishonour on you, as his parent, his guide, and instructor; and on me, who, too easily inferring the goodness of his morals from his ingenuous countenance and decent carriage, recommended him in terms, as if he was not to be over-praised. The father, perceiving the canon to grow warm upon the matter, put a stop to his expostulation, saying, with a smile, reverend sir, certainly you have few equals in Christian zeal, but I must undeceive you, and ask pardon for not doing it before: this same child of mine, whose irregularities have made such a noise, is no male, but as truly, in all respects, a female, as the woman who bore her; he then proceeded to relate the occasion of her leaving her home, and rambling in a man's habit. The good canon was amazed as such frantic doings, and courteously dismissed the carpenter ...

In all her several journeys with her master, she never made the least difficulty to lie in the same bed with other men, upon a case of necessity; but also making any advances to her bedfellow, though he were an Adonis. It is now about two years ago, that, attending upon the Podesta[44] and his son Antony, Lord of Santo Stephano at Florence, during their whole stay there, which was near two months, Giovanni was obliged to take part in the same bed, with the two other servants, wanton young fellows, whom they had taken along with them in that journey, and without any discovery to her prejudice; at which time, being upon a visit to a kinsman, during our vacation, I happened to put up at the very same inn; and, one of their servants having been sent away express, my servant, apprehending that he might disturb me, by coming into my chamber, where I had, some hours before, retired to sleep, betook himself to supply the place of the Podesta's absent servant. Not single day passed, during my stay here, but I was sure to be entertained with a brawling dialogue betwixt the Podesta and Giovanni, on account of the latter's being more free in his gallantries to the daughter of the house than became one who wore a livery ...

Among other charmers, he had the presumption to offer his addresses to a very lovely young gentlewoman, niece to the minister of the village; and prosecuted them with such ardour and success, that they both grew passionately in love with each other. The uncle, knowing the temptation of beauty, and the lubricity[45] of youth, kept a strict guard over his niece, till an advantageous match, which was in agitation, should be concluded; but Giovanni's person and blandishments preponderated against all other considerations; and, after eluding the uncle's attention, in several midnight interviews, Giovanni proposed to the young lady to carry her off at an appointed time, and that afterwards they should make for Rome; where, by means of an honest priest of his acquaintance, their passion should be confirmed and sanctified by the offices of the church: this overture was not only agreed to, but applauded as the greatest mark both of his love and virtue. To carry this scheme into execution, Giovanni had provided two horses, on which they were to set out very early one morning about the middle of June, in the year 1743. The evening before this important expedition, Giovanni's mistress, her discretion not being equal to her beauty, took her younger sister apart, and told her, that her uncle's rigid humours had now worn out her patience; that she had determined not to be mewed up at that rate any longer; and that Giovanni, who would do any thing for her, was to be her deliverer, having provided two horses against the dawn of day, on which they were to post away to Lucca, and from thence to Rome, where they were to be married. This mettlesome girl commended the project to the skies; but added, that she also, having long been tired of living with such an old cuff, would take this charming opportunity of freeing herself from him, and accompany her in an adventure, which carried so much spirit with it. The elder, too late sensible of her indiscretion, conjured her not to harbour any such thought, as being her uncle's favourite, and having good expectations from him; but the younger being one of those, who what they will, they will unalterably, was not to be cajoled, and flatly told her sister, that, if she made any farther difficulties against her being one of the party, their uncle should hear of it before he slept, and then, where is your journey to Rome? This so stunned the lady-errant, that she had not a word to say for some time; and after a pause, changing the key, said she would open the matter to Giovanni, who, she hoped, would agree to what she seemed so bent upon. Giovanni was too much taken up with the thoughts of the approaching exploit to give way to sleep, and was upon the spot before the time, where he found Maria; for love having kept Maria not less wakeful, and her solicitude about her sister suggesting to her that every moment was precious; she immediately informed him of her sister's determination, and the consequences of a refusal. Giovanni, who had complaisance, without reserve, for the youthful females, very cheerfully answered, Aye, with all my heart; it were pity a girl of so much mercury should stay behind; so, mounting them both upon the two horses, she put herself to the fatigue of accompanying them on foot. Their first rout was to Lucca, which lies at no great distance from Librafratta, but making a circuit to avoid Pisa, where her two fellow-travellers had a general acquaintance; before their short refreshment at Lucca was ended, Giovanni, who was used to dispatch, had provided a chaise ready at the door, into which she hurried the two nieces, whilst she contentedly placed herself in the common post behind. With this vehicle, these three adventurers proceeded towards Sienna, but with more haste than good speed; for, at a place called Il Pocchetto, a few miles from Sienna, whether by the weight of these three persons, or that the calash itself was old and crazy, whatever was the cause, it broke down, to the unspeakable consternation of the fare; but Giovanni, an expert traveller, quickly got it mended, and away they drove to retrieve the delay. Having seen these unfortunate creatures so far in their way, let us return to the priest, uncle to Maria and Priscilla. Upon missing his nieces, it must be thought that he flew into a violent rage, which yet he could vent only in words; but being informed, that they had been seen on the Lucca road, in company with Giovanni, he instantly dispatched away his chaplain, a young blade ... assisted by two servants of the Podesta, with a promise of suitable rewards, if they brought back his nieces, and secured Giovanni, in order to his being made an example for his audacious villainy, in imposing on the credulity of girls of a reputable family, to seduce them from their wardship. On this pursuit they posted away to Lucca, which the fugitives had left, long before their arrival. However, having intelligence that such a company had taken the Sienna road, they, without so much as baiting, spurred on, being animated by the scent they had gotten; and as the refreshment at Lucca had taken up some time, and the repairing the broken calash at Poghetto a great deal more, they came up with their chace at Staggia. The chaplain, to make short work of it, called out to the servants to fire upon Giovanni, who, having perceived them at some distance, had leaped down from behind the calash. The servants, pursuant to their leader's command, presented their pieces at Giovanni, who having a masculine spirit, as well as masculine desires, not at all daunted at such a threatening sight, drew a pistol which hung at her belt, and presented it towards the chaplain. This unexpected resolution put them to a stand, and both sides continued watching each other's motions, whilst the poor girls were shrieking, and wringing their hands; 'till Giovanni, considering that her sex would secure her from any very bad consequence of this affair, and that one girl's running away with two others might, in a court of justice, if it should go that length, be slightly passed over as a frolic, rather than severely animadverted upon as a crime, thought it advisable to surrender; and, turning contemptuously from the commanding officer to the servants, who were known to her, she delivered up her pistol, telling them that they were welcome to do their office. The chaplain, however, irritated at her petulance, if jealousy or avarice were not rather the motives to such an inhumanity, after her submission, stormed at one of the servants ... and threatened him with an oar in the galleys, if he delayed a moment; whereupon he let fly, aiming at Giovanni's thighs, upon a supposition that a wound in those parts would be the least hurtful, and hit the poor creature in the left thigh, four inches above the knee; the same shot killing a fine pointer of the Podesta's, and fracturing a leg of a boy of about twelve years of age, who happening to come by, had stopped, as it was very natural, to see what was the matter. The chaplain, as chief of the expedition, was not wanting to spread his success in every place through which he conducted his fair captives, on their return to their uncle, who, to prevent another elopement, went to Lucca, and initiated them into a conservatory of recluse ladies. As for Giovanni, who had fallen to the ground with pain and loss of blood, and the wounded boy, they were, by the compassion of the country folks, conveyed to the hospital of Poggibonsi, from whence, their case being dangerous, they were, within a short space, removed to our hospital della Scala. Giovanni's youth, dejection, and docility had so endeared her to the curate of Poggibonsi that he recommended her to several persons of credit at Sienna; and she, on her part, committed some things to his care, which, if her wound should prove her death, were to be his, as an acknowledgment of his so seasonable kindness, and a recompense for his prayers, which she, with a flood of tears, requested. Besides this, Paolo Marchi, a regular of distinguished piety, wrote a very affectionate letter, in his behalf, to Maria Colomba, purveyor to the nuns of the order of the Immaculate Conception of the Blessed Virgin at Sienna. Accordingly, Giovanni arrived at the hospital della Scala on the sixteenth of June, 1743, and was laid in the seventieth bed, being entered in the register of patients, from his own mouth, by the name of Giovanni, son of Francisco Bordoni, freeman of Rome, and aged twenty-four years old. Here I must observe with pleasure, as an instance of the candour and humanity of my countrymen, that, of all to whom the unfortunate Giovanni sent the recommenda-tory letters, not one failed to come, or send, with the most liberal offers of assistance; among the rest Maria Colomba showed a most vivid spirit of Christianism, by which she adds a lustre to her religious employment. My servant, Giambattista Giustiniani, hearing of such a patient, was led, by curiosity, to go and have a sight of him, imagining he might know him, being of the same class.

It is no wonder that he called Giovanni to mind, upon sight, having been quartered in the same inn for above forty days, and bed-fellows the greatest part of that time. Upon my coming home in the evening, Giambattista informed me that Giovanni, the Podesta Pucci's roguish servant, lay ill in the hospital of a wound, and desired, above all things, that I would be so good as to come and see him ... In the meantime Giovanni's wound grew extremely painful, and brought a high fever upon her, which was also accompanied with a difficulty of respiration, occasioned by an accretion of the Pus, or humours about her breast; from which a conjunction of symptoms, her recovery was apprehended to be doubtful; in this extremity, a leathern contrivance, of a cylindrical figure, which was fastened below the abdomen of her detestable imposture, became so troublesome, that she loosened it, and laid it on her pillow; and now, brought to a sense of the heinousness of her courses, she disclosed her secret to the charitable Maria de Colomba, who suffered not a day to pass without bringing or sending her some cordials. She told her that she was not only a female but a virgin, conjuring her, at the same time, to let no person whatever know it until her death, and then to declare it publicly, that she might be buried in a woman's habit, and with the garland on her head, an honorary ceremony observed among us in the burial of virgins. She breathed her last, a few days after this confidence, in her twenty-fifth year. Such was the end of this young woman, after a disguise of above eight years, during which she lived, undiscovered, as a man servant, in different families; it is, indeed, a proof of singular address and self-government, that in such a length of time, she should preserve her secret from detection, and be proof against any inclination or love for a man, though living continually in the utmost freedom with them, and often lying in the same bed; a passion universally natural to young women, and so vehement in its actings, as to violate the institutes of the cloister, or elope from the coercion of parents; but, on the other hand, here was effrontery and folly in the abstract, to fall in love with those of her own sex; to amuse them with passionate addresses; to kindle in them desires without the power of gratification; to mind neither dangers nor fatigues, and at last to lose her life in these fantastical pursuits. The leathern machine, which was hid under the pillow, fell into the hands of the surgeon's mates in the hospital, who immediately were for ripping it up, concluding that it contained money, or something else of value, but they found it stuffed only with old rags: the servants first suspected Giovanni's sex, by her prominent breasts, when they came to remove her body from the bed on which she died; and, making this known to the chief mates, they not only discovered her to be a woman, but also a virgin, the hymen being entire without the least laceration. Pietro Tsacchi, a native of Aruzzo, one of these mates, and a youth of great hopes, came to me very early on the morning of the twenty-eighth of June, and told me with a blush, that a patient was dead, in the hospital, of a wound in the thigh by a musket-ball, who, upon the denudation of her body, proved to be a woman, with a fine sound hymen, and other tokens of an untouched virginity; and that, if I would take the trouble, my own eyes would verify his account. Such a phaenomenon incited my curiosity, so that I set out with him; but finding the body of the deceased laid out in her proper habit, with the virginal garland on her head, and flowers strewed all over her clothes, I deferred examining her till the afternoon, when the officers of justice were to sit upon her, according to the established custom, when anyone dies of wounds in the hospital. Accordingly, taking along with me James Berti, my dissector, and Giambattista Giustiniani, my servant, we severally certified to the town-clerk, that we had seen her daily, for six weeks successively, in a man's dress at Florence; but, proceeding to an examination of her body, it appeared that some of the younger mates had made an incision in her belly, which they had sewed up again, and this to discover, forsooth, if she was not pregnant ...

The body, being again clothed in her funeral vestment, was carried to the church, where it was laid out, in order to its interment; which being turbulently opposed by the multitudes, which flocked, from all parts of the city, to get a sight of her, the corpse was brought back, though chiefly in deference to some religious, who would have her to be nothing less than a saint, having preserved her chastity inviolate, amidst the strongest temptations; some of these also asserting, that she might be the daughter of a Venetian nobleman; and, accordingly, an epistolary account of her, dated at Sienna, the first of July, and printed at Florence, places her in this honourable light. These reverend gentlemen certainly took the matter by a wrong handle, a woman's sanctity not consisting only in preserving her chastity inviolate, but in uniform purity of manners, in which, how far Catherine excelled, is manifest from every preceding line; accordingly, I urged that her making love, and with uncommon protervity,[46] to women, wherever she came, and her seducing at least two young women to run away from their uncle, were flagrant instances of libidinous disposition; proceedings incompatible with any virtuous principle, or so much as decency.

But the condition of this pretended young man, and the occasion of her disguise (both of which were cleared up soon after, by account from Rome) being at that time unknown, it was the more advisable to comply with the people's ferment.

About nine o'clock the next morning, I went again to the hospital, and caused an incision to be made in the body, and the parts of generation to be dissevered with the nicest exactness, which were carried to my house to be thoroughly examined by a regular dissection . . .

The clitoris of this young woman was not pendulous, nor of any extraordinary size, as the account from Rome made it, and as is said, to be that of all those females, who, among the Greeks, were called *Tribades*, or who followed the practices of *Sappho*; on the contrary, hers was so far from the usual magnitude, that it was not to be ranked among the middle-sized, but the smaller . . .

Remarks upon the foregoing dissertation

The wits, and even the learned men of Italy, have been long distinguished for their inclination to discourses of this nature, which are frequently interpreted in such a manner as to do no great honour to their abilities, and still less to their morals. But it may be they are, in this respect, a little hardly treated; since, in a warm country like theirs, where impurities of all sorts are but too frequent, it may very well happen that such strange accidents may, from time to time, arise as highly to excite both their wonder and their attention, rather from their skill in anatomy, and their acquaintance with human nature, than from any bad habits or vitiated inclinations in themselves.

As for the case of this young woman, it is certainly very extraordinary, and may therefore justify, at least in some measure, the pains which this learned and industrious man has taken about her. But it does not appear that he has assigned any cause whatever, or so much as advanced any probable conjecture on this extravagant turn of her lewdness, notwithstanding it surprised him so much. Yet this we might reasonably have expected from a treatise written by one of the faculty, and one who, without any scruple, professes that it had taken up so much of his thoughts.

It should seem, that this irregular and violent inclination, by which this woman rendered herself infamous, must either proceed from some error in nature, or from some disorder or perversion in the imagination. As to the first of these, the author seems to have removed all doubt; since, from the account he gives of the dissection of the body, it is very evident that there was nothing amiss; and we have good reason to believe, that he meant to insinuate so much at least to his readers, by insisting so long upon a particular circumstance. We ought, therefore, to acquit nature of any fault in this strange creature, and to look for the source of so odious and so unnatural a vice, only in her mind; and there, indeed, if closely attended to, it will be found that more monstrous productions are to be met with than have excited the pens of such as have addicted themselves to write of strange births, and such like prodigies.

It seems therefore most likely that this unfortunate and scandalous creature had her imagination corrupted in early youth, either by obscene tales that were voluntarily told in her hearing, or by privately listening to the discourses of women, who are too generally corrupt in that country. Her head being thus filled with vicious inclinations, perhaps before she received any incitements from her constitution, might prompt her to those vile practices, which begun in folly, were continued through wickedness; nor is it at all unreasonable to believe, that, by degrees, this might occasion a preternatural[47] change in the animal spirits, and a kind of venereal fury, very remote, and even repugnant to that of her sex.

Something of the like kind is reported to have happened many years ago to a very vicious woman, in a country that it is not necessary to name. This woman was the wife of an apothecary, very dissolute in her manners, and, as some thought, a little distracted in her head. Her husband bore with her a long time, out of respect to her family, and for the sake of the fortune he had with her. But at length she took a freak of this kind in to her head, which had very fatal consequences to an innocent and deserving person, and which also brought upon the offender herself a part at least of that shame and punishment which she deserved.

This vile woman, knowing that her husband had received a very large sum of money, took the advantage of his absence, broke open the place where he kept it, and having got it into her possession, procured men's clothes, in which she made herself escape. As soon as she found herself in a place of security, she provided an equipage, and assumed the name of a young gentleman who was her relation, by which, without any suspicion, she introduced herself into the best companies, and by a suitable behaviour, maintained the cheat for some time perfectly well; a thing so much the more practicable, as hers was an imposture absolutely new and strange.

It fell out, at some place of public diversion, that she heard a gentlewoman, the most famous of her time for the sweetness of her voice, and her admirable skill in music, perform a cantata, accompanied with a lute. Upon this, it came into her head to make love to her, which she did with all the exterior marks of the warmest passion. But the gentlewoman, though the person of this creature was far from being disagreeable, had a natural aversion to her, and could never be brought to have any liking for her; though neither she, nor anybody else, had the least suspicion of the imposture.

Her friends, however, who looked upon this as a very extraordinary match, pressed her to lay hold of so favourable an opportunity of settling herself handsomely in the world, and becoming the wife of a person who was able to maintain her in splendour, and who, from the name thus impudently assumed, was generally believed to have a great estate. All the excuses she could make could not divert her relations from the prosecution of this design; and at last, though with much reluctance, they so far vanquished her distaste, as to engage her to accept of this husband; and that too in a shorter time than ought to have been taken in a matter of such importance. But they were so afraid that the family of the young gentleman, for whom this woman was taken, should hear of the matter, and prevent the marriage, that they hurried it on with an indiscrete zeal, which they soon repented.

It was a length, therefore, publicly celebrated, and with great magnificence; which is, perhaps, one of the highest marks of impudence with which the world was ever acquainted. But, as may be easily believed, the villainous secret was soon discovered, and the execrable offender secured. The noise that this story made, brought the apothecary to the first knowledge of what was become of his wife; who, after she had undergone such an examination, as was necessary to render her pretended marriage, in the course of a judicial proceeding, absolutely null and void, was put into his power, with so much of the money as remained unsquandered in this wild adventure.

As for the unfortunate gentlewoman, who was the victim of her friend's good wishes, whose character was perfectly unspotted, and who was esteemed for her beauty, and admired for her virtue, as much as for the excellency of her voice, and delicate hand upon the lute, she was so deeply affected with the shame that attended this affair, which, however, brought not the least imputation upon her, that it threw her into a violent disorder of mind, from which a hectic fever arose, that killed her in a short time.

As for the monster who had been the author of this misfortune, her husband very prudently caused her to be confined as a lunatic; and in that condition she some years after breathed her last, to the great satisfaction of her spouse, and of her own family, who thought themselves, in some measure, dishonoured by her infamy.

This shows, as well as the case which occasioned the mentioning of it, that there is an amazing violence in these vicious irregularities, which has this happy consequence, that they are quickly betrayed, and in most countries chastised with that severity which they deserve; and, without doubt, the only reason that can justify the making things of this sort public, is to facilitate their discovery, and thereby prevent their ill consequences, which indeed can scarce be prevented any other way.

It is therefore very expedient, whenever a treatise of this kind is committed to the press, that it should be accompanied with such reflections as may render it manifest, that it comes abroad with a good intent, and with a real view of correcting, not a latent design of corrupting the morals of youth; and, for this reason, it may not be improper to hint at a few particulars that are extremely worthy of notice.

The first is, that it behoves people to be highly cautious, as to that kind of discourse which they hold in the presence of very young people of either sex; since, though it is very very easy to foresee that lewd or lax conversation must have bad effects, yet it is not altogether so easy to comprehend what very bad effects may follow from it; of which this discourse, and these remarks, afford sufficient instances.

In the next place, it affords (if that were at all necessary) a new argument for suppressing those scandalous and flagitious[48] books, that are not only privately but publicly handed about for the worst purposes, as well as prints and pictures calculated to inflame the passions, to banish all sense of shame, and to make the world, if possible, more corrupt and profligate than it is already. We are very certain that all things of this sort must have a very bad tendency; but surely it would lay some kind of restraint, even upon those who are most forward in these things, if they considered, that they know not what might be the consequences, and that they may become inconsiderately the instruments of much greater wickedness than they design.

We may add to all this, that from hence may be borrowed a very just reason for punishing more severely, or at least not making so light of a practice not altogether uncommon, which is that of women appearing in public places in men's clothes; a thing that manifests an extreme assurance, and which may have many ill consequences, and those too of very different kinds. This, by the Mosaic law, is considered as a capital offence, which deserves so much the more reflection, as it will be be found, upon a strict enquiry, that most of the laws in that code, are founded upon the most perfect knowledge of human nature. It is also looked upon as a great crime by our law, as well for political as moral reasons; and therefore it is very strange, that, merely to indulge an idle whim, or a foolish humour, the best, or at least the most innocent reasons that can be suggested for it, this should be looked on with an eye of indifference, and rather as a species of levity than of guilt.

To dispense with laws from necessity, or for the sake of some public convenience, may be excusable, and even reasonable; but, to suffer such laws as our ancestors instituted from the wisest motives, and for the most salutary purposes, to fall into desuetude,[49] and even contempt, to gratify the lovers of diversions; in favour of which, even their best advocate is able to say no more, than, than that they are silly diversions, is not a little strange and surprising, and must give a singular idea of those alterations in our policy and manners, which have arisen from our politeness, and our desire to copy foreigners in everything, not excepting those follies, of which the wisest people amongst them profess themselves ashamed.

A Discovery of a Very Extraordinary Nature

Donoghue lists a number of cases of female husbands reported in newspapers (1993: 65–73). Lord Hardwicke's Marriage Act (1753) stipulated that all weddings had to be publicly registered and tightened up the requirement for parental consent (if the bride was under 21). The story reported here is expanded in the August issue. Text from *Gentlemen's Magazine* (10 July 1766). For other examples of this genre see *The Counterfeit Bridegroom. Being a Comical and Pleasant Relation of a young Woman in the Borough of Southwark, who being in wants of a Husband, by a strange mistake, married a young Woman in Man's Apparel ...* (1720) and Henry Fielding's *The Female Husband* (1746).

A discovery of a very extraordinary nature was made at Poplar, where two women had lived together for six and thirty years, as man and wife, and kept a public house, without ever being suspected; but the wife happening to fall sick, and die, a few years before she expired, revealed the secret to her relations, made her will, and left legacies to the amount of half what she thought they were worth. On application to the pretended, she at first endeavoured to support her assumed character, but being closely pressed, she at length owed the fact, accommodated all matters amicably, put off the male, and put on the female character, in which she appeared to be a sensible well-bred woman, though in her male character she had always affected the plain plodding alehouse-keeper. It is said they had acquired in business money to the amount of £3000. Both had been crossed in love when young, and had chosen this method to avoid further importunities.

The Adulteress

The Adulteress (1773) was an anonymous modern version of Juvenal's *Sixth Satire*. A short extract from the preface has been included.

With JAMES and CHARLES rank
   lechery came in,
And virtue then gave place at court to
   sin:
New modes of lust e'en CHARLES
   himself devis'd,
And ROCHESTER both nurs'd them,
   and chastis'd:
Then did the Court chaste marriage-
   rites profane,
And purer virtue breath'd in Drury-
   lane . . .

Women and Men, in these unnat'ral
   times,
Are guilty equal of unnat'ral crimes:
Woman with woman act the manly
   part,
And kiss and press each other to the
   heart.

Unnat'ral crimes like these my satire
   vex;
I know a thousand *Tommies*[50] 'mongst
   the sex:
And if they don't relinquish such a
   crime,
I'll never give their names to be the
   scoff of time.
   But here, *Sweet Girls*, my
   indignation fires,
When Man with Man into the shade
   retires;
And when that justice damns them
   and their crimes,
The noble monsters of these
   monstrous times
Repair to majesty, and piteous plead
A wretch's cause – whom virtue
   deem'd to bleed

[In the days of Juvenal] 'The men and women were equally as lewd, flagitious, and luxurious. There is not a new fashion or a new vice. Pandora opened her box upon us at first, and the evils rise and fall in different latitudes as the people are laborious or effeminate, virtuous or vicious.'

GLOSSARY

Note: NCD indicates a definition from *A New Canting Dictionary: comprehending all the terms, antient and modern, used in the several tribes of Gypsies, beggars, shoplifters, highwaymen, foot pads, and all other clans of cheats and villains . . .* (1725).

ANDROGYNE. In classical Greek has the meaning 'man-woman'. Like 'hermaphrodite' the word suggests either a middle or double state with regard to the biological sex of the person. Androgyny is often used in preference to 'hermaphroditism' to suggest the possibility of a spiritual harmony emerging from an equality and balance between the sexes. In so far as the combination of opposites may result in a higher purity, the concept was often deployed in alchemy and in mystical works concerned with wholeness and integration (see C.G. Jung).

BUCK. 'As *A bold Buck*, is sometimes used to signify a forward daring person of either sex. *She wants to go buck*, expressed of a wanton woman, who is desirous of male-conversation. (NCD).

BUGGERY. In Old French the term *bougre* signified a heretic and a sodomite; the world is found in the Old Bulgarian *bulgarinu* and Medieval Latin *bulgarus*. Buggery is first defined as the crime of sodomy in the law of 1533 (25 Henry VIII c. 6).

CATAMITE. Like the name Ganymede, designated a servant, slave, or minion. The term is used in many Renaissance texts.

CROSS-DRESSING. The modern, politically correct term for transvestism.

CULLY. 'A fop, a rogue, a fool, or silly creature, who is easily drawn in and cheated by whores and rogues' (NCD).

CRUSTY-BEAU. 'One that lies with a cover over his face all night, and uses washes, paint, &c' (NCD).

EFFEMINACY. Lacking, virility or courage; soft, decadent, luxurious. The word shifts between censure of a personal trait or group of them, to a debilitating cultural condition. The Molly House provided a meeting place for effeminate men, who mimicked women and called each other by women's names.

EUNUCH. One who has been castrated.

FAGGOT. 'To bind hand and foot; as *Faggot the Culls*; *i.e.* 'Bind the men' (NCD).

FAGGOTS. 'Men mustered for soldiers, not yet listed' (NCD).

FIDDLE-FADDLE. 'Mere silly stuff, or nonsense; idle, vain discourse' (NCD).

FLOGGING-CULLY. 'An old lecherer, who, to stimulate himself to venery, causes himself to be whipped with rods' (NCD).

FERULA. 'An instrument of wood used for correction of lighter faults, more sensibly known to school-boys than to ladies' (*The Fop Dictionary*, 1700).

FRICATRICE. A lewd woman, a lesbian.

GANYMEDE. In Greek mythology, Zeus' cupbearer. The term came to be used for a passive homosexual, or to designate the sovereign's (sexual) favourite.

HERMAPHRODITE. from Hermaphroditos, the deity produced from the fusion of Hermes and Aphrodite (or Mercury and Venus). Anatomically the body appears to have male and female sexual parts, in different degrees. Perfect hermaphrodites have fully developed parts of both sexes but are not as a consequence 'self-sufficient' in the sexual act. In most cases hermaphrodites could marry provided they made a permanent choice of their sex. Mannish women were an obsession in tracts concerning hermaphrodites and may be linked with early constructions of lesbian culture.

INGLE. Used primarily in Renaissance texts to denote a servant boy, minion or catamite.

LESBIAN. Love between females. From Lesbos, an island in the Aegyptian, where the Greek erotic poet Sappho and her circle flourished.

MAGGOT. 'A whimsical fellow, full of strange fancies and Capricios. Maggoty, freakish' (NCD).

MOLLY. An effeminate man who engaged in sex with other men. Their meeting places , or Molly Houses, were raided at the beginning of the eighteenth century. The term probably derived from *mollis*, the Latin term for soft or effeminate.

Wayne Dynes has pointed out that 'The Greek equivalent of mollis is malakos. In I Corinthians 6:9, the Greek word is used unequivocally to anathematize the passive male homosexual' (*Homolexis: A Historical and Cultural Lexicon of Homosexuality*).

PATHIC(K). The passive and usually effeminate partner in same-sex acts.

PEDERASTY. Loving and/or sexual relations between a man and a boy. Sometimes describes the power difference between pupil and teacher. Not to be confused with the complex field of paedophilia (chiefly heterosexual relations with children, consensual or otherwise).

SAPPHO. Famous love poet of ancient Lesbos. 'Sapphic' is commonly used to mean 'lesbian'.

SODOMY. The 'crime against nature' - usually anal sex (buggery) between men; bestiality.

STONES. Testicles.

THIRD SEX. Used of eunuchs and individuals who engage in same-sex activities.

TOMMIES. Lesbians.

TRANSSEXUAL. One undergoing psychological and surgical treatment in pursuit of a change of sex.

TRANSVESTITE. One who chooses to wear the clothes of the other sex

TRIBADE. A lesbian.

YARD. Penis.

NOTES

1 Anatomies

1   *Some Yeares Travels into Africa* ... (1638) was a fantastic compendium of the strange and the wonderful margins of the 'olde knowne world' (17).
2   Sexual pleasure, or the pursuit of it.
3   Sexual acts, copulation.
4   Fourteenth-century traveller. See *The Voyages and Travels of Sir John Mandeville, Knight.*
5   Ctesias (late fifth century BC). Greek doctor at the Persian court. He was the author of a history of Persia in twenty-three books, and a book on India.
6   First century AD Roman poet. Famous for epigrams on Roman social life; recurring themes in his poetry which were considered obscene included homosexuality, oral stimulation and masturbation.
7   Lovers.
8   Fastening the sexual organs with a clasp or fibula.
9   The foreskin which covers the *glans penis* or *glans clitoridis.*
10 Desire, lust.
11 God of procreation.
12 Sometimes used of women, in derogatory sense ('lewd'); perhaps linked, through its etymology ('to rub') with tribadism (sex between women).
13 The common view that men's and women's bodies corresponded; the woman was essentially a man turned inside out. See Laqueur (1990).
14 I.e. spayed. A *spado* was a eunuch.
15 Manner of walking.
16 Sammu-ramat, mother of Adad-nirari III (reigned 810–783 BC). Reputed to have built the hanging gardens of Babylon.
17 Ammianus Marcellinus (*c.* AD 330–95) continued the historical work begun by Tacitus. See *The Roman Historie, containing such Acts and occurents as passed under Constantius, Iulianus.* Translated by Philemon Holland (1609).
18 See Christopheri Helvici's *Theatrum Historicum* or *The Historical and Chronological Theatre of Christopher Helvici* (1687), p. 5. He also notes in his calendar the destruction of Sodom and Gomorrha; the birth of Sappho is noted at p. 59c under 'Famous Men'.
19 Greek historian of the late first century BC. Several volumes of his monumental historical writings have survived.
20 See *Etymologion Linguae Latinae.*

21 Lucian of Samosata (*c.* AD 115–180).

22 Oxford and Cambridge.

23 Roman writer on natural history, author of *Naturalis Historia* in thirty-seven books.

24 The fashion for castrated singers is first recorded in 1552.

25 See his *Saturnalia*, ch. 52.

26 Ancillon refers us to Camerar, *Medit. Histor.*, tom 1, lib 5, cap. 19.

27 Legendary warrior-women.

28 Greek historian (*c.* 490–425 BC).

29 French writer (1533–92) famous for his *Essays*.

30 See *The Essayes or Morall, Politike and Millitarie Discourses* (1603), Bk 2, Ch. 29, pp. 405–6.

31 A doctrine held by Arius of Alexandria in the fourth century BC.

32 The period of legal infancy or immaturity.

33 Having an abnormally enlarged clitoris.

34 Soothsayers, who divined from observation of the entrails.

35 An unclean prodigy, or monster.

36 Priests.

37 In his *Observationes Medicae*. Parsons quotes from the Latin text in a footnote.

38 A number of monstrous births and preternatural phenomena were recorded (as short articles) in the *Transactions*.

39 *Lusus naturae* or sport of nature. It was believed that nature, bored with producing the same objects, sometimes played with creation, allowing the birth of mixed, deficient or excessive forms. The result was a monster.

40 Chest.

41 Hips.

42 Rubbing.

43 Situated near the groin.

44 Diemerbroeck (1609–74) wrote an influential study of the plague (1644) and an anatomical treatise (1672).

45 Classical anatomist. For Galen's inversion of the body see Laqueur (1990: 25–8).

46 Gaspard Bauhin (1560–1624). Professor of anatomy and botany.

47 Levinus Lemnius, sixteenth-century physician. See *The Secret Miracles of Nature* (1658) ch. 9, pp. 28–9.

48 Author of a book on sexual reproduction and anatomy.

49 Greek philosopher (*c.* 515–540 BC).

50 Twelfth-century Arabic philosopher and medical writer.

51 For background on female semen see Jacquart and Thomasset (1988: 61–71).

52 Christian theologian and philosopher, famous for his *Confessions* and *City of God*.

53 A fabulous people in Libya with monstrously large feet.

54 Men with dogs' heads.

55 See *De Conceptu et Generatione Hominis* (1554) and *The Expert Midwife* (1637), a version of his *Habammenbuch* (1583).
56 Sixteenth-century writer on anatomy.
57 Johannes Riolanus's *A Sure Guide; or the best and nearest way to Physick and Chyrurgery* was translated by N. Culpeper in 1657.

2 Crimes and Punishment

1 Henry VIII's act of 1533 made 'the detestable and abominable vice of buggery committed with mankind or beast' punishable by hanging until death.
2 It was important to decide whether anal penetration had taken place. In cases of attempted penetration, the pillory, imprisonment or fines could be levied rather than hanging until death.
3 A number of biblical sources are cited at this point. Leviticus 18:22, 23, 25 may serve as an example: 'Thou shalt not lie with mankind as with womankind: it is abomination. Neither shalt thou lie with any beast to defile thyself therewith: neither shalt any woman stand before a beast to lie down thereto: it is confusion ... And the land is defiled: therefore I do visit the iniquity thereof upon it, and the land itself vomiteth out her inhabitants.'
4 I.e. to confirm their religious allegiance.
5 Roman Catholics who refused the authority of the Church of England.
6 James Butler, 2nd Duke of Ormonde?
7 Penis.
8 I.e. valid.
9 A boy employed to carry a torch or lamp.
10 Prison.
11 Kissed.
12 The ordinary was the chaplain of Newgate prison. He prepared condemned prisoners for death.
13 Gregory Turner was not apprehended by the constables.
14 Norton suggests that the term meant that his penis 'was a ripe candidate for being treated for venereal disease' (62).
15 A house of correction for prisoners.
16 Hector Boethius (also known as Boece and Boyis), *c.* 1465–1536. Early Scottish historian, author of *Scotorum historiae a prima gentis origine* (1527).
17 An emblem of 'authority'.
18 The bones which enclose the brain; the skull.
19 Those who proclaim the superiority of contemporary science and technology against the authority of the classical traditions of 'ancient' thought.
20 One who pays for his provision at Oxford University.
21 'An officer or servant who buys provisions for a College ...' *OED*.

22 Rebuked or lectured.

23 Former.

24 Medical treatment.

25 Officers responsible for discipline and other minor offences.

26 Messengers.

27 University slang for the place where academics debated serious issues.

28 A mock-heroic or mock-pathetic poem; droll or ridiculous.

29 Having the characteristics of both sexes.

30 Query, or enquiry.

31 Willing or unwilling.

32 'Let it be done'.

33 A standard reference work, dating from 1607.

34 1722, and several later editions.

35 From *frig* 'to rub or chafe . . . FUCK' (*OED*).

3 Representations

1 Barbers.

2 Ancient painter whose works were famously true to life.

3 King James and his favoured companion.

4 Asylum for the insane.

5 Mythical king of Phrygia who was tortured by being placed in water he could not drink; fruit was offered him, but it always escaped his grasp.

6 A soft, fine silk material.

7 A loose dressing-gown.

8 Dressed up finely.

9 Head-dress.

10 A word rich in connotations: (a) a spectre female demon; (b) a slut, a lewd woman; (c) a bundle of rags fastened to the end of a stick; (d) a scarecrow (*OED*).

11 Worthless, exhausted.

12 Country term for an old woman. Gaffer signifies an old man.

13 Breaking wind.

14 A worker, or artisan, between an apprentice and a master.

15 Between natural and supernatural.

16 Established to enforce moral standars. See Bristow (1977).

17 Sewer, or drain.

18 A Roman Catholic, traitor, and suspected sodomite, who died in 1705.

19 Edmund in *King Lear* noted that a 'dull, stale, tired bed' went to the creating of 'a whole tribe of fops / Got 'tween asleep and wake'.

20 Pego, penis.

21 Conflation of *fricare* (to rub) and fricatrice (a lewd woman).

22 A Ganymede, a boy kept for 'unnatural' purposes.

23 A small man.

24 A castrated cock; a eunuch.

25 A weak person; an invalid.

26 A husband who interferes in women's matters; a scolding baby's nurse.

27 Rags; swaddling clothes worn by an infant.

28 Zealous followers of Sodom.

29 Servant; Zeus's cup-bearer; a boy kept for 'unnatural' sex.

30 A go-between; male procurer.

31 Fuck.

32 A card game.

33 Compare the censure expressed here with that in *Reasons for the Growth of Sodomy*, above.

34 I.e like an infant.

35 An influential Catholic.

36 A meek wife.

37 Copulate.

38 Brothel.

39 During the Trojan war.

40 Young hen.

41 Wig.

42 Physiognomy, i.e. face, expression.

43 Frill (usually on the breast).

44 As Satan.

45 John Oldham, seventeenth-century poet and satirist. See his *Satyrs upon the Jesuits* I.

46 Servant used for sexual favours.

47 The younger, or 'passive' partner in sodomy.

48 Seventeenth-century writers.

49 Oliver Cromwell.

50 Magazines of the time.

51 Fell in love with his own image in a pool; a self-admirer.

52 An actor of classical Roman times.

53 Hercules's favourite youth.

54 The man Bickerstaffe had attempted to seduce.

55 An affected person; a fop.

56 Seventeenth-century dramatists.

57 A hangman.

58 Scrofula, often affecting the lymphatic glands.

59 He quotes extensively from Charles Churchill's *The Times*.

60 Warburton, editor of Pope's poems.

4 Sapphic Texts

1 The mud of the Nile was endowed with fantastic powers of fertility.
2 Carriages.
3 Curious pictorial representation using branches and foliage; grotesque designs.
4 Masqueraders; i.e. those who confuse or bewilder by their appearance.
5 Actors, especially in a dumb-show.
6 Behest, bidding.
7 A festering sore. Also used in political or moral senses.
8 Scorning, or being contemptuous of.
9 Carcanet; necklace or collar.
10 First.
11 Clothes worn by an infant.
12 Tribade, lesbian.
13 Feasting, entertaining.
14 Intoxicated.
15 The notes suggest three senses for Mascula 'I. That this word means that she was a Tribas. 2. That it denotes the inclination she had for the sciences, instead of handling spindle and distaff. 3. The courage she had to precipitate herself at Leucate.'
16 In the same issue of *The Spectator*, Addison commented 'this translation is written in the very spirit of Sappho, and as near the Greek as the genius of our language will possibly suffer. Longinus has observed, that this description of love in Sappho is an exact copy of nature, and that all the circumstances which follow one another in such an hurry of sentiments, notwithstanding they appear repugnant to each other, are really such as happen in the phrenzies of love.'
17 Iphis's mother.
18 'Some Readings have it Key-hole, but not so properly, the nuns having no locks to their doors. I therefore in this case make use of crevice' (Samber's note).
19 Trifles, unimportant matters.
20 'A Discipline, is a sort of cat of nine tails with which they whip themselves in monasteries' (Samber's note).
21 'This word in French means Trifles' (Samber's note).
22 'Some readings have it *Flogging*, but the term being too vulgar, I am of their sentiment who read it *Flagellation*' (Samber's note).
23 'The Order of Feuillants was established in the year 1565 by John de la Barriere. They follow the rule of St Benedict, and St Bernard; formerly they went unshod with sandals. They wear fine white stuff, they are called Feuillants, from Feuille a leaf, because they carry in their arms a branch with leaves' (Samber's note).
24 'We have no word in English to signify what this word Fratraille does in

French, which means a *Frierly-Crew*' (Samber's note).

25   Goddess of justice.

26   God of medicine.

27   Pet, favourite.

28   Citizen, usually in a mild derogatory sense.

29   Harlot; mistress.

30   Three classical poets.

31   Rochester was infamous as a sexual libertine. He was probably author of *Sodom, or the Quintessence of Debauchery*.

32   Among the several origins of the name Miraare offered: (1) Myrrha the daughter of *Cynara* 'a woman of such an inordinate appetite, that she lay with her father, and had a son by him'; (2) Myrrhina 'a famous courtesan of *Athens*, who first practised and taught in that city *Sappho*'s manner and the *Lesbian* gambols'; (3) 'an old *Teutonick* word ... which the people of *Franconia* ... bestow'd on every tall masculine woman among their nobility ...'; (4) 'impure or wicked'; (5) 'or else is the Foeminine of *Mirus, Wonderful* or *Monstrous*'.

33   '*Coritan* are a people of *Northamptonshire*' (King's note).

34   'Woman with woman'.

35   Two of Sappho's mistresses.

36   Woman or hag.

37   Chapter XII contains 'the curious History of Miss Forward'; the early discoveries she made at the boarding school .

38   A whimsical fancy.

39   For more on the issue of French servants see Hecht (1954).

40   'From behind', i.e the buttocks. Also a logical term (compare *a priori*).

41   A small dog. 'Pug' was also used of harlots, courtesans, demons and imps.

42   Overflowing, boiling over.

43   Excrement, i.e. foul language.

44   A governor, or chief magistrate.

45   Slipperiness, lewdness.

46   Waywardness.

47   A category between the natural and the supernatural. Monstrous births and sports of nature were considered to be preternatural.

48   Wicked, infamous.

49   Disuse.

50   Lesbians.

BIBLIOGRAPHY

Adburgham, A. (1972). *Women in Print: Writing Women and Women's Magazines from the Restoration to the Accession of Victoria*. London: George Allen and Unwin.

Addy, J. (1989). *Sin and Society in the Seventeenth Century*. London: Routledge.

Ballaster, R. (1992). *Seductive Forms: Women's Amatory Fiction from 1684 to 1740*. Oxford: Clarendon Press.

Barker-Benfield, G.J. (1992). *The Culture of Sensibility: Sex and Society in Eighteenth-Century Britain*. Chicago: University of Chicago Press.

Bingham, C. (1971). 'Seventeenth-Century Attitudes toward Deviant Sex', *Journal of Interdisciplinary History* 1: 447–68.

Boucé, P.G. (ed.) (1982). *Sexuality in Eighteenth-Century Britain*. Manchester: Manchester University Press.

Bray, A. (1988). *Homosexuality in Renaissance England* (1982). London: Gay Men's Press.

Breasted, B. (1971). '*Comus* and the Castlehaven Scandal', *Milton Studies* 3: 201–4.

Bremner, J. (1989). *From Sappho to de Sade: Moments in the History of Sexuality*. London: Routledge.

Bristow, E.J. (1977). *Vice and Vigilance: Purity Movements in Britain since 1700*. Dublin: Gill and Macmillan.

Burford, E.J. (1973) *The Orrible Synne: A Look at London Lechery from Roman to Cromwellian Times*. London: Calder and Boyars.

Burg, B.R. (1980). 'Ho Hum, Another Work of the Devil: Buggery and Sodomy in Early Stuart England', *Journal of Homosexuality* 6: 69–78.

—— (1984). *Sodomy and the Pirate Tradition: English Sea Rovers in the Seventeenth-Century Caribbean*. New York and London: New York University Press.

Butler, J. (1990). *Gender Trouble: Feminism and the Subversion of Identity*. London: Routledge.

Cardindale, S. and H. Smith (1990). *Women and the Literature of the Seventeenth Century: An Annotated Bibliography Based on Wing's Short-Title Catalogue*. New York: Greenwood Press.

Castle, T. (1979). '"Amy, Who Knew My Disease": A Psychosexual Pattern in Defoe's *Roxana*', *English Literary History* 46: 81–96.

—— (1986). *Masquerade and Civilization: The Carnivalesque in English Culture and Fiction*. London: Methuen.

Cavin, S. (1985). *Lesbian Origins*. San Francisco: Ism Press.

Clark, S. (1985). '*Hic Mulier, Haec Vir*, and the Controversy over Masculine Women', *Studies in Philology* 82: 158–83.

Cohen, E. (1989). 'Legislating the Norm: From Sodomy to Gross Indecency', *South Atlantic Quarterly* 88: 181–217.

Cole, F. (1930). *Early Theories of Sexual Generation*. Oxford: Oxford University Press.

Cruikshank, M. (ed.) (1982). *Lesbian Studies: Present and Future*. New York: The Feminist Press.

Davenport-Hines, R. (1990). *Sex, Death and Punishment: Attitudes to Sex and Sexuality in Britain since the Renaissance*. London: Collins.

DeJean, J. (1989). *Fictions of Sappho, 1565–1937*. Chicago and London: University of Chicago Press.

Dekker, R.M. and Lotte C van de Pol. (1989). *The Tradition of Female Transvestism in Early Modern Europe*. London: Macmillan.

Dollimore, J. (1991). *Sexual Dissidence: Augustine to Wilde, Freud to Foucault*. Oxford: Clarendon Press.

Donoghue, E. (1993). *Passions between Women: British Lesbian Culture 1668–1801*. London: Scarlet Press.

Downing, C. (1991). *Myths and Mysteries of Same-Sex Love*. New York: Continuum.

Dugaw, D. (1989). *Warrior Women and Popular Balladry, 1650–1850*. Cambridge: Cambridge University Press.

Dynes, W. (1985). *Homolexis: A Historical and Cultural Lexicon of Homosexuality*. New York: Gai Saber Monograph.

Earle, P. (1989). *The Making of the English Middle Class: Business, Society and Family Life in London, 1660–1730*. London: Methuen.

Epstein, J. (1990). 'Either/Or – Neither/Both: Sexual Ambiguity and the Ideology of Gender', *Genders* 7: 101–42.

—— and K. Straub (eds) (1991). *Body Guards: The Cultural Politics of Gender Ambiguity*. London: Routledge.

Faderman, L. (1981). *Surpassing the Love of Men: Romantic Friendship and Love Between Women from the Renaissance to the Present*. London: The Women's Press.

Ferguson, M. (ed.) (1985). *First Feminists: British Women Writers 1578–1799*. Bloomington, Indiana: Indiana University Press.

Feroli, T. (1994). 'Sodomy and Female Authority: The Castlehaven Scandal and Eleanor Davies's *The Restitution of Prophecy* (1651)', *Women's Studies* 24: 1–19.

Ferris, L. (ed.) (1993). *Crossing the Stage: Controversies on Cross-Dressing*. New York and London: Routledge.

Fidelis, M. (1988). *The Well-known Troublemaker: A Life of Charlotte Charke*. London: Faber.

Foucault, M. (1990). *The History of Sexuality. Volume 1. An Introduction* (first published 1976). Harmondsworth: Penguin.

Foxon, D. (1963a). 'Libertine Literature in England, 1660–1745', *The Book Collector* 12: 21–36.

—— (1963b). 'John Cleland and the Publication of the *Memoirs of A Woman of Pleasure*', *The Book Collector* 12: 476–87.

Friedli, L. (1987). '"Passing Women". A Study of Gender Boundaries in the Eighteenth Century'. In G.S. Rousseau and R. Porter (eds), *Sexual Underworlds of the Enlightenment*. Manchester: Manchester University Press, 234–60.

Gagen, J. (1954). *The New Woman: Her Emergence in English Drama, 1600–1730*. New York: Twayne Publishers.

Garber, M. (1992). *Vested Interests: Cross-Dressing and Cultural Anxiety*. New York and London: Routledge.

Gerard, K. and G. Hekma (eds) (1987) *The Pursuit of Sodomy in Early Modern Europe*. New York: Haworth.

Gilman, S. (1989) *Sexuality: An Illustrated History*. New York: Wiley.

Goldberg, J. (1992). *Sodometries: Renaissance Texts: Modern Sexualities*. Stanford, CA: Stanford University Press.

——— (ed.) (1994). *Reclaiming Sodom*. New York and London: Routledge.

——— (ed.) (1994). *Queering the Renaissance*. Durham and London.

Greenberg, D.F. (1988). *The Construction of Homosexuality*. Chicago: University of Chicago Press.

Harvey, E.D. (1989). 'Ventriloquizing Sappho: Ovid, Donne, and the Erotics of the Feminine Voice', *Criticism* 31: 115–38.

Hecht, J.J. (1954). *Continental and Colonial Servants in Eighteenth-Century England*. Northampton, MA: *Smith College Studies in History* 40.

Hekma, G. (1994). 'The Homosexual, the Queen and Models of Gay History', *Perversions* 3: 119–38.

Herrup, C. (1996). 'The Patriarch at Home: The Trial of the 2nd Earl of Castlehaven for Rape and Sodomy', *History Workshop Journal* 41: 1–18.

Hitchcock, T. (1996). 'Redefining Sex in Eighteenth Century England', *History Workshop Journal* 41: 73–90.

Hobby, E. (1988). *Virtue of Necessity: English Women's Writing 1649–88*. London: Virago.

——— (1992). 'Katherine Philips: Seventeenth-Century Lesbian Poet'. In Hobby and White (eds), *What Lesbians Do in Books*. London: The Women's Press, 183–204.

Hunt, L. (ed.) (1993). *The Invention of Pornography, 1500–1800*. New York: Zone Books.

Jacquart, D. and C. Thomasset (1988). *Sexuality and Medicine in the Middle Ages*. Oxford: Polity Press.

Jones, A.R. and P. Stallybrass (1991). 'Fetishizing Gender: Constructing the Hermaphrodite in Renaissance Europe'. In Epstein and Straub (eds), *Body Guards*, 80–111.

Jones, V. (1990). *Women in the Eighteenth Century: Constructions of Femininity*. London: Routledge.

Jordanova, L. (ed.) (1986). *Languages of Nature: Critical Essays on Science and Literature*. London: Free Association Books.

Katz, J.N. (1994). 'The Age of Sodomitical Sin, 1607–1740'. In Goldberg (ed.), *Reclaiming Sodom*, 43–58.

Kearney, P.J. (1981). *The Private Case*. London: Jay Landesman.

Kehoe, M. (ed.) (1986). *Historical, Literary and Erotic Aspects of Lesbianism*, New York: Harrington Park Press.

Kelly, V. and D. von Mucke (eds) (1994). *Body and Text in the Eighteenth Century*. Stanford: Stanford University Press.

Kimmel, M.S. (ed.) (1990). *Love Letters between a Certain late Nobleman and the Famous Mr Wilson*. New York and London: Harrington Park Press.

King, T.A. (1994). 'Performing "Akimbo" Queer Pride and Epistemological Prejudice', in Meyer (ed.) *The Politics and Poetics of Camp*, 23–50.

Kopelson, K. (1992). 'Seeing Sodomy: Fanny Hill's Blinding Vision', *Journal of Homosexuality* 23: 173–83.

Laqueur, T. (1990). *Making Sex: Body and Gender from the Greeks to Freud*. Cambridge, MA: Harvard University Press.

Landry, D. (1990). *The Muses of Resistance: Laboring-Class Women's Poetry in Britain, 1739–1746*. Cambridge: Cambridge University Press.

Lipking, L. (1988). 'Sappho Descending: Eighteenth-Century Styles in Abandoned Women', *Eighteenth-Century Life* 12: 40–57.

Lucas, R.V. (1988). '*Hic Mulier*: The Female Transvestite in Early Modern Europe', *Renaissance and Reformation* 12: 65–84.

Maccubbin, R.P. (1985). *'Tis Nature's Fault: Unauthorised Sexuality during the Enlightenment*. Cambridge: Cambridge University Press.

MacDonald, R.H. (1967). 'The Frightful Consequences of Onanism: Notes on the History of a Delusion', *Journal of the History of Ideas* 28: 423–31.

Marcus, L.S. (1983). 'The Milieu of Milton's *Comus*: Judicial Reform at Ludlow and the Problem of Sexual Assault', *Criticism* 25: 293–327.

Meares, R. (1993). *The Metaphor of Play: Disruption and Restoration in the Borderline Experience*. Northvale, NJ and London: Jason Aronson.

Mengay, D.H. (1992). 'The Sodomitical Muse: Fanny Hill and the Rhetoric of Crossdressing', *Journal of Homosexuality* 23: 185–98.

Messenger, A. (1986). *His and Hers: Essays in Restoration and Eighteenth-Century Literature*. Lexington, KY: University Press of Kentucky.

Meyer, M. (ed.) (1994). *The Politics and Poetics of Camp*. New York and London: Routledge.

Mills, J. (1991). *Womanwords: A Vocabulary of Culture and Patriarchal Society*. London: Virago.

Moore, L. (1992). '"Something More Tender Still Than Friendship". Romantic Friendship in Early-Nineteenth-Century England', *Feminist Studies* 18: 499–520.

Norton, R. (1992). *Mother Clap's Molly House: The Gay Subculture in England 1700–1830*. London: Gay Men's Press.

Page, D.L. (1955). *Sappho and Alcaeus: An Introduction to the Study of Ancient Lesbian Poetry*. Oxford: Oxford University Press.

Pearson, J. (1988). *The Prostituted Muse: Images of Women and Women Dramatists 1642–1737*. Hemel Hempstead: Harvester Wheatsheaf.

Porter, R. and L. Hall (1995). *The Facts of Life: The Creation of Sexual Knowledge in Britain, 1650–1950*. New Haven and London: Yale University Press.

Rousseau, G.S. (1985). 'The Pursuit of Homosexuality in the Eighteenth Century: "Utterly Confused Category" and/or Rich Repository?' In Maccubbin (ed.) *'Tis Nature's Fault*, 132–68.

———— and Porter, R. (eds) (1980). *The Ferment of Knowledge*. Cambridge: Cambridge University Press.

———— and Porter, R. (eds) (1987). *Sexual Underworlds of the Enlightenment*. Manchester: Manchester University Press.

Quaife, G.R. (1979). *Wanton Wenches and Wayword Wives: Peasants and Illicit Sex in Early Seventeenth-Century England*. London: Croom Helm.

Raymond, J. (1986). *A Passion for Friends: Towards a Philosophy of Female Affection*. London: The Women's Press.

Saslow, J.M. (1986). *Ganymede in the Renaissance: Homosexuality in Art and Society*. New Haven and London: Yale University Press.

Schofield, M.A. and C. Macheski (eds) (1986). *Fetter'd or Free? British Women Novelists, 1670–1815*. Athens: Ohio Univerisity Press.

Sedgwick, E.K. (1990). *Epistemology of the Closet*. Berkeley and Los Angeles: University of California Press.

Semple, L. (1994). 'The Seven Ages of Sappho', *Perversions* 3: 5–41.

Senelick, L. (1990). 'Mollies or Men of Mode? Sodomy and the Eighteenth-Century London Stage', *Journal of the History of Sexuality* 1: 33–67.

Shapiro, S. (1987). 'Amazons, Hermaphrodites and Plain Monsters: The "Masculine" Woman in English Satire and Social Criticism from 1580–1640', *Atlantis* 13: 66–76.

———— (1988). '"Yon Plumed Dandeprat": Male "Effeminacy" in English Satire and Criticism', *Review of English Studies* 39: 400–12.

Shepherd, S. (1981). *Amazons and Warrior Women: Varieties of Feminism in Seventeenth-Century Drama*. Brighton: Harvester.

Smith, H.L. (1982). *Reason's Disciples: Seventeenth-Century English Feminists*. Urbana, IL: University of Illinois Press.

Smith, S. (1987). *A Poetics of Women's Autobiography: Marginality and the Fictions of Self-Representation*. Bloomington and Indianapolis: Indiana University Press.

Stallybrass, P. and A. White (1986). *The Politics and Poetics of Transgression*. London: Methuen.

Staves, S. (1982). 'Kind Words for the Fop', *Studies in English Literature* 22: 413–28.

Still, J. and M. Worton (1993). *Textuality and Sexuality: Reading Theories and Practices*. Manchester: Manchester University Press.

Stone, L. (1977). *The Family, Sex and Marriage in England, 1500–1800*. London: Weidenfeld and Nicolson.

Tannahill, R. (1980). *Sex in History*. London: Hamish Hamilton.

Taylor, C. (1989). *Sources of the Modern Self. The Making of Modern Identity*. Cambridge: Cambridge University Press.

Thomas, D. (1969). *A Long Time Burning: The History of Literary Censorship in England*. London: Routledge and Kegan Paul.

Thompson, R. (1979). *Unfit for Modest Ears: A Study of Pornographic, Obscene and Bawdy Works Written or Published in England in the Second Half of the Seventeenth Century*. London: Macmillan.

Todd, J. (1980). *Women's Friendship in Literature*. New York: Columbia University Press.

——— (ed.) (1987) *A Dictionary of British and American Women Writers 1660–1800*. London: Methuen.

——— (1989). *The Sign of Angellica: Women, Writing and Fiction, 1600–1800*. London: Virago.

Traub, V. (1992). 'The (In)significance of Lesbian Desire in Early Modern England'. In Zimmerman (ed.) *Erotic Politics*, 150–69.

——— (1996). 'The Perversion of "Lesbian" Desire', *History Workshop Journal* 41: 23–49.

Trumbach, R. (1977). 'London's Sodomites: Homosexual Behaviour and Western Culture in the 18th Century', *Journal of Social History* 11: 1–33.

——— (1985). 'Sodomitical Subcultures, Sodomitical Roles, and the Gender Revolutions of the Eighteenth Century: The Recent Historiography', *Eighteenth-Century Life* 9: 109–21.

——— (1989). 'The Birth of the Queen: Sodomy and the Emergence of Gender Equality in Modern Culture, 1660–1750'. In Vicinus et al. (eds) *Hidden from History* (1991), 129–40.

——— (1990). 'Sodomy Transformed: Aristocratic Libertinage, Public Reputation and the Gender Revolution of the 18th Century'. In Kimmel (ed.) *Love Letters between a Certain Late Nobleman and the Famous Mr Wilson*, 105–124.

——— (1991). 'London's Sapphists: From Three Sexes to Four Genders in the Making of Modern Culture'. In Epstein and Straub (eds), *Bodyguards*, 112–41.

Turner, J.G. (1993). *Sexuality and Gender in Early Modern Europe: Institutions, Texts, Images*. Cambridge: Cambridge University Press.

Vicinus, M. (1992). '"They Wonder to which Sex I belong": The Historical Roots of the Modern Lesbian Identity'. *Feminist Studies* 18: 467–97.

Vicinus, M., M.B. Duberman and G. Chauncey Jr. (eds) (1991) *Hidden from History: Reclaiming the Gay and Lesbian Past* (1989). Harmondsworth: Penguin.

Wagner, P. (1990). *Eros Revived: Erotica of the Enlightenment in England and America*. London: Paladin.

Weeks, J. (1985). *Sexuality and its Discontents: Meanings, Myths & Modern Homosexualities*. New York and London: Routledge.

Wheelwright, J. (1989). *Amazons and Military Maids: Women Who Dressed as Men in the Pursuit of Life, Liberty and Happiness*. London: Pandora.

White, C. (1970). *Women's Magazines 1693–1968*. London: Michael Joseph.

Woodward, C. (1993). '"My Heart So Wrapt": Lesbian Disruptions in Eighteenth-Century British Fiction', *Signs* 18: 838–65.

Zhang, J.Z. (1993). 'Defoe's "Man-Woman" Roxana: Gender, Reversal, and Androgyny', *Etudes Anglaises* 46: 272–88.

Zimmerman, S. (ed.) (1992). *Erotic Politics: Desire on the Renaissance Stage*. New York and London: Routledge.

INDEX

Abelard, 174

Achilles, 147

Adam, 44, 177

Addison, J., 142, 184

Adonis, 125, 225

adoption, 33, 34

affectation, 117–19, 138, 148, 160, 163

Africa, 37, 48, 104, 236

Amazons, 27, 144

America, 83

Amptil, 55, 56

amputation, 114

Anabaptist, 79

anatomy, 13–48

ancestors, 47, 129, 163, 234

Ancillion, C., 21, 121

androgyne, 35, 43, 45

androgyny, 6

Arabia, 16, 17, 26

aristocracy, 8

aristocrats, 7

Aristotle, 117

army, 23, 27, 28, 41, 203

Asia, 37, 48, 141, 144

Assyrian, 23

Astell, M., 176, 182

Athens, 28

Atherton, Bishop, 62–4

avarice, 32, 227

Averroes, 42, 43

babies, 132

bachelors, 87, 126–31, 187

Bacon, F., 9, 13, 52–3

baptism, 41, 46

Barker, J., 202

Batavia, 31

Bauhin, C., 41

Bayle, 29, 31

Bayle, P., 183

beards, 15, 23, 26, 38–40, 83, 144

Bedlam, 129

benediction, 22

Berlin, 26

Bickerstaffe, I., 162–8

Bigg, W., 55

Bingham, C., 53

blasphemy, 119, 151

Borneo, 31

boys, 23, 28, 39, 41, 45, 56–7, 66, 68,
     72, 76, 93–7, 111–13, 116, 124, 126,
     135, 136–37, 141, 143, 147, 158–60,
     170, 178, 184–186, 227–8

Branson, R., 50, 109–14

Bray, A., 6

Breasted, B., 53

breasts, 20, 38, 39, 130, 157, 217, 229

Bremner, J., 183, 184

bribery, 50, 89

Bristow, J., 52

Broadway, T., 51, 53, 56, 58

Brown, W., 71

Buckingham, Marquess of, 52, 125,
     146, 154

buggery, 59, 62, 78, 104–6, 108–9, 115,
     119, 148

Burg, B.R., 53

burlesque, 100

buttocks, 20, 26, 84, 216

Cain, 168

Cambridge, 100

cannibals, 16
Cape of Good Hope, 15, 17
Capitalism, 3
Castlehaven, Earl of, 51, 53–63
castration, 14, 15, 18, 21–34, 83, 117, 149
catamites, 52, 124, 134, 168
Catholicism, 51, 53, 55, 75
Cavin, S., 183, 184
celibacy, 126, 172–3, 214
chaplains, 61, 227
Charing-Cross, 36, 148
chastity, 16, 22, 24–5, 163, 166, 168, 178, 180–1, 206, 208, 230, 236
children, 9, 17, 24–5, 27, 28, 31, 33, 35–42, 44–7, 60, 65, 74–6, 81, 83, 107, 111, 113, 120, 129, 132, 136–7, 151, 161, 166, 193–4, 197, 199, 203–4, 225
Christianity, 26, 30, 51, 60, 63, 73, 79, 80, 102, 109, 122, 133, 163, 225
Church of England, 61, 75, 80
Churchill, C., 169–72
circumcision, 16
Clap, Mother (Margaret), 72–3
Clark, S., 175, 177, 179
Cleland, J., 158–60, 216–20, 222
climate, 10, 16, 19, 160–1, 223
clitoris, 17, 21, 34, 37–8, 41, 43, 45, 47, 204, 206, 230
cock, 93–5, 117, 142, 165
Cohen, E., 6, 7, 9, 121
coition, 16, 42
coitus, 37, 39, 42, 46
Columbus, R, 46
Confricatrices, 37–8
Constantine, 33
conversation, 15, 71, 86, 102, 137, 141–2, 148, 155, 176, 214, 234
copulation, 17, 19, 42, 69, 106, 236
courage, 23, 34, 61, 126, 136, 197, 211

court, 1, 6, 28–31, 33, 61, 81, 112–14, 150, 164, 167, 168–9, 202, 223, 227, 236
covetousness, 24
cross-dressing, 8, 132–3, 175–81, 184–7, 212–5, 222–34
Ctesias, 16, 236

Dalton, J., 147
dancing, 20, 78–9, 136
daughters, 17, 41, 55, 60, 74, 133, 177, 185–6, 208–9, 213, 222–3, 225, 230
decency, 112, 115, 161, 224, 230
deconstruction, 1
deficiency, 13, 15, 34, 42–3
Defoe, D, 49, 50, 198
deformity, 17, 23, 32, 44, 178, 180–1, 203
DeJean, J., 183–4
Dekker and de Pol, 177, 179
depravity, 32, 60, 137, 139, 142, 148, 163, 221, 223
desertion, 27, 115
desire, 1, 2, 5, 8, 11, 13–14, 22, 38, 46, 50, 52, 62–3, 90, 109, 118–20, 126, 170, 181, 185, 186, 190, 195, 198, 200, 203, 205–6, 209, 212, 216, 218, 220–1, 234
devil, 52, 101–2, 109, 124, 144, 147, 173, 178, 202, 214
dialogical, 3
Diemerbroeck, 40
diet, 6, 130
dildo, 198–202, 212, 222, 228
dildos, 176
dispensation, 33
Dissenters, 80
domination, 3
Donoghue, E., 8, 18, 175–6, 183–4, 188, 198, 203, 215, 221, 234

drinking, 67–8, 74, 77–8, 80–1, 109,
  113, 124, 133, 146
drunkenness, 69, 70, 74, 81, 109, 113,
  133, 145
Dryden, J., 154, 184–7
Dublin, 62, 64, 107, 114
Duffus, G., 67–9
Dugaw, D., 176

education, 136, 204–5, 213
effeminacy, 7, 10, 15–16, 23–4, 30, 52,
  117, 119–21, 124, 126, 130–41, 148,
  180, 236
ego-psychology, 4
Egypt, 16, 18, 37, 47
Eloisa, 174
Enlightenment, 2, 10
erection, 17, 20, 38, 39
essentialism, 5, 117
Ethiopia, 17, 37, 46, 47, 149
Eton, 137
eunuchs, 2, 10, 14, 15, 18, 21–34, 83,
  117, 120, 121, 139, 141, 172–3
Europe, 26, 48, 125, 169
Eusebius, 30, 31
excrement, 26
exhibitionism, 2
exposure, 63, 68, 89, 92, 115, 139, 148,
  163, 208

Faderman, L., 8
fashion, 14, 21, 118–19, 121, 139, 149,
  202, 236
fathers, 29, 33, 55, 86, 88, 90, 106,
  132–4, 136–7, 160, 166, 171, 184–5,
  192, 194, 209, 223–5
favours, 21, 23, 28, 30, 100, 134
Ferdinand I, 40
Feroli, T., 53
Fielding, H., 235

Flanders, 41
flogging, 18, 20, 84–5, 115. See also
  whipping.
Florida, 17, 35
fops, 7, 117, 118–19, 121, 124–5, 134–5,
  147, 149–51. See also effeminacy.
fornication, 119, 146
Fortescue, J., 104, 105, 106
Foucault, M., 3, 6, 118, 121
Foxon, D., 15, 158, 188, 216
France, 19, 22, 26, 27, 38, 107, 118,
  125–6, 138–9, 141, 146, 150, 157,
  162, 166, 176, 198, 211, 220–2
Freud, S., 4, 5
French, W., 85–104
fribble, 121, 153
frication, 39
Fricatrices, 17, 39
Friedli, L., 18, 34
friendship, 8, 28, 29, 54, 68, 84–5,
  87–8, 91, 96, 98, 100, 103, 107, 140,
  145, 164, 168, 173, 175, 177, 181, 188,
  190, 200, 202–5, 213, 232

Galen, 40
Ganymede, 125, 141, 147, 159, 169,
  170
Garber, M., 176, 177, 179
Garrick, D., 153, 162–8
gay identity, 1
generation, 15, 23, 25, 35, 36, 40, 42,
  44, 45, 47, 49, 109, 126, 128, 140,
  148, 178, 230
German, 41
Germany, 41, 107
girls, 23, 37–8, 41, 45, 76, 78, 81, 104,
  109, 133, 137, 143, 159, 174, 184, 189,
  192, 196, 201, 209, 213–14, 218,
  222–4, 226–7
gluttony, 24, 123

God, 22, 31, 44, 54–5, 59, 60–3, 66,
    109, 114–15, 122–4, 126–7, 129, 133,
    139, 146, 161, 171–2, 178, 192–5,
    202–3, 207, 213, 225, 236
Gomorrah, 114, 125, 152, 168
gossipping, 126, 132
Gothic, 153, 156
Gray's Inn, 53
Greek, 25, 27, 30, 37, 40, 42, 141, 149,
    166, 168, 209, 230, 236
Griffin, W., 75–6
Guinea, 14–15

hair, 26, 38–9, 138, 143, 147, 159–60,
    187, 189, 192, 213
hanging, 50, 60–2, 71, 72, 75, 76, 80,
    96, 214
Harvey, E.D., 183–4
Hercules, 164
heretics, 6
hermaphrodism, 6
hermaphrodites, 2, 10, 14, 17–21,
    34–48, 117, 120–1, 150, 179, 182
Herodotus, 28
Herrup, C, 53
Hervey, Lord, 150–1
hetrosexual, 1, 2, 4, 177, 187
hetrosexuality, 1–5, 10, 177, 212, 216
Hitchcock, T., 177
Holland, 49, 104, 114
Holy Scripture, 26
homosexuality, 1, 3–9, 10, 120–1, 131, 236
honour, 24, 31–2, 54, 60–1, 84, 108,
    126, 135–6, 141, 150, 156, 170, 172,
    178, 188, 192, 200, 230
Hungary, 41
husbands, 27–8, 41, 56, 58, 60, 70–1,
    80, 83, 127, 132–3, 174, 176, 179,
    184, 186, 203–4, 210, 216, 231–4
Hylas, 164, 170

idleness, 6, 119, 122–4, 145, 161, 234
impotence, 24, 151
impotency, 7. See also sterility
incest, 124
India, 180
Indians, 17
Indies, 31
indolence, 120, 137
infibulation, 16
ingle, 152
Ireland, 55, 62, 64, 83, 106–8, 165
ischia, 38
Italy, 19, 21, 27, 36, 53, 83, 93, 100, 107,
    118, 120, 139, 140–1, 150, 164, 180,
    198, 223, 230

Jacquart and Thomasset, 34
jealous, 24, 30, 78, 186
jealousy, 23, 29–30, 60, 133, 227
Jesuits, 152
Jews, 16, 23, 147, 167
Jones, R., 168
Joseph, 23
Juno, 29, 36, 186, 187
jurisprudence, 3
Juvenal, 206, 236

Katz, J., 6, 121
Kedger, G., 77–8
Kenrick, W., 162–8
Kent, 104
King, T.A., 7
kissing, 21, 30, 67–8, 72, 74, 76–9,
    92–3, 95, 100, 110, 113, 120, 125,
    138–41, 147, 159, 160, 182, 189, 196,
    217–19, 236
Kopelson, K., 158

labia, 38
lad, 103, 113, 116, 158. See also boys.

Laqueur, T., 2, 34

Latin, 9, 22–3, 25, 118, 136, 150, 168, 202, 207, 209

law, 1, 14, 23, 32–4, 36, 51, 53–5, 83, 88, 95, 99, 105–6, 108, 114–16, 126–7, 129, 163, 167, 194, 210, 234

Lawrence, G., 73–5

Leader, N., 67–9

lechery, 13, 17, 139, 147, 151, 171, 221, 235

legitimacy, 3

Lemnius, 42

Leo, 33

lesbian, 8, 175, 176, 177, 209, 223. *See also* sapphic.

lewdness, 31, 72, 79, 83, 132, 144, 166, 234–5

libertine, 7, 8, 51

Lipking, 183, 184

Lucas, 177, 179

Lucian, 23, 29, 32, 176, 181–3

lust, 16–19, 24, 55, 83, 124, 130–1, 134–5, 152, 171, 200–1, 205–6, 221, 224, 235

lusus naturae, 14, 37

luxury, 4, 17, 32, 119, 122–3, 141–2, 146–7, 169

macaronis, 167

Macrobius, 27

Macroclitorideae, 35, 43

male-misses, 160

manhood, 21, 26, 34, 117, 121, 141, 146, 169, 171, 173, 182, 214, 223

manners, 16, 23, 139, 153–7, 160, 162, 167, 180, 192–3, 209, 230–1, 234

Marcellinus, 23–4, 31

Marcus, L.S., 53

Marcuse, H., 5

marriage, 5, 17, 21–2, 30, 34, 41, 53, 55–6, 58, 65, 71–2, 74–5, 76, 80–1,

106, 126–9, 133, 137, 167, 175, 182, 184, 187–8, 203, 206, 209, 226, 232, 235

Marten, J., 14–18

Martial, 16, 206

masculinity, 6, 8, 15, 18, 20–1, 38–9, 41–2, 45, 131, 134, 144, 154–5, 157, 177–8, 180, 198, 213, 227

masquerades, 142, 145, 161

masturbation, 204–7, 212, 216–20

Meares, R., 9

medicine, 177, 202

melancholy, 13, 25, 87, 107, 148

Mengay, D.H., 216

metamorphosis, 38, 40, 157, 212, 213

Methodists, 214

Meyer, M., 3, 134

military, 34, 146

mimicry, 72, 103, 131, 132, 142, 156

modesty, 21–2, 85, 112, 123, 132–3, 140, 163, 180–1, 201, 217–18

mollies, 7, 50, 72–3, 75, 77–80, 117–21, 130–4

monastery, 192

monsters, 9, 25, 32, 35, 43–5, 117, 127, 133, 135, 145, 162–3, 178–9, 186, 207, 233

monstrous, 10, 13–14, 19, 26, 35–6, 44, 114, 121, 126–7, 143, 160, 164, 177–8, 231

Montaigne, 29

Moors, 83

mothers, 40, 55, 81, 106–7, 118, 134, 137, 146, 151, 160, 184, 187, 203

mouth, 33, 141, 160, 210

murder, 50, 86, 115, 163

mutilation, 23, 25–6

mutiny, 27

Naples, 40

Nebuchadnezzar, 23
Nero, 30, 152
Ninus, 23
Noah, 44, 195
Norton, R, 52, 66–7, 72, 80, 106, 118, 131, 150, 162
nuns, 2, 176, 187–97, 207, 228
nursery, 135–7, 221

Oates, T, 51, 134
opera, 21, 120–1, 141, 162, 164
opium, 16, 25
Orpheus, 165
Ovid, 206, 222
Oxford, 85–6, 88, 91, 93–4, 100

Pallas, 15
pantomime, 119–20, 142, 168
Papal Dominions, 19
parents, 26, 28, 41, 136, 173, 186, 197, 209, 229
Paris, 39
Parmenides, 42
parsons, 132, 171, 202, 212
Parsons, J., 14, 34, 121
passion, 30, 89, 160, 174, 179, 181–6, 189, 191, 202–3, 208–9, 225, 229, 232
Pathick, 106, 153
Patiphor, 23
patriarchy, 2, 175
Patroculus, 147
Pembroke College, 100
penis, 14–16, 37–40, 45–7, 112, 117, 198, 204, 206, 212
performativity, 3
Persia, 16, 23, 144, 236
perversion, 4
perversity, 3
phallus, 14, 176, 177

piety, 22, 31, 123, 228
pillory, 50, 67, 69, 71, 73, 106, 115–16, 139, 171
plague, 109, 115, 123, 144, 160, 169
Plato, 84, 166
Pliny, 26, 32
Pope, A., 120, 131, 151, 174
Porter, R., 119
post-structuralism, 3, 4, 5
power, 2–5, 10, 18, 23, 29, 33–4, 36, 39, 54, 62, 86, 91, 97, 118, 139, 163, 175, 178, 193, 198, 215–17, 218, 229, 232
prepuce, 16–17
Presbyterian, 108
preternatural, 36
pretty gentleman, 121, 153–7
Priapus, 16, 124
pride, 6, 16, 52, 122, 138, 140, 149, 151, 154, 161, 170, 213, 224
priests, 142, 146
private, 2, 23, 50–1, 61, 66, 77, 80–1, 91, 110, 122, 137, 142, 173, 179, 199, 222
privilege, 4, 33, 176
procreation, 4, 44, 127, 170, 213, 222
prodigies, 35, 41, 231
prostitutes, 216
Protestantism, 55, 61, 80
psychiatry, 3
Psychoanalysis, 4
public, 2, 18, 26, 30, 32, 46, 49–51, 53, 64, 68, 73, 82–3, 86, 89, 97, 99, 102, 109, 120, 124, 128, 135, 137, 139, 142, 148, 150, 163, 169, 171, 173, 194, 197, 199, 209, 232–5
punishment, 27, 29, 51, 67, 83, 92, 94, 104–6, 114–16, 133, 139, 152, 163, 169, 173, 185, 209, 231, 234

Quakers, 214

queer, 1, 3

race, 3, 16, 44, 103, 123, 133, 138, 144–5,
    152, 157, 172, 198
rakes, 7
rape, 51, 53–4, 58–60, 67, 83, 167
Renaissance, 1, 6
repentance, 61, 122, 172
resistance, 3, 9, 56, 146, 217
Rochester, 51, 206, 222
Rodin, T., 69–70
Rome, 19, 30, 35, 141, 145, 152, 159,
    166, 206, 222–3, 225, 230
Rousseau, G.S., 10, 51, 119
Royal Society, 37, 38
Rueffe, J., 45

sacred, 2, 22, 30, 101, 108, 173
Samber, R., 188
sapphic, 8
Sapphic texts, 175–235
Sappho, 183–4, 208, 223, 230
scandal, 35, 50, 53, 81, 134, 163, 210
school, 77, 84, 135–7, 154, 177, 185, 196,
    210–11
Scotland, 17
scrotum, 26, 38–9, 40, 45
Sedgwick, E.K., 2, 4–6, 13, 50, 52
seed, 13, 15, 128
semen, 17, 42–3
Semiramis, 23, 144
Semple, L., 183–4
Senelick, L., 121, 134, 153, 162
sensibility, 6, 163, 210
servants, 20, 40–1, 52–3, 56, 58, 60,
    62, 77, 81–2, 85, 90, 92, 94–5,
    107–8, 112–13, 116, 155, 171, 177,
    202–4, 206, 214, 220, 223–9
Shakespeare, 142, 166
Shapiro, 18, 34, 177, 179

sin, 6, 7, 52–3, 55, 60, 69, 75–6, 114–5,
    121–2, 124, 139–41, 147–8, 152, 166,
    170, 173, 196, 202, 205, 210
singing, 21, 78, 83, 141–2, 164
Sinibaldus, 15
Skipwith, 55–8
slaves, 24, 33, 83, 135, 145, 152, 194, 212
sloth, 124, 193

tongue, 33, 67, 92, 95, 110, 165, 170
transvestite, 7
Traub, 177, 179
Tribades, 18, 37, 208, 230
Tribads, 208
Tropic of Capricorn, 16
Trumbach, R., 7–8, 131, 134, 215
Tulpius, 37
tumours, 37
Turkey, 16, 31, 53, 101, 147, 209
tyranny, 32, 128, 145

university, 25, 97, 85–104, 136–7
urine, 15, 25, 46
uterus, 35, 36, 40, 42–3, 45

vagina, 38, 40, 47
vanity, 21, 31, 134, 149
venereal, 39, 80, 134, 176, 206, 231
venery, 15–16, 19
Venette, 15
Venus, 15, 19, 124, 152, 176, 183, 187–8,
    224
Vicinus, M., 8
Virginia, 17
virgins, 176, 222, 228–9
virility, 14, 25–6, 34, 38–9, 40, 42–3,
    118, 182, 214
Vizzani, C., 222–34
voice, 15, 23, 38–9, 61–2, 83, 114, 134,
    142, 155, 157, 164, 174, 184, 232

voices, 13, 16, 20, 26, 72, 141
Vossius, 23
vulva, 37, 38, 46, 215

Wadham College, 49, 50, 85–104
Walpole, E, 106–8
Ward, N., 117, 121, 131
warfare, 34, 193
Weeks, J., 1, 3, 5
werewolves, 6
Wheelwright, J., 176
whipping, 30, 83, 104, 106, 114,
    194–6
White, A., 2, 9
Whittle, G., 80–2
whore, 57, 59
whores, 2, 39, 57, 70, 146–7, 158, 169,
    178, 201
wifes, 28, 30, 39, 41, 53, 58–60, 65, 68,

70, 75–6, 81–2, 93–7, 116, 136,
    145–6, 148, 166, 177, 182, 184, 200,
    203, 216, 231–2, 235
Wilson, Beau, 51
witchcraft, 119
woman-haters, 127, 130–1
womb, 13, 15, 24, 26, 117, 205, 221
women, old, 19, 143–6
Wright, T., 78–80

Xerxes, 28

youth, 18, 52, 65, 100, 103, 132, 136,
    140–1, 145, 152, 157, 164, 166, 184,
    187, 195, 211, 221, 223, 225, 229,
    231, 234

Zhang, J.Z., 175, 198
Zurich, 45